BIOMES OF THE EARTH

TROPICAL FORESTS

Michael Allaby

Illustrations by
Richard Garratt

CHELSEA HOUSE
PUBLISHERS
An imprint of Infobase Publishing

Tropical Forests

Chelsea House
An imprint of Infobase Publishing
132 West 31st Street
New York NY 10001

ISBN-13: 978-0-8160-5322-3
ISBN-10: 0-8160-5322-7

Library of Congress Cataloging-in-Publication Data

Allaby, Michael.
   Tropical forests / Michael Allaby; illustrations by Richard Garratt.
      p. cm.—(Biomes of the Earth)
   Includes bibliographical references and index.
   ISBN 0-8160-5322-7
   1. Rain forest ecology—Juvenile literature. 2. Rain forests—Juvenile literature. I. Title. II. Series.
   QH541.5.R27A45 2006
   577.34—dc22   2005006747

Chelsea House books are available at special discounts when purchased in bulk quantities for businesses, associations, institutions, or sales promotions. Please call our Special Sales Department in New York at (212) 967-8800 or (800) 322-8755.

You can find Chelsea House on the World Wide Web at http://www.chelseahouse.com

Text design by David Strelecky
Cover design by Cathy Rincon
Illustrations by Richard Garratt
Photo Research by Elizabeth H. Oakes

Printed in China

CP FOF 10 9 8 7 6 5 4 3 2

This book is printed on acid-free paper.

From Richard Garratt: To Chantal,
who has lightened my darkness.

CONTENTS

CHAPTER 6
ECOLOGY OF TROPICAL FORESTS

CHAPTER 7
PEOPLES OF TROPICAL FORESTS

CHAPTER 8
BIODIVERSITY AND TROPICAL FORESTS

CHAPTER 9
THREATS TO TROPICAL FORESTS

CHAPTER 10
MANAGING TROPICAL FORESTS

CONCLUSION

PREFACE

Earth is a remarkable planet. There is nowhere else in our solar system where life can survive in such a great diversity of forms. As far as we can currently tell, our planet is unique. Isolated in the barren emptiness of space, here on Earth we are surrounded by a remarkable range of living things, from the bacteria that inhabit the soil to the great whales that migrate through the oceans, from the giant redwood trees of the Pacific forests to the mosses that grow on urban sidewalks. In a desolate universe, Earth teems with life in a bewildering variety of forms.

One of the most exciting things about the Earth is the rich pattern of plant and animal communities that exists over its surface. The hot, wet conditions of the equatorial regions support dense rain forests with tall canopies occupied by a wealth of animals, some of which may never touch the ground. The cold, bleak conditions of the polar regions, on the other hand, sustain a much lower variety of species of plants and animals, but those that do survive under such harsh conditions have remarkable adaptations to their testing environment. Between these two extremes lie many other types of complex communities, each well suited to the particular conditions of climate prevailing in its region. Scientists call these communities *biomes*.

The different biomes of the world have much in common with one another. Each has a plant component, which is responsible for trapping the energy of the Sun and making it available to the other members of the community. Each has grazing animals, both large and small, that take advantage of the store of energy found within the bodies of plants. Then come the predators, ranging from tiny spiders that feed upon even smaller insects to tigers, eagles, and polar bears that survive by preying upon large animals. All of these living things form a complicated network of feeding interactions, and, at the base of the system, microbes in the soil are ready to consume the energy-rich plant litter or dead animal flesh that remains. The biome, then, is an integrated unit within which each species plays its particular role.

This set of books aims to outline the main features of each of the Earth's major biomes. The biomes covered include the tundra habitats of polar regions and high mountains, the taiga (boreal forest) and temperate forests of somewhat warmer lands, the grasslands of the prairies and the tropical savanna, the deserts of the world's most arid locations, and the tropical forests of the equatorial regions. The wetlands of the world, together with river and lake habitats, do not lie neatly in climatic zones over the surface of the Earth but are scattered over the land. And the oceans are an exception to every rule. Massive in their extent, they form an interconnecting body of water extending down into unexplored depths, gently moved by global currents.

Humans have had an immense impact on the environment of the Earth over the past 10,000 years since the last Ice Age. There is no biome that remains unaffected by the presence of the human species. Indeed, we have created our own biome in the form of agricultural and urban lands, where people dwell in greatest densities. The farms and cities of the Earth have their own distinctive climates and natural history, so they can be regarded as a kind of artificial biome that people have created, and they are considered as a separate biome in this set.

Each biome is the subject of a separate volume. Each richly illustrated book describes the global distribution, the climate, the rocks and soils, the plants and animals, the history, and the environmental problems found within each biome. Together, the set provides students with a sound basis for understanding the wealth of the Earth's biodiversity, the factors that influence it, and the future dangers that face the planet and our species.

Is there any practical value in studying the biomes of the Earth? Perhaps the most compelling reason to understand the way in which biomes function is to enable us to conserve their rich biological resources. The world's productivity is the basis of the human food supply. The world's biodiversity holds a wealth of unknown treasures, sources of drugs and medicines that will help to improve the quality of life. Above all, the world's biomes are a constant source of wonder, excitement, recreation, and inspiration that feed not only our bodies but also our minds and spirits. These books aim to provide the information about biomes that readers need in order to understand their function, draw upon their resources, and, most of all, enjoy their diversity.

ACKNOWLEDGMENTS

Richard Garratt drew all of the diagrams and maps that appear in this book. Richard and I have been working together for many years in a collaboration that succeeds because Richard has a genius for translating the weird electronic squiggles I send him into clear, simple artwork of the highest quality. As always, I am grateful to him for all his hard work. I also wish to thank Elizabeth Oakes for her fine work as a photo researcher.

I must thank Frank K. Darmstadt, executive editor at Chelsea House. Frank shaped this series of books and guided them through all the stages of their development. His encouragement, patience, and good humor have been immensely valuable.

I am especially grateful to Dorothy Cummings, project editor. Her close attention to detail sharpened explanations that had been vague, corrected my mistakes and inconsistencies, and identified places where I repeated myself. And occasionally Dorothy was able to perform the most important service of all: She intervened in time to stop me making a fool of myself. No author could ask for more. This is a much better book than it would have been without her hard work and dedication.

Michael Allaby
Tighnabruaich
Argyll
Scotland
www.michaelallaby.com

INTRODUCTION

What are tropical forests?

The air is heavy with moisture. Water drips from every leaf and runs down the trunk of every tree. The weather feels sticky, even oppressive, but the shade cast by the trees towering overhead means the air is warm rather than hot. High above, the crowns of adjacent trees meet to form an almost continuous closed canopy, but with a few gaps through which the sunshine passes all the way to the forest floor, where bright patches of sunlight give the forest a dappled look.

The trees reach to the sky, competing with each other for sunlight, and smaller trees grow between the giants. Some are saplings waiting for a chance to grow tall. They will get their chance when one of the big trees dies and falls, opening up a sunlit space that the young tree can fill with a spurt of rapid growth.

Other trees and shrubs prefer the shade. They thrive in a dimmer light and fill some of the space on the floor. It is not too difficult to walk through the forest, however. The floor is fairly open and travelers can weave their way between the trees.

Many of the trees are festooned with climbing plants, *lianas* or *lianes* that begin their lives in the deep shade at the base of a large tree. As they grow they cling to the bark of the tree, extending upward until they reach the crown, where their leaves are exposed to full sunlight. Lianes are woody plants, just like the trees that support them, and their narrow stems are sometimes more than 200 feet (61 m) long. They can completely enclose a tree so its trunk is hidden, and when the tree dies it remains standing until it has fully decomposed, held together by its jacket of lianes.

Climbers are rooted in the ground, but the trees support other plants that live on the outside of their branches and in the hollows where branches join the main trunk. Called *epiphytes*—*epi* is the Greek word for "upon," and *phyte* is from *phyton,* meaning "plant"—they use their roots only to anchor themselves, obtaining the water and nutrients they need from the rain that falls on their leaves. Many orchids are epiphytes.

There are big, showy flowers everywhere. Trees have flowers of their own, some of them growing directly from the trunk, as well as the flowers belonging to their climbers and epiphytes. Flowers that rely on insects, bats, or birds for pollination need to put on a spectacular show. Their pollinators must be able to find them easily amid the confused tangle of plants. As well as size and color, some of the flowers use scent to attract insects, but it is not always the familiar delicate perfume that pervades a flower shop. Here there are flowers that stink of rotting meat. Humans may find it revolting, but the flies that pollinate the flower find it irresistible.

Colorful birds fly from tree to tree. Screeching monkeys leap from branch to branch. Bigger animals dwell on the forest floor, but they remain well hidden. Snakes lie in wait for prey or glide steadily and silently in pursuit of it. There are many species of frogs. Some live in pools of water high up in the trees, and many of the frogs are brightly colored—a warning that they are covered in extremely poisonous slime.

Huge, bright butterflies flitter from plant to plant. Processions of ants march along branches and return carrying pieces of leaf held above them like umbrellas. Other ants patrol at ground level. There are countless beetles, some of them large and some brilliantly colored, like jewels. There are giant centipedes, millipedes scurrying among the loose plant material on the forest floor, and spiders that lurk in the secret places, waiting for careless insects to come within their reach.

This is a tropical rain forest, a bewildering profusion of plants and animals growing riotously in the warm, wet climate where there are no seasons and one day is just like every other. More different species of living organisms live in forests like this than live in any other type of environment. There may be as many as 260 different species of trees all growing within one square mile (100 species/km²).

It is a tropical rain forest, but that is only one type of forest growing in the tropics. The description best fits a lowland forest, growing in a wide river valley, where the rainfall is heavy and approximately the same amount of rain falls in every month. Most tropical forests grow in a seasonal climate, however, where the rainfall is not spread evenly through the year.

The monsoon climate is the most extreme example of a seasonal variation in rainfall. There are two monsoon seasons. Almost all of the year's rain falls during one season—the wet monsoon—and practically no rain falls for the rest of the year, during the dry monsoon. Monsoons occur only in the Tropics, and so forests growing in a monsoon climate form another type of tropical forest. *Monsoon forest* must cope with alternating periods of extremely wet and extremely dry weather.

Obviously, a tropical forest is a forest that grows in the Tropics, and the Tropics enjoy a warm climate. It does not follow, however, that all tropical forests grow in a warm climate. Tropical climates are warm at sea level, but the air temperature decreases with height.

Forests that grow on tropical mountainsides—known as *montane* forests—experience lower temperatures, and the character of the forest changes so that there are different types of montane forest at different levels. A high rainfall means that the skies are often cloudy and tall mountains project into the clouds. Parts of the tropical mountains are shrouded in fog—in fact, cloud—for most of the time. This affects the vegetation, producing a characteristic type of *cloud* forest. Higher still, the cold winds stunt the growth of the trees, producing *elfin forest.*

Many tropical forests abound in different species, but others are dominated by a very few species of trees. In some areas there may be only one or two species growing over a large area. Mangrove forests, growing near coasts, contain very few tree species because few species can tolerate the conditions in which mangroves thrive. Bamboo forest also occupies large areas. Bamboos belong to the grass family, but some species can grow very tall, and in some areas bamboo forms dense thickets. In the mountains of tropical southern Asia, there are forests of rhododendron.

Tropical forest covers approximately 4.4 million square miles (11.5 million km²)—about 7 percent of the world's total land area. It is the forest that grows in the Tropics, but it is not one type of forest, but several.

CHAPTER 1

GEOGRAPHY OF TROPICAL FORESTS

Where are the Tropics?

Tropical forests grow in the Tropics, and the Tropics form a belt on either side of the equator bounded by lines of latitude. Latitude 23.45°N marks the tropic of Cancer and 23.45°S marks the tropic of Capricorn. Between these two lines of latitude there is one day in the year when the Sun is directly overhead at noon. The Sun is never directly overhead in latitudes any higher than the two Tropics.

The word *tropic* comes from the Greek *tropikos,* which means "turning." It refers to the fact that the Sun appears directly overhead a little farther from the equator each day, and when it reaches the Tropic it advances no farther and seems to turn back. Long ago, when the Tropics were first given their names, the Sun was in the constellations of Cancer and Capricorn on the days when it appeared overhead at 23.45°N and 23.45°S, respectively. Changes in the Earth's axis of rotation mean that it is now in the constellations of Gemini when it is at 23.45°N and Sagittarius when it is at 23.45°S.

The Earth turns on its own axis, making one revolution every 24 hours. It also orbits the Sun, taking a year to complete one orbit. Imagine that the Earth's path around the Sun follows the edge of a flat disk, with the Sun at its center. This disk is called the *plane of the ecliptic* and it is shown in the illustration. (The drawing on page 3 is not to scale, of course. Although the Sun is many times larger than the Earth, it is so far away that it appears quite small.) The diagram shows the Earth at four points in its orbit, but no matter where the Earth is, the Sun will appear directly overhead somewhere close to the equator.

Notice, though, that the Earth's axis of rotation is not at right angles to the plane of the ecliptic. If the Earth were

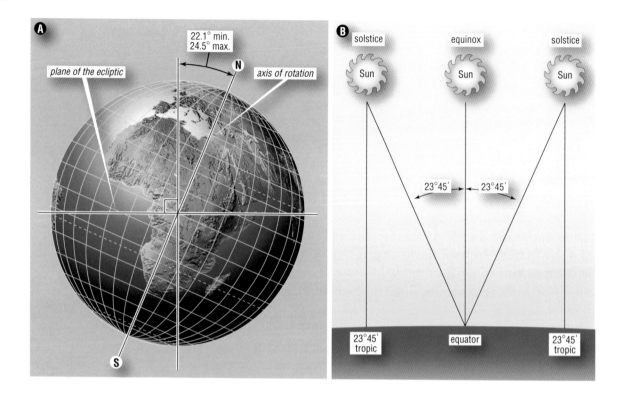

The tropic of Cancer lies at 23.45°N and the tropic of Capricorn at 23.45°S. The latitudes are determined by the angle of tilt between the Earth's rotational axis and a line drawn at right angles to the plane of the Earth's orbit.

upright, the Sun would be overhead exactly at the equator on every day of the year. In fact, the Earth's axis is at an angle of 23.45° to the vertical. The angle of tilt varies over a period of about 42,000 years from a minimum of 22.1° to a maximum of 24.5°, so at present we are almost in the middle of the cycle. The drawing on the left in the illustration shows the angle of tilt and the drawing on the right shows its consequence.

Look again at the drawing of the Earth in its orbit. Because the Earth is tilted, first one hemisphere and then the other receives more direct sunlight. Halfway between these two positions, both hemispheres are illuminated equally. The two extreme positions are called the *solstices*, and they fall on June 21–22 and December 22–23. The midway positions are called the *equinoxes*. These fall on March 20–21 and September 22–23.

As the Earth orbits the Sun, the tilt of the axis makes the height of the noonday Sun change. At the equinoxes the Sun is directly overhead at the equator, and therefore the Northern and Southern Hemispheres receive the same amount of sunlight. On those two days, everywhere in the world, the Sun remains above the horizon for 12 hours and below it for 12 hours—hence the name *equinox,* which means "equal night." At the summer solstice—June 21–22 in the Northern Hemisphere and December 22–23 in the Southern Hemisphere—the noonday Sun reaches its greatest height in the sky. At this time the Sun remains above the horizon for longer than it is below the horizon. The difference in the lengths of day and night increases with distance from the equator. In latitudes higher than the Arctic or Antarctic Circle—in the lands of the "midnight Sun"—the Sun does not sink below the horizon at the summer solstice. At the winter solstice the noonday Sun is lower in the sky than it is on any other day in the year, and beyond the Arctic or Antarctic Circle it does not rise above the horizon at all.

A line drawn at the equinox from a point on the equator directly to the Sun will follow the plane of the ecliptic. This is the central line shown in the left diagram. If a similar line is drawn from the point on the equator to the Sun at the solstice, the angle between this line and the equinoctial line will be 23.45° because that is the angle by which the axis is tilted. If a line is then drawn from the Sun to the point where it

The plane of the ecliptic is an imaginary disk whose circumference is the path of the Earth's orbit about the Sun.

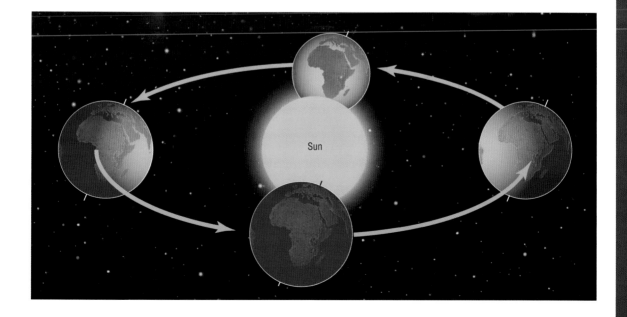

appears overhead at the solstice, that line will meet the surface at latitude 23.45°.

That is why the tropics of Cancer and Capricorn are at latitudes 23.45°N and 23.45°S respectively, and why the solstices, when the Sun is directly overhead at one or other Tropic, are Midsummer Day in one hemisphere and Midwinter Day in the other. Tropical forests grow in the lands lying between these latitudes.

Where tropical forests occur

A glance at a map of the world shows that the equator passes mainly over water. Oceans cover most of the Tropics, and this strongly affects the conditions under which tropical forests develop (see "Why it rains so much at the equator" on page 46). It might be expected, therefore, that luxuriant tropical forests would carpet all the land throughout the entire tropi-

The global distribution of tropical forest

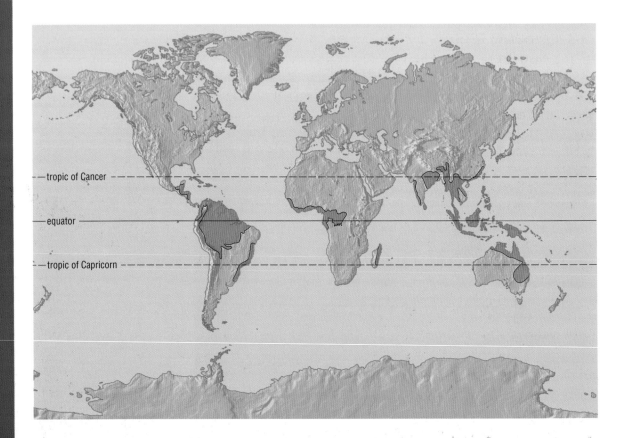

tropic of Cancer

equator

tropic of Capricorn

cal region, all the way from Cancer to Capricorn. In fact, they cover a very much smaller area than that.

Forests grow in all the lands lying inside the Tropics, but they have never covered all of the tropical land area. As the map shows, tropical forests occur in four regions: America and the Caribbean, Africa and eastern Madagascar, India and Malaysia, and Australia. It also occurs in some oceanic islands, such as the Hawaiian Islands. These regions are shown on the map. Approximately 57 percent of the total area of tropical forest is in the Americas, 25 percent is in Asia, and 18 percent is in Africa.

Tropical forests do not blanket all of the land lying in the Tropics. Montane forest grows in the mountains that run down the western side of Central America, but desert lies to the west of the Andes in South America. On the eastern side, the South American tropical forest gives way to tropical and temperate grassland.

Despite Africa's vast area, only a small part of West Africa supports tropical forest. The forest extends along the coast from Guinea and Sierra Leone in the west to the Congo Basin in the east. Tropical grassland—savanna—borders the forest. The Sahara lies beyond the grassland to the north. To the south of the forest there are areas of desert, including the Kalahari Desert, surrounded by grassland. Tropical forest is the natural vegetation in eastern Madagascar, but on the western side of the central mountains it is grassland and desert.

Most of tropical Asia is naturally covered by tropical forest. It occurs down the western side of India, in Sri Lanka, Myanmar (Burma), and from Thailand and Vietnam through Malaysia and Indonesia to Papua New Guinea and the smaller islands farther to the east. It also covers parts of northern and eastern Australia.

Not all of this is rain forest. Rainfall is heavy and spread fairly evenly through the year in Central America, the Amazon Basin, the Congo Basin, eastern Madagascar, and much of Southeast Asia. These are the areas where tropical rain forest occurs. Elsewhere the climate is seasonal. The total annual rainfall is heavy, but there are distinct wet and dry seasons associated with the summer and winter monsoons (see "Monsoons" on page 63). West Africa, India, Myanmar, parts of Southeast Asia, parts of Australia, and some of the Pacific islands have a monsoon climate.

Equatorial climates are rainy—but not everywhere. The Somali Republic, for example, in the northeastern corner of Africa known as the Horn of Africa, is largely desert or semi-desert, despite being within a few degrees of the equator. Most of Africa, central India, and Australia are too dry to support forests. In some places mountains capture the moisture in approaching air (see "Mountain climates" on page 70), leaving areas on the leeward side in their *rain shadow*. The interior of a continent may be too far from the ocean to receive much rain (see "Continental and maritime climates" on page 56). Even near coasts, approaching air may cross a cold ocean current, where much of its moisture condenses, so that the air is dry by the time it reaches land.

Climatic variations mean that tropical forest grows only in certain parts of the Tropics. It does not cover the whole of the region.

American tropical forests

The largest tropical forest in the world covers most of the Amazon region of Brazil; most of Guyana, Suriname, and French Guiana; parts of eastern Venezuela; and the western coastal regions of Colombia and Ecuador. The map of vegetation zones shows the extent of the forest, and the political map shows the location of the countries in which it lies. The forest covers the Brazilian Highlands in the east and in the west it climbs the slopes of the Andes. It merges with more open woodland in the state of Mato Grosso, in the south, but continues along the river valleys.

Known in Brazil as *selvas* (singular *selva*), the forest covers about 2.7 million square miles (7 million km²). About 60 percent of all the world's tropical rain forests are in South America. In addition, the tropical forests in Central America and the Caribbean Islands occupy about 196,000 square miles (509,000 km²).

Brazil owes its name to an extremely valuable red dye called brazil or brasile, obtained from the brazilwood tree

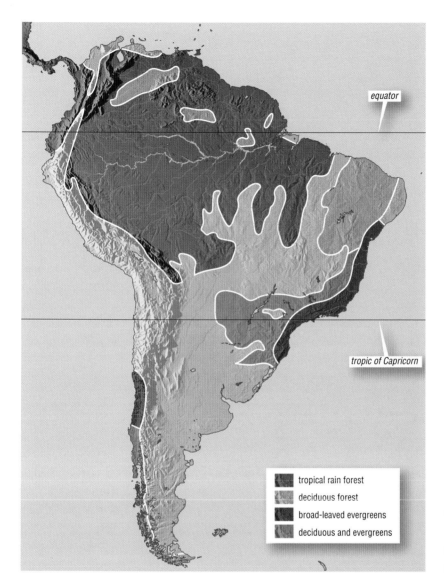

equator

tropic of Capricorn

- tropical rain forest
- deciduous forest
- broad-leaved evergreens
- deciduous and evergreens

Forests in South America. The lowland wet forests are sometimes called selvas.

(*Caesalpinia echinata*) that was abundant in the forests when the Portuguese first arrived in the 16th century. Mahogany (*Swietenia macrophylla*) is possibly the most famous of all the trees of the American tropics. It is widespread but occurs as scattered individuals rather than stands of trees, and today it is rarer than it once was, following centuries of exploitation.

The American forests produce both one of the world's lightest woods and the world's heaviest. Balsa wood, from

Northern South America and southern Central America, showing the countries and principal cities

Ochroma lagopus, weighs only 10 pounds per cubic foot (150 kg/m³). It is used for making models. Lignum vitae, from *Guiacum officinale,* weighs 80 pounds per cubic foot (1,250 kg/m³) and is used to make such items as mallet heads and bowling balls.

Swamps and marshes, called *igapós,* cover much of the lowland area. The undergrowth is dense but dominated by trees, some of which yield commercially valuable timber. The timber of *Calophyllum brasiliense,* for example, called *jacareúba* in

South America and *Santa Maria* in Central America, is used in heavy construction.

Away from the swamps, the *várzea* regions are flooded only once a year. This is where the rubber tree (*Hevea brasiliensis*) originated and where Brazil nuts are still collected from *Bertholletia excelsa* trees growing wild in the forest.

Palms are widespread, some as small trees growing in the shade of the forest giants, others as plants that creep across the forest floor, and many with fierce spines to deter plant-eating animals. Epiphytes are abundant and include Spanish moss (*Tillandia usneoides*)—not a moss, but a member of the same plant family (Bromeliaceae) as the pineapple.

Forests of a similar type extend northward through the eastern side of Central America. Figs (*Ficus* species) are common among the undergrowth and there are many lianes.

Montane forests occupy the higher ground and are the predominant type of forest in the interior of Guatemala and Honduras and in parts of Nicaragua, Costa Rica, and Panama. On the eastern side of Central America, facing the Caribbean, lowland rain forest gives way at higher elevations to evergreen montane forest and then to a forest abundant in tree ferns and mosses.

Cloud forest is common in the mountains above about 6,500 feet (1,982 m) and above about 4,900 feet (1,494 m) in southwestern Costa Rica. Above the cloud forest there are oak trees (*Quercus* species) and spurges (euphorbias), and above about 9,800 feet (2,990 m) the vegetation comprises evergreen shrubs, berries, heaths, and sphagnum moss.

As well as being the largest tropical forest, the South American forest also contains the greatest diversity of species. There are about 2,500 species of trees in the Amazon Basin, and in an area of about 1,900 square feet (204 m^2) near Manaus, Brazil, where the Negro and Amazon Rivers meet, scientists found plants belonging to 107 species in 37 different families. Of approximately 70,000 species native to South America, about 55,000 grow nowhere else—they are said to be *endemic*. Of the 43,000–48,000 species in Central America and the Caribbean region, about 20,000–25,000 are endemic.

African tropical forests

Africa is a dry continent. Deserts cover a large proportion of the total area and are surrounded by semiarid grassland. Nevertheless, tropical forests occupy about 780,000 square miles (2.02 million km^2), approximately one-third of the continent.

Tropical forests once covered a much larger area. Fires— some natural and some set by local people to clear land for farming—have destroyed part of the forest. When African forest is cleared, the climate becomes drier and grassland replaces the trees.

Lowland rain forest extends as a belt along the West African coast approximately from the mouth of the Senegal River, in Senegal, and then fills the Congo Basin. Throughout this region the climate is warm at all times of year and the

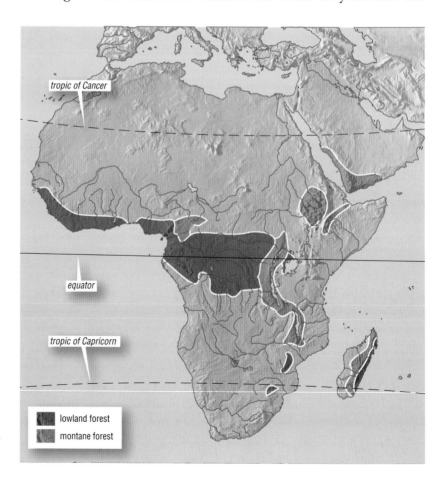

Lowland and montane forest in tropical Africa

annual rainfall exceeds about 60 inches (1,520 mm). The lowland forest ends in the mountains on the western side of the Great Lakes, but montane forest (see "Montane forest" on page 85) rises to about 4,000 feet (1,220 m). The map shows the area.

The African forest is less diverse than the tropical forests of South America and Asia, but it nevertheless supports a wide variety of plants and animals. The tallest trees in the lowland forest rise to about 200 feet (61 m) and include many that are important for their timber. Several species of *Khaya* yield African mahogany, and *Entandophragma* species yield sapele and utile. Obeche is the timber of *Triplochiton scleroxylon*. *Pericopsis elata* produces a timber called afrormosia and *Chlorophora excelsa* produces one called iroko. Both are widely used as substitutes for teak. Balsa is a South American wood, but the African forests produce a similarly light wood from the umbrella tree (*Musanga cecropioides*). The umbrella tree grows quickly in large forest clearings and its wood has many local uses, although it is not traded commercially. African forests also produce ebony, a hard black wood obtained from *Diospyros* species, especially *D. mespiliformis* (West African ebony, also called swamp ebony, Calabar ebony, and Lagos ebony) and *D. monbuttensis* (Yoruba ebony, also called walking stick ebony). *Diospyros* are medium-size trees that grow in the understory.

Many forest trees produce beautiful flowers, but the most gorgeous African tree is called flame of the forest or the flamboyant tree (*Delonix regia*), which produces scarlet flowers that completely cover its dome-shaped crown. The flame of the forest came originally from Madagascar, where in 1932 a missionary is believed to have discovered a single specimen that became the source of the many cultivated trees.

Above the rain forests, the montane forests include tree heaths (*Erica arborea* and several species of *Philippia*). There are also giant groundsels (*Senecio* species) and giant lobelias (*Lobelia* species), with thick, unbranched stems that make them resemble trees. Giant groundsels grow up to 20 feet (6 m) tall and giant lobelias can reach 27 feet (8 m).

Asian tropical forests

Tropical forest is the natural vegetation over about 864,000 square miles (2.2 million km^2) of Asia. It extends from Bhutan, Myanmar (Burma), and Bangladesh in the north, across parts of India, through Indochina and the Malay Peninsula, and across the islands of Indonesia and the Philippines. Lowland rain forest covers about 566,000 square miles (1.47 million km^2) of this total area, and about 774,000 square miles (2 million km^2) is closed broad-leaved forest—forest in which the crowns of the trees form a continuous canopy. The map shows the extent of the Asian forest.

The monsoon forests of India, Myanmar, Thailand, and Indochina gave the world teak (*Tectona grandis*), which is among the most valuable of all timbers. Nowadays teak is grown in plantations because centuries of exploitation have made it rare in all but the most inaccessible parts of the forest. Teak trees must have a dry season, so they will not grow in rain forests. Sal is the timber from *Shorea robusta*, a tree

Forests in tropical Asia and Queensland, Australia

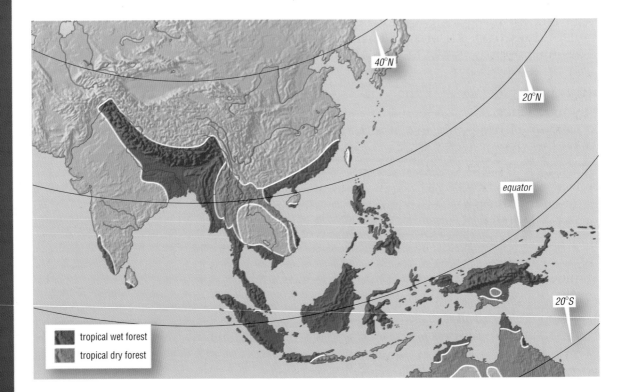

tropical wet forest
tropical dry forest

40°N
20°N
equator
20°S

used for general construction and second in importance after teak. Its bark yields a black dye and a resin that was formerly used in carbon paper and typewriter ribbons. Sal grows in the monsoon forests of India and Bangladesh.

Nowadays many of the most valuable rain forest trees of Asia belong to the genus *Shorea*. Some produce reddish timbers, such as red meranti, red seraya, and red lauan, which are used for light work and as veneers. Ramin, a lightweight wood used to make dowels and moldings, comes from *Gonystylus bancanus,* a tree that grows in the swamp forests of Malaya and Borneo. *Alstonia spatulata,* a tree from the rain forests of western Malaya, produces a wood that is even lighter than balsa (see "American tropical forests" on page 6), weighing only three to five pounds per cubic foot (47–77 kg/m^3).

The Asian forests yield many products in addition to timber. Bubblegum is made from chicle, a type of latex obtained from giant *Dyera costulata* trees that grow in Malaysia and Indonesia. Temporary dental fillings are made from gutta-percha, a rubbery latex from *Palaquium gutta,* a rain forest tree that grows throughout most of the region. Gutta-percha softens when heated, but then sets, becoming hard but not brittle. It was one of the first plastics and was formerly used to make electrical insulation and golf balls.

Most tropical forests contain no coniferous trees, but the Asian forests are the exception. The hoop pine or Moreton Bay pine (*Araucaria cunninghamii*) and klinki pine (*A. hunsteinii*), which grow in the forests of New Guinea, are closely related to the monkey puzzle tree, or Chile pine, of South America. East India copal or Manila copal is a resin used in some specialist paints and varnishes that is obtained from *Agathis dammara,* a coniferous tree related to *Araucaria* that grows in central Malaysia.

Asian forests also produce many fruits. Breadfruit (*Artocarpus altilis*), native to the Pacific Islands where it is a staple food in some places, is now widely cultivated. (The infamous mutiny on HMS *Bounty* in 1789 occurred while the ship was transporting breadfruit trees for cultivation in the West Indies.) The jackfruit (*A. scortechnii*), a relative of the breadfruit, is one of the world's largest fruits, some weighing 55 pounds (25 kg). Other Asian fruits include mangosteen (*Garcinia mangostana*), rambutan (*Nephelium lappaceum*), and durian (*Durio zibethinus*), native to Malaya. Durian smells strongly of sewage, but people who have acquired a taste for it consider it one of the world's most delicious fruits.

Tropical forests of New Guinea and Australia

Papua New Guinea comprises the eastern half of the island of New Guinea. The western half forms the Irian Jaya province of Indonesia. New Guinea is mountainous but, as the map shows, it is almost completely forested. Together, Irian Jaya and Papua New Guinea have an area of about 347,000 square miles (900,000 km^2), of which 267,000 square miles (692,000 km^2), or 77 percent, is forested.

Australia has a generally dry climate, except in the far north of the country, in Arnhem Land and the Cape York Peninsula, and down the eastern coast of Queensland, where the annual rainfall is 50 inches (1,270 mm) or more. For example, Darwin, Northern Territory, receives about 58 inches (1,476 mm), and Cairns, Queensland, receives about 85 inches (2,151 mm). The rainfall is highly seasonal, however, giving this part of Australia a monsoon climate (see "Monsoons" on page 63) with a wet summer and dry winter. Cairns receives only six inches (152 mm) of rain between the end of June and the beginning of October. Darwin receives only 0.6 inch (15 mm) during this period. The wet months are from November to April.

Despite its dry climate and poor soils, Australia's forests cover 20 percent of the total land area, occupying about 597,000 square miles (1.5 million km^2) in a country of about 3 million square miles (7.68 million km^2). Most of this is natural forest, but not all of it is tropical.

There are two areas in eastern Queensland where the forest is similar in composition to Malayan forest. Everywhere else the Australian forest is dominated by eucalyptus trees. There are about 450 species in the genus *Eucalyptus.* They dominate temperate as well as tropical forests and all of the trees form-

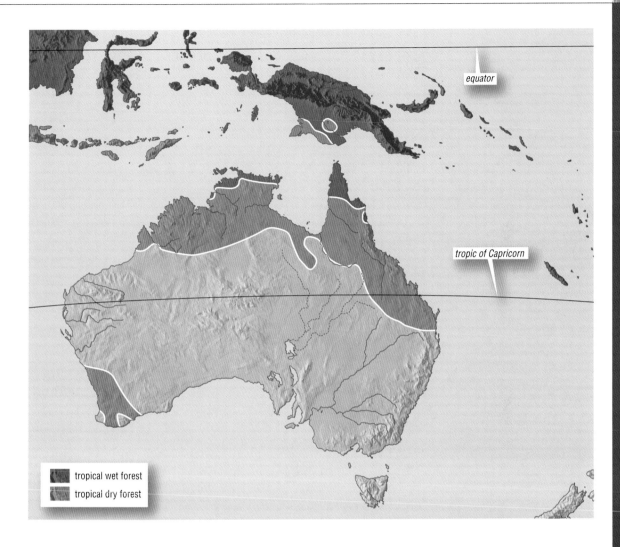

ing the forest canopy are usually eucalypts. The understory often contains acacias. About half of the approximately 1,200 species in the genus *Acacia* are native to Australia. Most acacias are evergreen trees and shrubs, often called wattles from their use by early settlers for building huts that were then plastered with mud ("daub and wattle"). They grow in the drier regions, where the tropical forest is more open and interspersed with grassland and cypress pines (*Callitris* species).

In Papua New Guinea the lowland rain forests extend to nearly 5,000 feet (1,500 m) up the sides of the mountains.

Forests of New Guinea and Australia

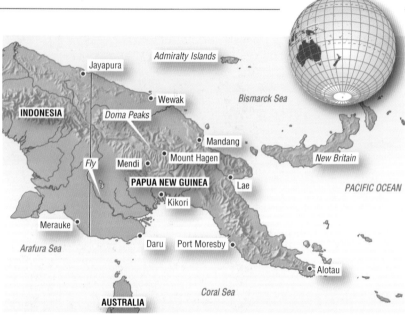

Papua New Guinea

The composition of the forest is very diverse. Botanists divide it into six regional types, each with its own characteristic trees. The Bismarck forest system, for example, includes kamerere trees (*Eucalyptus deglupta*), lancewood or malas (*Homalium foetidum*), New Guinea basewood (*Endospermum medullosum*), New Guinea walnut (*Dracocontomelum manniferum*), and many more.

At higher elevations the forest becomes more open and even more mixed. This montane forest includes stands of Moreton Bay or hoop pine (*Araucaria cunninghamii*) and klinki pine (*A. hunsteinii*). The tallest tree ever recorded growing in the tropics, measured in 1941, was a klinki pine 291.7 feet (88.9 m) tall. The Moreton Bay pine can reach 210–245 feet (64–75 m). These trees occur in the mossy upper montane rain forest, where they tower above the canopy, which is usually at about 100 feet (30 m).

Freshwater swamp forest occurs beside several rivers, often with terentang (*Campnosperma brevipetiolatum* and *C. auriculatum*). Sago palms (*Metroxylon sagu*) are also common. Mangrove forests grow along much of the coast and are especially extensive in the Gulf of Papua, near Madang and Lae, and in the estuary of the Sepik River, shown on the map.

Forests also grow on the wide, sandy beaches. These contain Burmese rosewood, also called Andaman redwood and amboyna wood (*Pterocarpus indicus*), used to make furniture; beefwood, also called bull oak and whistling pine (*Casuarina equisetifolia*); and Indian beech, also called karanja and thinwin (*Milletia pinnata*). There are also many palms growing beneath the taller trees. Bamboo scrub with tree ferns is widespread, mainly between 2,000 feet and 4,000 feet (600–1,200 m) on some steep mountainsides.

Where tropical forests grew long ago

All over the world, people use coal as a fuel. They are able to do so because coal is abundant and widely distributed. If people continue to use coal at the present rate, there is enough of it in North America to last for about 230 years. Europe has enough to last about 190 years, Russia for more than 500 years, and Asia and the Pacific region for about 145 years. That is a very large amount of coal. Antarctica also has huge reserves, although it is buried beneath the ice and it would be illegal to mine it.

The existence of so much coal reveals something interesting about the history of the world. Coal is made from plant material that failed to decompose (see the sidebar). It forms in swamps. Swamps occur in many parts of the world, and coal can form in them regardless of where they are, but swamps require a wet climate, and the wettest climates are found in the Tropics. Lowland tropical forests contain many areas of swamp forest and some of them are places where coal is forming today—although it will be many millions of years before it is ready to use.

Pennsylvania is one of the places where there are large deposits of coal. This means—and there can be no other explanation—that at one time parts of Pennsylvania were swampy and the climate was tropical. Britain, between latitudes 50°N and 60°N, also has large coal reserves. It, too, once enjoyed tropical weather.

Climates change over long periods. When Pennsylvania and Britain were accumulating the plant debris that would eventually become coal, they both had a tropical climate and

How coal forms

Leaves and dead branches that fall to the forest floor do not remain there for long. Scratch away the surface layer of plant material and you will find it is only a few inches deep. Beneath it there is soil, made from dead material that has decomposed.

Decomposition requires air, however. The beetles, insect larvae, fungi, bacteria, and other organisms that feed on dead plant matter need oxygen for respiration, and they obtain it from pockets of air trapped below ground. If the dead leaves, branches, and trees fall onto waterlogged ground and are then buried before they have time to decompose fully, the airless conditions may slow their decomposition and eventually halt it completely. Plant material will accumulate because it is being added faster than it decomposes. If the water rises to cover the deposit, mud will settle on top of it and the plant matter will be buried.

The weight of the overlying water and mud compresses the partly decomposed material, transforming it into *peat*. When dry, peat may be brown and fibrous or black and dense. It is used as a fuel in some parts of the world.

Over the years more mud settles over the top of the peat, increasing the pressure. The peat becomes drier as the water is squeezed out of it until it has become *lignite*, or *brown coal*. Further compression—making a layer of plant material originally 20 feet (6 m) thick into a layer about 1 foot (30 cm) thick—turns lignite into black, shiny *bituminous coal*, and compression beyond that turns it finally into *anthracite*. The qualities, or *ranks*, of different types of coal vary in the amount of energy released when they burn. Lignite, for example, yields about 1,820 kilocalories (1 kcal = 1,000 calories) for every pound burned (4,000 kcal/kg; 17 megajoules (MJ)/kg). Good-quality black coal yields about 3,860 kcal per pound (8,500 kcal/kg; 35 MJ/kg) and anthracite about 4,000 kcal per pound (9,000 kcal/kg; 38 MJ/kg).

Peat, lignite, bituminous coal, and anthracite are made from dead plant material. These are forming now, especially in parts of Asia, but most of the world's coal formed during the Carboniferous and Permian periods, more than 300 million years ago.

The necessary conditions for coal formation occur mainly in swamps that develop in shallow lakes and ponds. Consequently, coal is made predominantly from swamp plants.

were covered by tropical rain forest bounded by deserts to the north and south. An ice cap covered the South Pole, and by about 280 million years ago, glaciers and ice sheets covered much of the Southern Hemisphere, but the tropical weather continued in Pennsylvania and Britain.

These tropical forests were very different from those of today. None of the trees had flowers. Indeed, there were no flowers anywhere because flowering plants had not yet appeared. The forests were of huge tree ferns, lycopods related to present-day club mosses but growing up to 130 feet (40 m) tall, and horsetails up to 50 feet (15 m) tall.

Flowering plants became widespread during the Cretaceous period, 145 million–65 million years ago. During the early part of that period there were temperate forests in Antarctica and in northern Canada and Eurasia. Temperatures fell below freezing in winter, and there was snow, but the snow and ice melted in spring. Later in the Cretaceous period, the climate was warmer than it is today. There was no ice at either pole, and the climate was subtropical over much of the United States and Europe.

Climates change, but that is only part of the explanation. Continents also move (see "Continental drift and plate tectonics" on page 25) and when the raw material for coal formation was being laid down, the eastern United States and Canada, the southern tip of Greenland, and western Europe all lay close to the equator. The world had a warmer climate than it has now, but the reason some places had a tropical climate is that they were in the Tropics.

How old are the present-day tropical forests?

Forests have always grown in the Tropics, but the constant rearrangement of the continents (see "Continental drift and plate tectonics" on page 25) means that in the past, tropical forests grew in regions that no longer lie within the Tropics. Nor were those ancient forests much like present-day ones. The trees growing in them were not at all like modern trees.

The change that led to the development of today's forests occurred about 130 million years ago. That is when the first flowers appeared. Water lilies were the first plants to produce flowers, followed by buttercups and then by the first tree, a magnolia that closely resembled modern magnolias.

Flowering plants, or *angiosperms,* had a big advantage over the nonflowering plants around them. Until they appeared, all of the larger plants had to rely on the wind to carry their pollen from male to female individuals. For this to work, they had to produce vast quantities of pollen, almost all of which was wasted. In contrast, flowering plants produced special shoots, each of which had four whorls of modified leaves called *sepals, petals, stamens,* and *carpels.* The sepals are usually green and enclose and protect the other organs until they are ready to open. The stamens and carpels are respectively the male and female reproductive structures. Together they compose a flower.

Petals are often brightly colored, and many flowers are scented. Their coloring and perfume attract insects or other animals. When an animal visits the flower, it brushes against the stamens and pollen clings to its coat. At the next flower it visits, this pollen sticks to the carpel. This method of pollination is much more efficient than simply relying on the wind. Some flowering plants, such as grasses, are wind-pollinated and produce small, drab flowers. Scientists do not know how this condition came about. The wind-pollinated plants may never have developed flowers to attract animals, or they may be descended from plants that lost this feature.

Angiosperms possess other improvements over their predecessors. They are more efficient at transporting water and nutrients to their growing tips, and they produce seeds that are enclosed in a protective structure called the *ovary.* Nonflowering plants, such as conifers, produce seeds lacking this protection. These plants are called *gymnosperms,* from the Greek *gymnos,* "naked," and *sperma,* "seed." The prefix *angio-* is from *angion,* "container." Finally, many angiosperms enclosed their seeds in a fruit that animals found attractive and nutritious. The animals ate the fruit and either discarded the seeds or swallowed and later excreted them. In this way they dispersed the seeds more widely than would have been possible if the seeds had simply fallen to the ground.

Flowering plants were much better at reproducing themselves than any of the nonflowering plants. They spread rapidly, evolving into many different forms. Today there are about 260,000 species of angiosperms but only 721 species of gymnosperms.

During the time when the angiosperms were spreading to more and more parts of the world, the climate everywhere was warmer and wetter than it is today. The Tropics occupied the belt on either side of the equator, of course, but weather conditions like those of the Tropics extended much farther. Flowering plants came to dominate tropical forests that covered a very large area.

By 65 million years ago, most of the land that now lies in the Tropics had reached the Tropics, although India was still in the Southern Hemisphere and moving northward, toward southern Asia. Tropical forests covered all of the present-day Tropics. The climate was already starting to change, however. Very gradually, it was becoming cooler. Falling temperatures in high latitudes reduced the amount of water evaporating from the oceans. Consequently less cloud formed, and although the Tropics remained warm they became drier. The tropical forests were compressed into an increasingly narrow equatorial belt, and the rain forests survived only near the coasts and in hilly country—places where the rainfall remained high throughout the year. Deserts appeared in the subtropics, and between the rain forests and the deserts there was seasonal tropical forest composed of plants descended from rain forest ancestors.

Tropical rain forests, seasonal forests, and montane forests probably occupied their present regions by about 20 million years ago. This does not mean, however, that the tropical forests are 20 million years old. In the first place, forests are not static, remaining eternally unchanged. Plants die and different plants replace them, so the composition of the forest changes constantly. The forest may remain, but it is not necessarily the same type of forest. In the second place, the climate continued to change. The Tropics became still drier and the forests were driven into ever-smaller areas. The first of the ice ages had arrived.

Tropical forests during the ice ages

Soon after they first appeared, flowering plants spread through a warm world, when the difference between tropical and arctic temperatures was much smaller than it is today. As they established themselves, the plants changed, adapting evolutionarily to the climates in which they grew. Trees in middle and high latitudes became deciduous, shedding their leaves in the fall as a way of surviving the dry winters, while tropical trees remained evergreen. The world's forests were acquiring local characteristics that eventually made the tropical forests very different from temperate forests and made forests in one continent different from those in another.

The world's climate was slowly changing, however. The higher latitudes were growing cooler and the *temperature gradient*—the rate at which the temperature decreases between the equator and the poles—was becoming steeper. About 50 million years ago, ice sheets began to cover Antarctica. Antarctica is a large continent. Much of it is at a high elevation and therefore colder than the Arctic, most of which is covered by the ocean. Ice began appearing in the Arctic much later—about 3 million years ago.

Temperatures continued to fall and the polar ice sheets began to spread outward from the Arctic. The world had become a cold place, where from time to time the land as far south as the Great Lakes was buried beneath ice that was thousands of feet thick. The first of these *glaciations* or *ice ages* may have happened about 2.3 million years ago, although the evidence is sketchy.

Glaciations began and ended, separated by warmer intervals called *interglacials.* There have been four major glaciations in the last 800,000 years. Evidence for ice ages is gathered in different places and the dates do not coincide precisely, so what are probably the same events have different names in North America, Britain, and elsewhere. The last four glaciations are known in North America as the Nebraskan (800,000–600,000 years ago), Kansan (480,000–230,000 years ago), Illinoian (170,000–120,000 years ago), and Wisconsinian (75,000–10,000 years ago). Scientists have allocated names to the various periods in the Earth's history (see the sidebar "Geologic time scale" on page 33). All of these ice ages occurred during the Pleistocene epoch—the name means "most new," from the Greek *pleistos,* "most," and *kainos,* "new." The interglacial we live in today is the Holocene—meaning "entirely new," from *holos,* "entire" (see the sidebar).

Holocene, Pleistocene, and late Pliocene glacials and interglacials

Approximate date (1,000 years BP)	North America	Great Britain	Northwestern Europe
Holocene			
10–present	Holocene	Holocene (Flandrian)	Holocene (Flandrian)
Pleistocene			
75–10	Wisconsinian	Devensian	Weichselian
120–75	Sangamonian	Ipswichian	Eeemian
170–120	Illinoian	Wolstonian	Saalian
230–170	Yarmouthian	Hoxnian	Holsteinian
480–230	Kansan	Anglian	Elsterian
600–480	Aftonian	Cromerian	Cromerian complex
800–600	Nebraskan	Beestonian	Bavel complex
740–800		Pastonian	
900–800		Pre-Pastonian	Menapian
1,000–900		Bramertonian	Waalian
1,800–1,000		Baventian	Eburonian
Pliocene			
1,800		Antian	Tiglian
1,900		Thurnian	
2,000		Ludhamian	
2,300		Pre-Ludhamian	Pretiglian

BP means "before present" (present is taken to be 1950). Names in italic refer to interglacials. Other names refer to glacials (ice ages). Dates become increasingly uncertain for the older glacials and interglacials and the period before about 2 million years ago. Evidence for these episodes has not been found in North America; in the case of the Thurnian glacial and Ludhamian interglacial the only evidence is from a borehole at Ludham, in eastern England.

During the ice ages, the climate everywhere became drier. The ice never reached the Tropics and temperatures there remained tolerable for trees, but the rainfall decreased dramatically. Low temperatures in higher latitudes meant that less water evaporated from the Earth's oceans, so globally fewer clouds formed and less rain and snow fell. Less rain and snow meant that the ground was drier, so there was less water to evaporate from the ground surface. It was not only the continents that were covered by ice; so was a large area of the sea. It froze, reducing the area of exposed water surface and therefore reducing evaporation further.

Tropical trees cannot tolerate prolonged drought, and when the ice sheets advanced, the tropical forests retreated. Grasslands took their place, similar to the savanna grasslands of modern Africa. When the ice retreated and the interglacial climate brought more rain, the forests expanded once more, but they had to do so through the spread of their seeds from the areas where they had survived the ice age. Not all of the forest plants were able to achieve this, and each cycle of glaciation and interglacial saw some extinctions.

The coldest part of the most recent (Wisconsinian) ice age—known as the *last glacial maximum*—occurred about 20,000 years ago. Most scientists believe that during the last glacial maximum the tropical forests were confined to isolated areas, called *refugia,* where conditions were more tolerable. There were two large refugia in Africa, for example, one in what are now Cameroon and Gabon, and the other in the eastern part of the Democratic Republic of Congo, as well as smaller refugia in West Africa. Southeastern Asia appears to have been affected less severely. Its climate remained wet and the tropical forests survived intact over large areas. The forests began to expand once more from about 12,000 years ago, as the ice age approached its end and temperatures and rainfall increased.

There may be places where the forest is millions of years old, but most of the present tropical forest dates from the end of the last ice age and parts of it are only a few centuries old. A large part of the Amazon Basin was being farmed until the 17th century (see "Peoples of the American tropical forests" on pages 192–206). Parts of the Congo Basin and Asian forests were also cultivated at some time in the fairly recent past. Where the original tropical forest survives it is several thousand years older than the remaining undisturbed temperate forests. It also encloses the much older refugia from where the present plants spread.

CHAPTER 2

GEOLOGY OF
TROPICAL FORESTS

Continental drift and plate tectonics

Many of the most valuable tropical timbers come from trees
belonging to the family Dipterocarpaceae—the dipterocarps.
Some are small, but others, including trees belonging to the
genera *Dipterocarpus* and *Shorea,* are giants, commonly with
straight, cylindrical trunks up to 98 feet (30 m) long and 13
feet (4 m) in diameter. As well as timber, they produce resins
that are used to make varnishes.

As the map shows, the dipterocarps occur mainly in tropical Asia, where there are extensive forests composed almost

*Global distribution of
dipterocarp trees*

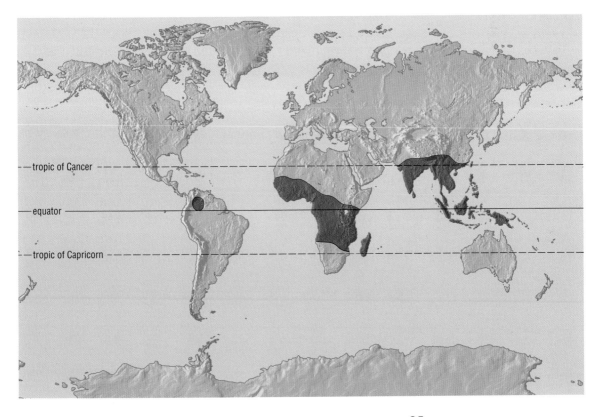

entirely of just one or two dipterocarp species. Other dipterocarps occur in Africa, where there are also fossils of dipterocarp trees that no longer grow there, and there is one species
that grows in the mountains of South America.

If all of these related trees arose in a particular region and
then diversified into the 16 genera and 530 species that exist
today, how did they cross the Indian Ocean between Africa
and Asia? How did they reach South America? These are tropical species that cannot survive without constantly warm
temperatures and rain that falls throughout the year. They
could not cross the Himalayas and then the Syrian, Arabian,
and Sahara Deserts in order to migrate overland between
Africa and Asia, and their seeds could not possibly be carried
so far—and far less could they cross the vast ocean to reach
South America.

The dipterocarps are not alone in having this peculiar distribution. Many other plant families, temperate as well as
tropical, pose the same question—not to mention rocks.
Plant seeds can travel and plants do migrate, but rocks do not
move around. How can it be, then, that rocks in the
Highlands of Scotland closely resemble rocks in eastern
Canada? Why are the rocks along the west coast of Africa so
similar to rocks on the east coast of South America that it
looks as though they were broken and then pulled apart?

These questions puzzled scientists for a long time, and the
more they discovered about the world the more the questions multiplied. There are even more fossil plants and animals distributed in this way than there are living species, and
the rocks containing the fossils share this *disjunct* distribution. Coal forms mainly in tropical swamps (see the sidebar
"How coal forms" on page 18), but it is found all over the
world. Parts of Devon, in the south of England, have sand-
stone rocks that can form only in a hot, dry desert.

There were many attempts to solve the riddle, some of
them based on the idea that the Moon was made from rocks
torn away from the Earth. According to this explanation, this
violent event might have left a deep depression that filled
with water to form the Pacific Ocean and the continents on
either side of the Pacific might have moved toward each
other to close the gap. The resulting stresses might then have

torn apart other continents, opening the Atlantic Ocean and explaining the fit between Africa and South America.

In 1912 the German meteorologist Alfred Wegener (see the sidebar) proposed the most thorough explanation for all

Alfred Lothar Wegener and continental drift

Since the first realistic maps of the world were published in the 16th century, many geographers had puzzled over the fact that the continents on each side of the Atlantic Ocean looked as though they might fit together. Some thought it mere coincidence, but others suggested ways a single continent might have split into two parts that then moved apart.

The German meteorologist Alfred Lothar Wegener (1880–1930) went much further. Wegener compiled a mass of evidence to support what he called "continental displacement." This phenomenon came to be called *continental drift.* He studied the scientific literature for descriptions of rocks that were similar on each side of the Atlantic. He found plants with limited distribution that are separated by vast oceans and fossil organisms that are also distributed in this way.

Finally he proposed that about 280 million years ago, during the Upper Paleozoic subera, all the continents were joined, forming a single "supercontinent," which he called *Pangaea* (from the Greek *pan,* meaning all, and *ge,* meaning Earth), surrounded by an ocean called *Panthalassa* (*thalassa* means ocean). He theorized that Pangaea broke apart and the separate pieces drifted to their present locations; the continents are still drifting.

In 1912 Wegener published a short book outlining his theory, *Die Entstehung der Kontinente und Ozeane* (The Origin of the continents and oceans). He was drafted into the German army in 1914 at the start of World War I but was wounded almost at once. He developed his ideas further while recovering in a hospital, and in 1915 he published a much longer edition of his book (it was not translated into English until 1924).

His idea found little support. Geologists at the time believed the *mantle*—the material beneath the Earth's crust—to be solid, and they could not imagine any way that continents could move. They also found that some of Wegener's calculations of the rate of continental displacement were incorrect.

But support for Wegener's idea began to grow in the 1940s, when for the first time scientists were able to study the rocks on the ocean floor. These studies indicated that the oceans had grown wider by spreading outward from central ridges, where underwater volcanoes were erupting, laying down new rock. Wegener's theory was generally accepted by the late 1960s, but by then Alfred Wegener was dead. He had died in 1930 during his third expedition to study the climate over the Greenland ice sheet.

these observations. He suggested that the continents move over the Earth and at one time they were all joined together as a single "supercontinent" that he called Pangaea, from the Greek *pan,* "all," and *ge,* "Earth." This idea came to be known as the theory of *continental drift.*

According to Wegener, the continents have always moved and they are doing so today. It was not until long after Wegener's death, however, that his idea came to be accepted. Geologists could think of no way for continents to move because they believed that the rocks beneath the surface, in the Earth's *mantle,* were solid. Then it was discovered that the rocks of the mantle are so hot and are held under such tremendous pressure that they behave like a very thick liq-

Continental drift. The three maps show the approximate positions of the continents 135 million years ago and 65 million years ago and their positions today.

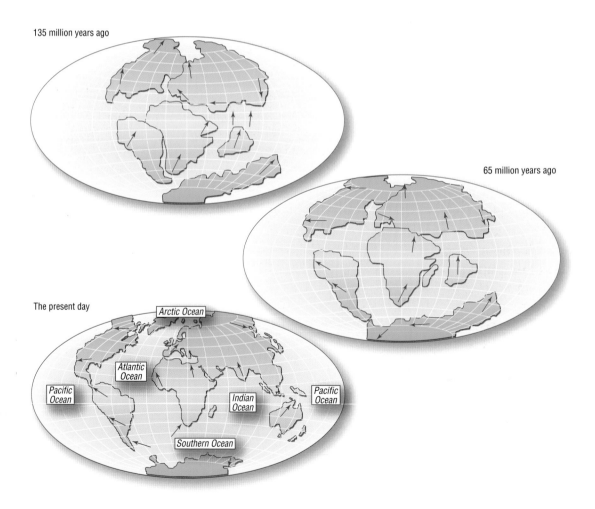

135 million years ago

65 million years ago

The present day

Arctic Ocean

Atlantic Ocean

Pacific Ocean

Indian Ocean

Pacific Ocean

Southern Ocean

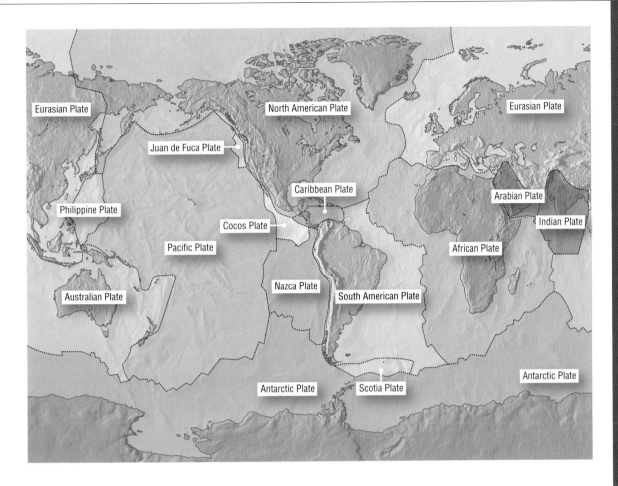

The major plates into which the Earth's crust is divided

uid. The rocks above them are cold and solid, forming a crust that is broken into pieces called *plates*. Currents flowing through the mantle drag these plates this way and that. As plates move apart, mantle material rises to the surface along a rift between them and solidifies. Where plates collide, one plate may slide beneath the other, returning to the mantle, and where continents collide the rocks crumple to form mountains. In other places, plates slide past each other. That is how continents drift, often turning around as they do so. The first of the three maps shows the world as it appeared about 135 million years ago, at about the time the first flowering plants appeared. The middle map shows the world 65 million years ago, when the North Atlantic Ocean was just starting to open, South and North America were not joined, and India had reached the equator. The third map shows the world as it is today. Millions of years from now, North America will collide with Asia, Britain will cross the Arctic Circle, and Australia will reach the equator.

The theory of continental drift has now become the theory of plate tectonics. A tectonic process is one related to the deformation of the crust or to structures produced by such deformation. There are seven major plates: the African, Eurasian, Pacific, North American, South American, Antarctic, and Australian plates. There are also several lesser plates: the Cocos, Caribbean, Nazca, Arabian, Indian, Philippine, and Scotia plates. In addition, there are minor plates, such as the Juan de Fuca plate, microplates, and fragments of former plates that have broken apart. The map shows the present location of the major and lesser plates.

How mountains rise and wear away

Forests that grow high on the sides of tropical mountains— montane forests—are quite different in character from the forests of the lowlands. One day, though, many millions of years from now—provided that the tropical forests survive— lowland forests will replace those montane forests. This will happen because eventually the mountains will disappear. Huge, imposing, and solid as they are, no mountain or mountain range lives forever. Mountains rise and then they wear away.

Mountain ranges form when two of the Earth's crustal plates collide. A section of continental crust may collide with a plate carrying an ocean basin, or one continent may slam into another. Continents are made from rock that is bulkier and less dense than the rock of the ocean floor. As a result, the crust is thicker beneath continents than it is beneath oceans. When a continental plate and oceanic plate collide, the denser oceanic crust slides beneath the continental crust. The technical term for this process is *subduction.*

As the oceanic crust moves beneath the continental crust, hot rock from the mantle rises to produce volcanoes that add rock to the continental crust. At the same time, the advancing continental crust scrapes sedimentary rock from the sur-

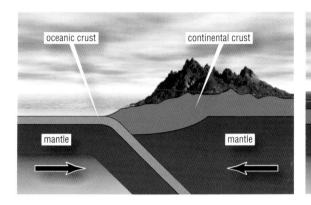
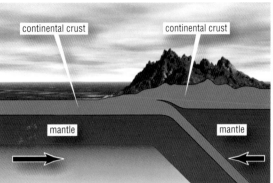

face of the oceanic crust. This material—a mixture of ocean sediment, continental crust, and newly added volcanic rock—is crumpled upward to form high mountains. The first part of the diagram illustrates what happens.

This is how the Andes of South America formed. The Nazca plate is moving eastward and beneath the South American plate, which is moving westward. The collision probably began about 50 million years ago, and it has accelerated over the past 10 million years. The two plates are still moving toward each other, and the Andes Mountains are still growing higher.

It was also around 50 million years ago that India, traveling northward on the Indian plate, crashed into the southern edge of the Eurasian plate. When continents collide, it is impossible for one plate to be subducted beneath the other because both plates are equally buoyant. Instead, the two sections of continental crust crumple upward, usually with one plate riding over the other. This produces very high mountain ranges. The collision between India and Eurasia raised the Himalaya Mountains, and the collision has not ended. India is still moving northward at a rate of 1.5–2 inches (4–5 cm) a year, and crumpling has shortened the Indian plate by about 600 miles (1,000 km). As a result, the Himalayas, like the Andes, are still growing higher.

Several strands of evidence convince geologists that this is the way mountain ranges form, but the most persuasive clues come from the fossils found in the mountain rocks. Louis Agassiz (1807–73), the Swiss-American scientist who proved that glaciers had once covered much of Europe and North

Mountain building. Left: Where continental and oceanic crust collide, oceanic crust is subducted into the mantle and lighter continental crust is crumpled to form mountains. Right: Where continents collide, one section of continental crust sinks beneath the other and crustal rocks from both continents are crumpled upward.

Forests cover the valleys and lower slopes, but tropical South America is mountainous. The granite mountains of the Serra dos Orgãos, not far from Rio de Janeiro, Brazil, rise above the Atlantic Forest.
(Courtesy of Frans Lanting/Minden Pictures)

America, began his career by studying fossils of fish that he found in the rocks of his native Switzerland, high in the Alps. There are likewise fossilized seashells high up in the Himalayan rocks, and some of the rocks of the Andes once lay on the ocean floor or near the coast.

Once rocks have been raised up to form mountain ranges, they are exposed to the wind and rain, to freezing temperatures in winter, and to the blazing sunshine of summer. Water seeps into cracks, then freezes, expanding as it does so and widening the crack until fragments of rock break free. Rain carries some of these fragments away, rolling them down the mountainside, where they knock particles from other rocks and lose particles themselves. The wind hurls some of these particles against rocks, smashing them into ever smaller pieces and wearing away the exposed rock faces. Rainwater is slightly acid, and the acid slowly eats into the rocks, releasing soluble compounds and leaving the rocks scarred and weakened.

Geologic time scale

Eon/ Eonothem	Era/ Erathem	Sub-era	Period System	Epoch/ Series	Began Ma*
Phanerozic	Cenozoic	*Quaternary*	Pleistogene	Holocene	0.11
				Pleistocene	1.81
		Tertiary	Neogene	Pliocene	5.3
				Miocene	23.03
			Paleogene	Oligocene	33.9
				Eocene	55.8
				Paleocene	65.5
	Mesozoic		Cretaceous	Upper	99.6
				Lower	145.5
			Jurassic	Upper	161.2
				Middle	175.6
				Lower	199.6
			Triassic	Upper	228
				Middle	245
				Lower	251
	Paleozoic	Upper	Permian	Lopingian	260.4
				Guadalupian	270.6
				Cisuralian	299
			Carboniferous	Pennsylvanian	318.1
				Mississippian	359.2
			Devonian	Upper	385.3
				Middle	397.5
				Lower	416
		Lower	Silurian	Pridoli	422.9
				Ludlow	443.7
				Wenlock	428.2
				Llandovery	443.7
			Ordovician	Upper	460.9
				Middle	471.8
				Lower	488.3
			Cambrian	Furongian	501
				Middle	513
				Lower	542
Proterozoic	Neoproterozoic		Ediacaran		600
			Cryogenian		850
			Tonian		1000
	Mesoproterozoic	Stenian			1200
			Ectasian		1400

(continues)

(continued)

Eon/ Eonothem	Era/ Erathem	Sub-era	Period System	Epoch/ Series	Began Ma*
			Calymmian		1600
	Paleoproterozoic	Statherian			1800
			Orosirian		2050
			Rhyacian		2300
			Siderian		2500
Archean	Neoarchean				2800
	Mesoarchean				3200
	Paleoarchean				3600
	Eoarchean				3800
Hadean	Swazian				3900
	Basin Groups				4000
	Cryptic				4567.17

Source: International Union of Geological Sciences, 2004.

Note: *Hadean* is an informal name. The Hadean, Archean, and Proterozoic eons cover the time formerly known as the Precambrian. *Quaternary* is now an informal name, and *Tertiary* is likely to become informal in the future, although both continue to be widely used.

*Ma means millions of years ago.

This *erosion* of the rocks is called *weathering,* and in time they are worn away completely. Jagged mountains gradually become more rounded and lower until they are gentle hills, cloaked with vegetation. The rock from which the mountains were made is ground into tiny particles and carried away. Some of the rock grains settle on land and become soil. Rivers transport most of the rock back to the ocean, where it settles on the seabed, eventually to become sedimentary rock that one day may be lifted high into the air once more by a new collision between plates.

It takes a long time, of course, but the Earth is ancient and what may seem a long time is no more than a brief interlude in its long history. Geologists divide the Earth's history into distinct episodes called *eons*. Eons are divided into *eras,* and eras into *sub-eras, periods,* and *epochs*. We are now living in the Holocene epoch of the Pleistogene period, of the Quaternary sub-era, of the Cenozoic era, of the Phanerozoic eon. The table sets out the complete geologic time scale from the formation of the Earth to the present day.

Tropical soils

When European explorers saw tropical rain forests for the first time, their senses must have been almost overwhelmed by the richness of the plant life. Although they were familiar with the forests of home, when they reached tropical America, Africa, and Asia, they saw forests with a far greater variety of trees, trees that were taller than European trees, and everywhere there were climbing plants and epiphytes. To their eyes, the tropical forests were like vast, luxuriant, and highly productive versions of European forests.

Before long, conquerors followed the explorers, and once they had secured territories in the names of their own nations, colonists began to arrive. The colonists planned to live permanently in the new territories and to do that they needed to secure their food supply. They set about clearing the land in order to grow crops and raise livestock, and they did so in the confident anticipation of high yields.

It was a perfectly reasonable outcome to expect. Temperate forests grow on fertile soils. The best farmland in Europe was created from forest soils. When the trees and undergrowth are cleared and the land is plowed, the soil will yield abundant harvests. The colonists supposed that the tropical forests, being much more luxuriant, were sustained by soils that were even more fertile than those of Europe. Such luxuriant growth implied warm temperatures throughout the year, high rainfall, and fertile soils. There was no doubt about the warm temperatures and high rainfall—they could feel those for themselves—and there was no obvious reason to doubt the fertility of the soil.

The farmers cleared the forest, sowed their crops, and watched the vigorous, rapid growth. A few months later they gathered bumper harvests. After a year or two, however, crop yields began to fall. There was no obvious reason for the decline, but it continued year after year until the farmers found themselves unable to grow any crops at all unless they applied vast amounts of animal manure and composted crop wastes as fertilizers and soil conditioners. Surrounded by forest that was as lush as ever, the farmed land was turning into something close to desert.

What the farmers had failed to appreciate is that a tropical forest is very different from a temperate forest, and the difference is due to the climate. The warm temperatures and high rainfall that make the plants grow fast also provide ideal conditions for insects, fungi, bacteria, and all the animals that feed on them. There were clues that the settlers might have spotted. In a temperate forest there is a fairly deep layer of leaves, twigs, and other plant material covering the ground. In the tropical forest this layer is much thinner. The farmers might have noticed that the trees they felled had roots that were much shallower than those of temperate trees and that often spread sideways as a dense mat growing just below the ground surface. Farmers might also have noticed that when their animals defecated, the dung did not lie on the ground for days the way it does in temperate regions. Within minutes it was covered in insects and it vanished within hours. Indeed, any dead plant or animal material that fell to the ground began to decay at once.

The settlers could hardly avoid noticing the butterflies that alighted on their faces and the sweat bees (bees belonging to the family Halictidae, which are attracted to perspiration) that could cover any exposed skin. They must have seen the columns of army ants that devoured any animal in their path. The colonists soon realized that the luscious beauty of the forest was closely linked to decay, but they failed to appreciate what this meant.

In a temperate forest, the decomposed remains of plant and animal wastes become incorporated into the soil. The fertility of a temperate soil is maintained by this constant replenishment. Decomposition is too rapid for this in the Tropics. The nutrients released by decomposition are absorbed at once into the roots of plants. That is why the trees have shallow roots: They are obtaining their nutrients from just below the surface. This also means that little of the nutrients enters the soil; many tropical soils are basically infertile.

Approximately two-thirds of all the plant nutrients in a temperate forest reside in the soil and one-third in the plants themselves. In a tropical forest about half of the nutrients reside in the soil and half in the vegetation. The difference sounds small, but it is highly significant. The abundant harvests that the settlers enjoyed in the early years used up the nutrients stored in the soil. When they cleared the forest to make space for their fields, the farmers removed the large store of nutrients held in the vegetation. They removed more of the nutrient store with each harvest. Thus it is hardly surprising that their crop yields began to decline after a few years. The adjacent forest continued to flourish because the

Laterite

Tropical soils are often red or yellow, as a result of the presence of oxides and hydroxides, chiefly of iron and aluminum. These compounds sometimes form hard lumps or continuous layers of a rock called *laterite.* The name is from *later,* the Latin word for "brick."

Most laterite is porous and claylike in texture. The surface is dark brown or red, but if the laterite is broken, the interior is a lighter red, yellow, or brown. Laterite is fairly soft while it remains in the soil, but it hardens when it is exposed to air. It has been mined as a source of iron and nickel. Bauxite, the most important aluminum ore, is very similar to laterite. In some lateritic soils aluminum combines with silica to form the mineral kaolinite, also known as China clay, which is used in the manufacture of fine porcelain and as a whitening agent or filler in paper, paints, medicines, and many other products.

Laterite forms in well-drained soils under humid tropical conditions. The high temperature and abundant moisture accelerate the chemical reactions that break down rock—the process called *chemical weathering*—and many of the dissolved products of those reactions drain out of the soil and are lost. The remaining compounds are concentrated because of the removal of others. In a strongly lateritic soil, iron oxides and hydroxides may account for nearly half of the weight of soil and aluminum oxides and hydroxide for about 30 percent. There may be less than 10 percent silica—the most common mineral in many soils.

Lateritic soils are found in India, Malaysia, Indonesia, China, Australia, Cuba, and Hawaii and in equatorial Africa and South America. There are similar soils in the United States, but these are not true laterites.

nutrients stored in the vegetation were rapidly recycled whenever dead plant and animal material fell to the ground.

Tropical soils are often red due to their high concentration of iron oxide—rust. Before long, the iron, together with aluminum, was forming *laterite* (see the sidebar) and the soil in many places was becoming as hard as concrete.

How soils age

Tropical soils are the oldest of all soils, and most of their original stock of nutrients has long gone, leaving them greatly depleted. They are ancient, and that is why they are less fertile than temperate soils.

The nutrients that sustain plants originate in the mineral particles from which all soils are made, but as soils grow older, little by little they lose their nutrients. Tropical soils are often deep, so that the underlying rock lies much farther below the surface than it would in a temperate soil. Their depth makes the soils easy to till, but it is a sign of their age and does not mean they are fertile. Many tropical soils are very acidic, contain few mineral nutrients, and lose organic matter very readily. Some plants prefer an acid soil but many do not, and the more acidic the soil becomes, the fewer plant species it will sustain. Crop plants such as corn, wheat, fruits, and vegetables fail if the soil becomes very acid.

Soil begins to form when the action of the weather makes cracks in the surface of solid rock and breaks off tiny fragments that accumulate in the cracks. Rainwater dissolves chemical compounds from the rock, and plants are able to anchor themselves among the particles and obtain nourishment from the dissolved compounds. When the plants die, their remains attract fungi and bacteria, and together these supply organic matter that mixes with the mineral particles. A soil at this stage in its development is only an inch or two deep. It is a young soil.

As more plants establish themselves and the weathering of the rock continues, the layer of soil gradually becomes deeper, and as it does so it begins to acquire a definite structure. Digging vertically through it exposes a section, called a *soil*

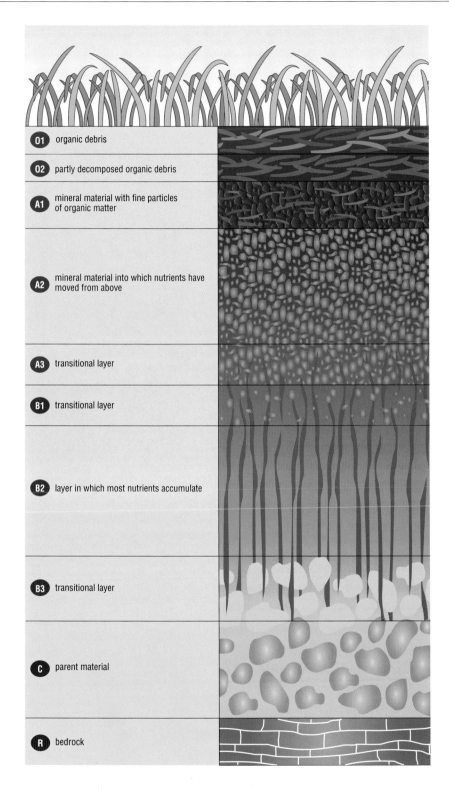

Profile of a fertile soil showing the horizons

profile, with distinct layers, called *horizons.* Soil scientists label these horizons "O," "A," "B," "C," and "R," recording several subdivisions of each. The illustration shows the principal horizons, giving a summary of what each horizon contains. The *parent material* comprises partly weathered rock fragments derived from the bedrock below.

Dissolved compounds, including plant nutrients, are moving constantly through the soil. They drain downward from the O and A horizons into the B horizon, where they accumulate. They also move upward from the C into the B horizon and from there into the A horizon. Compounds also leave the soil altogether, carried away by the rainwater, eventually into rivers and from there to lakes and the sea. This movement of nutrients is called *leaching.*

Over many years the leaching of nutrients alters the character of the soil, causing the soil to age. The soil in the drawing is an ideal soil, typical of a valuable farm soil that originally developed beneath a temperate forest. It is a mature soil. Soil will not develop in this way unless the climate favors plant growth. Desert soils fail to accumulate organic matter and consequently they never develop clearly defined horizons. Soils of the subarctic and arctic develop very slowly because the growing season is so short. They remain young for much longer than temperate soils.

As aging continues, leaching removes most of the nutrients from the A horizon, so the contrast between the A and B horizons becomes extreme. The soil is then old. It supports only a few species of plants—the aggressive ones that are able to seize such nutrients as the soil provides.

Weathering continues to release nutrients in the C horizon. These are drawn upward, eventually to the A horizon, and then they, too, are leached away. Eventually the C horizon is fully weathered, the A horizon is very thin, and the soil consists almost entirely of a B horizon, but one from which soluble nutrients have been lost. The soil is then classed as "senile."

The soil no longer supplies enough nutrients to sustain the large demand of the aggressive plants, and they fail and disappear. Plants with more modest needs begin to flourish and the vegetation becomes much more diverse. It consists, though, mainly of shallow-rooting species that absorb nutrients from decomposed organic matter at the surface. This is the final stage in soil development, and it is the stage at which many tropical soils have arrived.

How soils are classified

Farmers have always known that soils vary. There are good soils and poor soils, heavy soils containing a large proportion of clay, sandy soils that dry out rapidly, and light, loamy soils that retain moisture and nutrients. Loam is a mixture of sand, silt, and clay—mineral particles of different sizes. In the latter part of the 19th century Russian scientists were the first to attempt to classify soils. They thought that the differences between soils were due to the nature of the parent material—the underlying rock—and the climate. They divided soils into three broad classes. *Zonal* soils were typical of the climate in which they occur, *intrazonal* soils were less dependent on climate for their characteristics, and *azonal* soils were not the result of climate. Azonal soils include windblown soils and those made from silt deposited by rivers on their floodplains. Individual soil types were placed in one or other of these broad groups. This system remained in use until the 1950s, and some of the Russian names for soils are still widely used, such as Chernozem, Rendzina, Solonchak, and Podzol.

American soil scientists were also working on the problem, and by the 1940s their work was more advanced than that of their Russian colleagues. By 1975 scientists at the United States Department of Agriculture had devised a classification they called "Soil Taxonomy." It divides soils into 10 main groups, called orders. The orders are divided into 47 suborders, and the suborders are divided into groups, subgroups, families, and soil series, with six "phases" in each series. The classification is based on the physical and chemical properties of the various levels, or *horizons,* that make up a vertical cross section, or *profile,* through a soil. These were called "diagnostic horizons."

National classifications are often very effective in describing the soils within their boundaries, but there was a need for an international classification. In 1961 representatives from the Food and Agriculture Organization (FAO) of the United Nations, the United Nations Educational, Scientific and Cultural Organization (UNESCO), and the International Society of Soil Science (ISS) met to discuss preparing one. The project was completed in 1974 and is known as the FAO-UNESCO Classification. Like the Soil Taxonomy, it was based on diagnostic horizons. It divided soils into 26 major groups, subdivided into 106 soil units. The classification was updated in 1988 and has been amended several times since. It now comprises 30 reference soil groups and 170 possible subunits. The FAO has also produced a World Reference Base (WRB), which allows scientists to interpret the national classification schemes.

Obviously, soils vary widely. As any farmer will tell you, the soil in one part of a field can be quite different from the soil in another part of the same field. Nevertheless, soil scientists, called *pedologists,* have devised systems for classifying soils. The sidebar outlines the history of soil classification.

Movement of water through tropical soils

Rainfall at the equator is frequent and usually heavy, but that is not how it feels on the forest floor. Down there the air is so humid it is difficult to keep anything dry, but the rain does not beat down because the canopy of leaves acts like an umbrella. The rain falls onto the leaves and drips from them onto the leaves lower down. Some of the rain trickles down tree trunks and creepers and eventually drips onto the ground. During its descent, enough of the water evaporates to keep the air permanently moist.

Water that reaches the ground gently is able to drain away by soaking vertically downward into the soil. Heavy rain drains differently, pounding the surface so hard that it breaks up small lumps of soil into tiny particles. These are the particles that make the water brown when storms turn an ordinarily placid river into a raging torrent. Just below the soil surface, the particles settle out of the water and fill up all the spaces between soil lumps, forming a layer the water cannot penetrate. Instead of draining vertically, the rainwater then fills natural hollows and flows across the surface, washing some of the surface soil into the nearest river. This is a major cause of soil erosion on hillsides that have been cleared of trees (see "Threats to tropical forests" on page 214).

While the plants shelter the ground, water drains downward. The sidebar explains what it is that makes a soil porous, and why a porous soil is not necessarily permeable. Water passes through the soil until it meets a layer of hard-packed clay or rock that it cannot penetrate. Unable to descend further, the water accumulates above this impermeable layer, filling all the tiny spaces between soil particles until the soil is completely sodden. If you were to dig a hole down into this soil, the bottom of the hole would fill with water—you would have dug a well. Such water, lying underground but

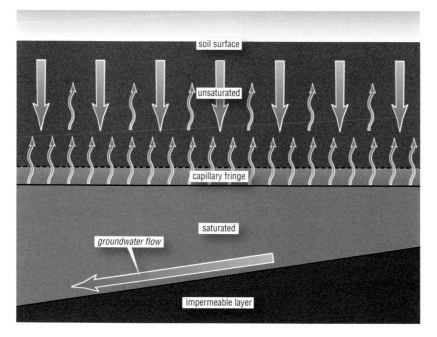

soil surface

unsaturated

capillary fringe

saturated

groundwater flow

impermeable layer

Movement of water through the soil. Water sinks downward from the surface through the upper layer of unsaturated soil. Water in the saturated layer flows downslope over the underlying impermeable rock or clay. At the upper surface of the saturated layer, water moves upward by capillarity through a capillary fringe.

unable to descend below a certain level, is called *groundwater,* and it continues to flow downhill, but very slowly because it is moving through the soil. The diagram shows the groundwater in the saturated layer. The arrows indicate the direction in which the water is moving.

The upper margin of the saturated layer is known as the *water table.* This is not a smooth, level surface, like the surface of a pond, because it is located in the soil itself, and between the saturated and unsaturated layers there is a *capillary fringe,* in which water is moving in both directions.

Water rises through the capillary fringe and is then drawn upward through the unsaturated layer due to *capillary attraction,* also called *capillarity.* Capillarity occurs because water molecules are attracted to one another and also to the molecules at solid surfaces. Their mutual attraction pulls water molecules into the spherical shape that allows them to be as close together as possible. It is why a drop of water is spherical and why, when water is held in a narrow tube, its surface bulges upward.

As the first diagram (1) shows, the attraction between water molecules and molecules in the sides of the tube makes

Porosity and permeability

When soil particles pack together, their irregular shapes mean there are small spaces between them. These spaces are called *soil pores,* and the total percentage of the space they occupy—the *pore space*—in a given volume of soil is known as the *porosity* of that soil.

The size and shape of soil particles determines the size of the soil pores, but without necessarily affecting the total amount of pore space. Sand grains are relatively large and usually very angular in shape. They do not fit together neatly, and consequently sand and sandy soils have large pores. Clay, on the other hand, consists of microscopically small, flat-sided particles that lie in sheets, stacked one on top of another with extremely small pores between them. But the difference in size of the particles means that the total pore space may be similar for both soils. In that case, both soils are equally porous.

They are not equally water permeable, however. *Permeability* is a measure of the speed with which water or air is able to move through a soil. Air does not stick to soil particles, so the air-permeability of a soil depends only on the total pore space. Water does stick to soil particles, however, coating each particle with a film approximately one molecule thick that is tightly bound to the surface. If the soil pores are very small the water adhering to particles may reduce their size even more, slowing the movement of water through the soil and therefore reducing the permeability of the soil.

Permeability is classified by the rate at which water moves through the soil. The usual classification is given in the following table.

Class	Rate of movement	
	(inches per hour)	(millimeters per hour)
Slow:		
Very slow	less than 0.05	less than 1.25
Slow	0.05–0.20	1.25–5.08
Moderate:		
Moderately slow	0.20–0.80	5.08–20.32
Moderate	0.80–2.50	20.32–63.50
Moderately rapid	2.50–5.00	63.50–127.00
Rapid:		
Rapid	5.00–10.00	127.00–254.00
Very rapid	more than 10.00	more than 254.00

water climb the tube, and the attraction between water molecules drags more water behind it. This alters the shape of the surface, and the water molecules immediately rearrange

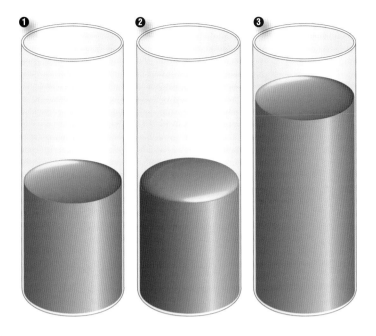

Capillarity. Water is shown held in a narrow tube. 1. Attraction between water molecules and molecules in the tube makes water climb the sides of the tube. 2. The center rises to restore the most economical shape. 3. Water now rises farther up the sides.

themselves to restore the bulge (2), which is as close to spherical as the tube allows. The center of the water has now risen, and so the water at the sides climbs a little higher up the tube (3). Water will continue to rise in this way until the weight of the column of water is equal to the attractive force pulling it upward.

Capillarity occurs only in very narrow tubes because the weight of the water soon exceeds the force exerted by capillary attraction. Soil pores (see the sidebar) are connected, and they form passages through the soil that are narrow enough to allow water to move by capillarity. Consequently, water drains vertically downward through the soil by gravity, but then rises by capillarity through the capillary fringe and from there to the surface.

CHAPTER 3

TROPICAL FOREST CLIMATES

Why it rains so much at the equator

Equatorial regions are among the rainiest places on Earth. Belém, Brazil, for example, at latitude 1.45°S, receives an average of about 96 inches (2,438 mm) of rain a year. Cayenne, the capital of French Guiana, in the northeast of South America, is a little farther from the equator, at 4.9°N, but even wetter, with an average annual rainfall of 126.1 inches (3,203 mm). San Francisco, in contrast, at 37.78°N, receives an average 22 inches (561 mm) of rain a year.

All three cities are close to the ocean. San Francisco is on the coast, of course, as is Cayenne, but Belém is a few miles inland, although it lies beside the wide Tocantins River. Clearly, it cannot be the distance from the sea that makes two of these cities so much rainier than the third. In fact, it is the combination of high temperatures and an abundance of water that produces the high equatorial rainfall.

As the Earth moves in its orbit around the Sun, the tilt of its axis means that first one hemisphere and then the other faces the Sun. In the hemisphere that is tilted toward the Sun and enjoying summer, the Sun rises higher in the sky than it does during winter. The Sun is never directly overhead in San Francisco, however. On Midsummer Day in the Northern Hemisphere, when the noonday Sun reaches its highest point in the sky, the Sun is directly overhead at the tropic of Cancer—and it is Midwinter Day in the Southern Hemisphere. Immediately after Midsummer Day—also known as the *summer solstice*—the Sun appears to move toward the equator on its journey to the opposite hemisphere. It crosses the equator at the spring and autumn *equinoxes,* the days when the Sun is above the horizon for precisely 12 hours and below it for 12 hours everywhere on Earth.

The tropics of Cancer in the north and Capricorn in the south lie at latitudes 23.45°N and 23.45°S. Imagine that the Earth's orbit about the Sun marks the edge of a flat disk with the Sun at its center—this imaginary disk is known as the *plane of the ecliptic*. The Earth's axis is tilted 23.45° from a line perpendicular to this plane. That is why the two Tropics are where they are and why the region lying between them— between 23.45°N and 23.45°S—receives more sunshine than any other part of the Earth.

Some of the sunshine reaching the atmosphere is reflected back into space by clouds and light-colored surfaces, but a little more than half of it passes through the air and is absorbed by the surface. The warmed surface then warms the air in contact with it. As its temperature rises, the air expands. This makes it less dense and allows denser, cooler air to sink beneath it, pushing it upward.

Water evaporates into the warm air near the surface, but as the air rises it grows steadily cooler (see the sidebar "Adiabatic cooling and warming" on page 57) and the water vapor begins to condense into liquid droplets—clouds. Condensation warms the air by releasing latent heat. Latent heat is the energy that water molecules need to absorb in order to break free from the bonds that hold them locked together as ice or in small, highly mobile groups as liquid water. The energy is absorbed from the surrounding medium, but it does not alter the temperature of the water itself; *latent* means "hidden." Precisely the same amount of latent heat is released when water vapor condenses, when ice melts, and when ice sublimes directly into water vapor.

Warming due to the release of latent heat makes the air continue rising, and more water vapor condenses. The clouds grow bigger and the cloud droplets grow into raindrops. Because the Tropics receive more sunshine than anywhere else, this process is more vigorous there than in any other part of the world.

Rising air also moves away from the Tropics. This movement of air transports warmth from equatorial regions all the way to the poles and allows cooler air to move toward the equator. This constant motion is known as the *general circulation of the atmosphere* (see the sidebar).

General circulation of the atmosphere

The tropics of Cancer in the north and Capricorn in the south mark the boundaries of the belt around the Earth where the Sun is directly overhead on at least one day in the year. The Arctic and Antarctic Circles mark the boundaries of regions in which the Sun does not rise above the horizon on at least one day of the year and does not sink below the horizon on at least one day in the year.

A beam of sunlight illuminates a much smaller area if the Sun is directly overhead than it does if the Sun is at a low angle in the sky. The amount of energy is the same in both cases, but the energy is spread over a smaller area directly beneath the Sun than it is when the Sun is lower. This is why the Tropics are heated more strongly than any other part of the Earth and the amount of heat falling on the surface decreases with increasing distance from the equator (increasing latitude).

The Sun shines more intensely at the equator than it does anywhere else, but air movements transport some of the warmth away from the equator. Near the equator, the warm surface of the Earth heats the air in contact with it. The warm air rises until it is close to the tropopause, which is the boundary between the lowest layer of the atmosphere (the troposphere) in which air temperature decreases with height, and the layer above (the stratosphere), where the temperature remains constant with increasing height. The height of the tropopause is around 10 miles (16 km), and at this height the air moves away from the equator, some heading north and some south. As it rises, the air cools, so the high-level air moving away from the equator is very cold—about –85°F (–65°C).

This equatorial air subsides around latitude 30°N and S, and as it sinks it warms again. By the time it reaches the surface it is hot and dry, so it warms this region, producing subtropical deserts. At the surface, the air divides. Sometimes called the horse latitudes, this is a region of light, variable winds or no winds at all. Most of the air flows back toward the equator and some flows away from the equator. The air from north and south of the equator meets at the Intertropical Convergence Zone (ITCZ), and this circulation forms a number of vertical cells called *Hadley cells,* after George Hadley (1685–1768), the English meteorologist who first proposed them in 1735.

Over the poles, the air is very cold. It subsides, and when it reaches the surface it flows away from the poles. At about latitude 50–60°N and S, air moving away from the poles meets air moving away from the equator at the polar front. The converging air rises to the tropopause, in these latitudes about seven miles (11 km) above the surface. Some flows back to the poles, forming polar cells, and some flows toward the equator, completing Ferrel cells, discovered in 1856 by the American climatologist William Ferrel (1817–91).

Warm air rises at the equator, sinks to the surface in the subtropics, flows at low level to around latitude 55°, then rises to continue its journey toward the poles. At the same time, cold air subsiding at the poles flows back to the equator. The diagram below shows how this circulation produces three sets of vertical cells in each hemisphere. It is called the "three-cell model" of the atmospheric circulation.

If it were not for this redistribution of heat, weather at the equator would be very much hotter than it is, and weather at the poles would be a great deal colder.

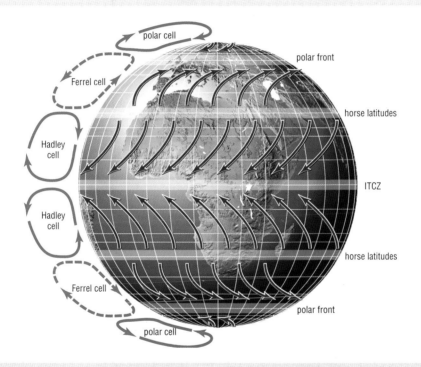

General circulation of the atmosphere. Warm air rises over the equator, moves away from the equator at high altitude, and subsides over the Tropics; there it divides, some flowing back toward the equator and some flowing away from the equator. This forms a series of Hadley cells. Cold air subsides over the poles and flows away from the poles at low level. This forms a series of polar cells. Air rises where Hadley-cell air flowing away from the Tropics meets polar-cell air flowing toward the equator. The air flows toward the equator at high altitude, descending where it meets high-level Hadley-cell air. This forms a series of Ferrel cells.

Even with the large amount of sunshine they receive, the Tropics would not have a wet climate if there were not a virtually limitless supply of water—but there is. The equator crosses the Pacific, Indian, and Atlantic Oceans. It runs across South America and Africa, but for most of the way it crosses warm water. Consequently, evaporation is vigorous almost everywhere, and satellite photographs usually show patches of dense cloud forming a belt around the Earth close to the equator.

Those are the clouds that give Belém, Cayenne, and most other places in the equatorial region their high rainfall.

Trade winds

The clouds over the equator form a belt—though one with plenty of clear sky between clouds—in an area of permanently low pressure, called the *equatorial trough.* The equatorial trough is not precisely at the equator, but moves with the seasons between approximately 25°N and 15°S. It also moves from year to year, following changes in the temperature at the sea surface and always coinciding with the highest surface temperature. Consequently, the equatorial trough also coincides with the *thermal equator,* the line around the Earth where the temperature is highest. Its average position, and the position of the thermal equator, is about 5°N. The warmest region on Earth is not the geographic equator, but the thermal equator.

Pressure is low along the equatorial trough because that is where winds flowing toward the equator from both hemispheres meet. Where the winds converge, air is swept upward, and it is their convergence that produces the low surface pressure. The belt where the winds converge is known as the *Intertropical Convergence Zone* (ITCZ).

The converging winds are called the *trade winds,* a name that was first used in 1650 to describe any wind that "blows trade"—that is, blows constantly along the same track; *trade* is an old word for "track." Since early in the 18th century the term *trade wind* has been restricted to the tropical trade winds. These blow from approximately latitude 30° in both hemispheres, from the northeast in the Northern

Hemisphere and from the southeast in the Southern Hemisphere. They do not blow everywhere in the Tropics or blow all the time, but they are the most reliable winds on Earth.

It was seafarers who discovered and named the trade winds. In the days of sailing ships they were of obvious importance, but dangers lurk to the north and south of them. At around latitude 30°N and S, about where the trade winds originate, there are times and places when the wind does not blow at all and ships could be becalmed. Sailors called these the *horse latitudes*. Ships often carried cargoes of horses, and if the vessel was becalmed, supplies of drinking water could run low. Some of the horses might then die and be thrown overboard. There were similar dangers close to the equator, inside the ITCZ, where the areas of calm were called the *doldrums*. These were more dangerous because their location varied unpredictably, but between July and September the doldrums sometimes extend all the way across the Atlantic, making the timing of voyages critical. Food stores could run low on a ship that was becalmed, and until modern times sailors had no means of making seawater drinkable.

The reliability of the trade winds made scientists curious. The first to attempt an explanation was the English astronomer Edmond Halley (1656–1742) in 1686, and in 1735 the English meteorologist George Hadley (1685–1768) proposed an improved version of Halley's explanation. Hadley suggested that warm air rises over the equator, moves at high altitude to the North and South Poles, and then sinks to the surface and flows back toward the equator. As it moves, Hadley suggested, the rotation of the Earth deflects the air to the west, so it approaches the equator as the northeasterly and southeasterly trade winds. We now know that air rising over the equator does not travel directly all the way to the poles. The circulation Hadley proposed occurs only in the Tropics, where the cells are known as *Hadley cells* in acknowledgment of his discovery (see the sidebar "General circulation of the atmosphere" on page 48).

Hadley was more nearly right about the trade winds, however. In the 19th century the American climatologist William Ferrel (1817–91) completed the explanation. The *Coriolis*

Walker circulation

Sir Gilbert Walker (1868–1958) was a British meteorologist, at one time head of the Indian Meteorological Service, who made a close study of the Indian monsoons. This led him to a wider study of tropical climates, and in 1923 he proposed a modification to the Hadley-cell circulation, which was subsequently found to be correct.

Air rises over the equator, moves away from the equator at high altitude, subsides to the surface around latitude 30°N and S, and returns to the equator at low level. This circulation comprises the Hadley cells, of which there are about four in summer and five in winter. Walker suggested that in addition to this *meridional* (north-south) flow there is a small but continuous *latitudinal* (east-west) movement. The latitudinal movement also forms cells, known as *Walker cells*. These are shown in the illustration.

Air in the Walker circulation rises in the vicinity of Indonesia and over the western Pacific and eastern Indian Oceans. Towering clouds develop in the rising air and produce heavy rainfall. At high altitude the rising air divides into two streams, flowing eastward and westward. Streams from adjacent cells converge and subside. At the surface, the air diverges again and converging air from adjacent streams rises.

The Walker circulation produces areas of low pressure and heavy rainfall over tropical South America, Africa, and Indonesia, and areas of high pressure and low rainfall

effect, which causes moving air (and water) to swing to the right in the Northern Hemisphere and to the left in the Southern Hemisphere due to the Earth's rotation, has no effect at all close to the equator. Ferrel found that it is not the rotation of the Earth that deflects the winds, but their *relative vorticity,* which is the tendency of moving air and water to turn about a vertical axis. Occasionally, the trade winds cross the equator. When this happens, the relative vorticity acts in the opposite direction and the winds blow from the northwest or southwest, rather than the northeast or southeast.

Between them, Edmond Halley, George Hadley, and William Ferrel succeeded in explaining the reason for the trade winds—almost. In 1923 Sir Gilbert Walker discovered an additional reason not only for the trade winds' reliability, but also for the otherwise curious fact that they are especially reliable on the eastern sides of the Atlantic, Pacific, and Indian

over the eastern sides of the oceans. This distribution of pressure generates an east-to-west flow of air close to the surface, strengthening the trade winds. Every few years the pattern changes over the Pacific, producing an El Niño weather phenomenon.

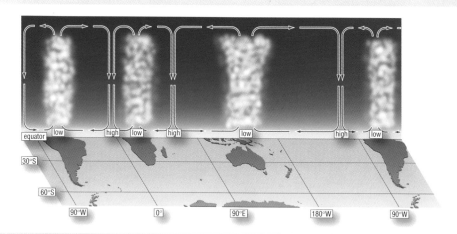

Walker circulation. As well as moving away from and toward the equator, air also circulates latitudinally. It is this circulation that produces towering rain clouds.

Oceans (see the sidebar). There they blow at an average speed of about 11 MPH (18 km/h) in the Northern Hemisphere and 14 MPH (22 km/h) in the Southern Hemisphere, driven by high pressure on the eastern side of the Hadley cells and low pressure on the western side.

In their long journey across the oceans, the trade winds gather a great deal of moisture. When they converge in the ITCZ, the air that rises is close to saturation. That is why the clouds forming in the rising air tower to such heights, and it is why the rainfall over equatorial regions is so high.

Dry seasons and rainy seasons

Close to the equator, the weather changes little through the year. At Belém, for example, February is the coldest month, with an average daytime temperature of 86°F (30°C), and the warmest month is October, when the average daytime temperature is 89°F (32°C). This is a difference of only 3°F (1.7°C) between "summer" and "winter." At Cayenne the difference is 7°F (3.9°C). These differences are much smaller than those between the average temperatures by day and night—14–16°F (8–9°C) at Belém and about 10–17°F (6–9°C) at Cayenne. There can be no real summer and winter in places where the daily temperature range is much greater than the seasonal temperature change.

There are differences in rainfall through the year, however. September, October, and November are drier than other months at Belém, and very little rain falls at Cayenne from the beginning of August to the end of November. This is the difference that distinguishes the climates of the equatorial rain forest, where it rains at least half of the days in every month, and the tropical rain forest, where there are some months in which rain is less frequent than that. Belém has an equatorial rain for-

Extreme positions for the Intertropical Convergence Zone (ITCZ) in January and July. Note that the ITCZ is always in the Northern Hemisphere over most of the Atlantic Ocean and the eastern Pacific Ocean.

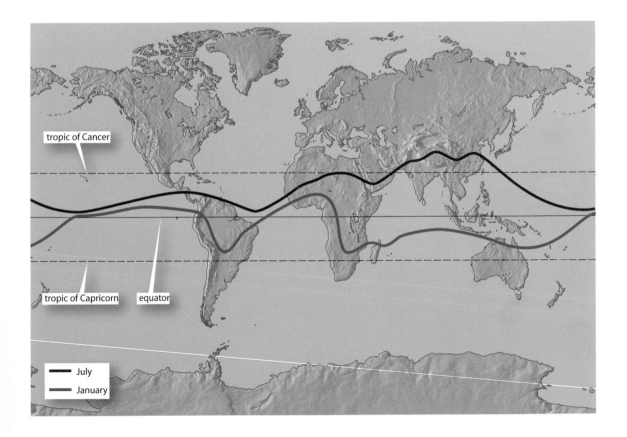

tropic of Cancer

tropic of Capricorn   equator

July
January

est climate, and Cayenne, where it rains on an average of only 11 days in November, nine days in August, and four days in September and October, has a tropical rain forest climate.

By August, the ITCZ (see "Trade winds" on page 50) has crossed the equator into the Southern Hemisphere. With it have gone the huge clouds that form in the rising air at the convergence and drench the forest in torrential downpours. Cayenne, at 4.9°N, is then out of range of these storms, and its rainfall decreases sharply. The ITCZ moves quite far to the south in South America, as the illustration shows, and Belém, at 1.45°S, is far enough from it to experience a reduction in rainfall, but the reduction is small. The map shows the ITCZ as a sharp line, but this is misleading. It is a wide belt and despite moving with the seasons, it remains over some areas, or very close to them, throughout the year. Belém is in such an area, but Cayenne is not. Places that remain inside the ITCZ all year have an equatorial rain forest climate and those adjacent to them, but outside the ITCZ in some months, have a tropical rain forest climate.

This limitation means that true tropical rain forest, already restricted to the lowlands, occupies only about 7 percent of the total land area of the planet. It never has been as extensive as some people suppose. Approximately two-thirds of this forest is equatorial rain forest and the remainder is tropical rain forest.

Between the edge of the tropical rain forest and the tropics of Cancer and Capricorn the climate does have seasons. They are marked not by large changes in temperature but by changes in rainfall. Rather than the cold and warm seasons of temperate latitudes, the two tropical seasons are wet and dry. Sena Madureira, Brazil, at latitude 9.1°S and near the edge of the Amazon Basin, is far enough from the ITCZ in winter to experience a distinct dry season. The map shows its location, and also those of Belém and Cayenne. Sena Madureira has an annual rainfall of about 81 inches (2,062 mm), and rain falls on at least half of the days in each month between December and March—the Southern Hemisphere summer. Rain is much less frequent in winter. It rains on a total of only 10 days during July and August, the driest months, and the rainfall in those months amounts to only 2.7 inches (68 mm).

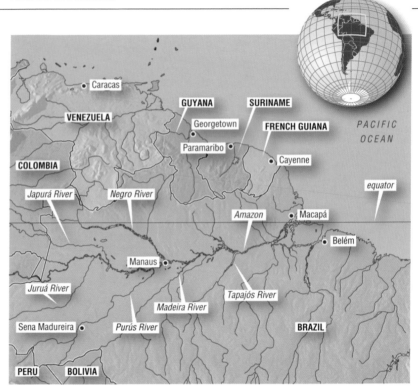

Map showing the locations of Cayenne, French Guiana, and Belém and Sena Madureira, Brazil

The difference between wet and dry seasons increases with distance from the equator—but really with distance from the ITCZ. Darwin, Australia, is at latitude 12.47°S, just inside the summer limit of the ITCZ. It receives about 57 inches (1,448 mm) of rain between October and April but only 1.3 inches (33 mm) during winter, from May to September. Usually no rain at all falls in July and the amount falling in August is insignificant.

The contrast between wet and dry seasons is most extreme in regions with a monsoon climate (see "Monsoons" on page 63).

Continental and maritime climates

Equatorial and tropical rain forests grow in warm, wet climates that result from their low latitude and the high rainfall associated with the ITCZ. Most places in the tropical lowlands have a warm climate, but not all have a wet climate. Most of Australia, for instance, lies inside the Tropics, yet a large part of the interior is desert. The southern part of the Sahara is in the Tropics, and so are the northern sections of the Namib Desert in Namibia and the Atacama Desert in

Adiabatic cooling and warming

Air is compressed by the weight of air above it. Imagine a balloon partly inflated with air and made from some weightless substance that totally insulates the air inside. No matter what the temperature outside the balloon, the temperature of the air inside remains the same.

Imagine the balloon is released into the atmosphere. The air inside is squeezed between the weight of air above it, all the way to the top of the atmosphere, and the denser air below it.

Suppose the air inside the balloon is less dense than the air above it. Denser air will push beneath it and the balloon will rise. As it rises, the distance to the top of the atmosphere becomes smaller, so there is less air above to weigh down on the air in the balloon. At the same time, as the balloon moves through air that is less dense, it experiences less pressure from below. This causes the air in the balloon to expand.

When air (or any other gas) expands, its molecules move farther apart. The amount of air remains the same, but it occupies a bigger volume. As they move apart, the molecules must "push" other molecules out of their way. This uses energy, so as the air expands its molecules lose energy. Because they have less energy they move more slowly.

When a moving molecule strikes something, some of its energy is transferred to whatever it strikes, and part of that energy is converted into heat. This raises the temperature of the struck object by an amount related to the number of molecules striking it and their speed.

In expanding air, the molecules are moving farther apart, so a smaller number of them strike an object each second. They are also traveling more slowly, so they strike with less force. This means the temperature of the air decreases. As it expands, air cools.

If the air in the balloon is denser than air below, it will sink. As it sinks, the pressure on the air will increase, its volume will decrease, and its molecules will acquire more energy. Its temperature will increase.

This warming and cooling has nothing to do with the temperature of the air surrounding the balloon. It is called *adiabatic* warming and cooling, from the Greek word *adiabatos,* meaning "impassable," suggesting that the air is enclosed by an imaginary boundary through which heat is unable to pass.

Chile. The Atacama is the world's driest desert, where the average annual precipitation is about 0.4 inch (10 mm) and arrives as fog, not rain. It rains no more than two to four times a century.

The low rainfall of the Sahara and the Australian Desert is a consequence of the ITCZ. Air rises at the convergence, loses most of its moisture, and moves away from the equator (see the sidebar "General circulation of the atmosphere" on page 48). At about latitude 30° in both hemispheres, this very dry air meets air moving toward the equator and sinks all the way to the surface. It warms as it descends (see the sidebar "Adiabatic cooling and warming"), reaching the surface as hot, extremely dry air. The subsiding air produces a region of permanently high surface pressure. Air flows outward from centers of high pressure, thus preventing moister air from entering the region and producing a desert climate that extends well inside the Tropics.

The Namib and Atacama Deserts are different. Both these deserts lie along the western coasts of continents, although a coastal range of mountains separates the driest part of the Atacama from the ocean. Although the winds are generally from the east throughout the Tropics (see "Trade winds" on page 50), near the coasts the daily land and sea breezes are much stronger. Due to the fact that the land warms up much faster than the sea during the day and cools much faster at night, a wind blows from the sea by day and from the land by night. The illustration shows how this comes about.

Sea breezes should bring moist air over the land, but parallel to the coast there is an ocean current carrying cold water—the Peru (or Humboldt) Current off the coast of Chile and the Benguela Current off the coast of Namibia. Air is chilled as it crosses the current. Some of its moisture condenses to form fog, but, more important, the cool air remains close to the surface. It does not rise to produce clouds that might deliver rain.

The Galápagos Islands, about 650 miles (1,046 km) from the coast of Ecuador and, at 0.5°S, almost on the equator, also have this type of climate. They lie directly in the Peru Current, and despite being surrounded by vast expanses of ocean they receive only four inches (102 mm) of rain a year,

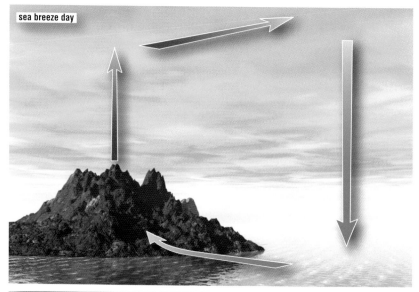

sea breeze day

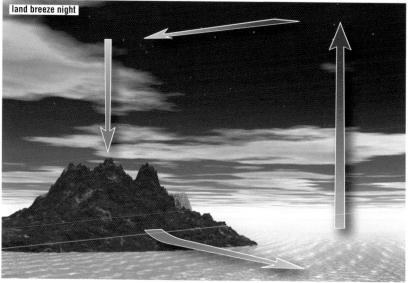

land breeze night

Land and sea breezes. During the day, warm air rises over the land and cool air flows from the sea to replace it. This is the sea breeze. At night the land cools. If its temperature falls below that of the sea surface, air flows from land to sea as a land breeze.

all of it falling between January and April. They are not alone in this junction of conditions. The Canary Islands, about 60 miles (100 km) from the North African coast, lie in the cold Canary Current. Las Palmas, the main city, receives only nine inches (229 mm) of rain a year.

Air that remains over the ocean for any length of time gathers moisture. Because the ocean warms up and cools down much more slowly than the land, air over the ocean is cooler than air over land in summer but warmer in winter. Air that remains over a continent develops quite different characteristics. It is dry, and hot in summer and cold in winter. In both cases, the temperature and amount of moisture in the air at a given altitude are much the same everywhere throughout what is known as an *air mass*.

There are distinct types of air mass. Continental air masses develop over continents, and maritime air masses develop over the oceans. They vary in temperature according to the latitude in which they formed, but the air masses affecting the Tropics are either tropical or equatorial, so they may be classed as continental tropical (abbreviated as cT), maritime tropical (mT), or maritime equatorial (mE). There is no continental equatorial type because oceans cover most of the equatorial region.

Once formed, air masses move away from their *source regions,* where they developed, bringing warm or cool, wet or dry weather to the lands they cross. Continental air brings extreme summer and winter temperatures and generally dry conditions. This is a *continental climate*. Maritime air brings mild winters, cool summers, and rain distributed fairly evenly through the year. This is a *maritime climate.*

As an air mass moves across a continent or ocean, its characteristics may change. Maritime air reaching North America from the Pacific Ocean loses its moisture and has become continental air by the time it reaches the Atlantic. By the time it reaches Europe it has once more become maritime air. Because air masses change, climates have degrees of *continentality* and *oceanicity*. Climate scientists calculate the continentality and oceanicity of the climates in particular places, either from records of the air masses affecting them or from their annual temperature range and latitude.

Convection and tropical storms

In the temperate regions of the world, rain often falls as drizzle or light showers. Close to the intertropical convergence zone (ITCZ), the weather is not like that. Violent storms deliver most of the rain, and on average there is at least one big thunderstorm a week.

Very special conditions are needed to produce a thunderstorm. Warm air that is almost saturated with moisture must be made to rise, while a strong wind at a height of about 10 miles (16 km) sweeps away the rising air.

Along the ITCZ, where the trade winds from both hemispheres meet (see "Trade winds" on page 50), warm air converges and rises. It is very moist air because the winds have traveled a long distance across the surface of the warm, tropical sea. The conditions are perfect for producing the towering clouds that can generate storms.

Water evaporates rapidly in the Tropics because of the high temperature of the air, which is heated by contact with the sea and land surface. As its temperature rises, the air expands and becomes less dense. Denser, cooler air subsides and moves beneath it, pushing the warm air upward and being warmed in its turn. Warm air is constantly rising and cool air is descending in a process called *convection* that transfers heat from the surface, where the Sun's warmth is absorbed, to air at higher levels.

As air rises, its temperature falls (see the sidebar "Adiabatic cooling and warming" on page 57). Molecules of water vapor move more slowly and spend more time close to one another when they meet. The water vapor starts to condense when the air reaches the *dew-point temperature,* which varies according to the amount of water vapor in the air. The height at which condensation begins—and therefore the height of the cloud base—is called the *lifting condensation level.*

Condensation releases latent heat (see the explanation in "Why it rains so much at the equator" on pages 46–50) as the hydrogen bonds form and water molecules give up the heat energy they absorbed when they broke the bonds and evaporated. Latent heat warms the surrounding air. It expands and rises higher, causing more condensation, more release of latent heat, and so on. Such air is said to be highly unstable (see the sidebar "Lapse rates and stability" on page 66).

The high-level wind sweeps rising air away from the cloud top, drawing more air upward and helping the cloud to continue growing. High in the cloud the temperature is so low, even over the equator, that many cloud droplets are below freezing temperature but nevertheless remain liquid. They are *supercooled*. The cloud also contains ice crystals. The wind carries some of these away from the top of the cloud. They vaporize as they enter drier air but often form a shape like a blacksmith's anvil.

The cloud is now huge. Clouds of this type are called *cumulonimbus*. Air rises through it in currents rushing upward at up to 100 MPH (160 km/h). Ice crystals and raindrops fall downward, dragging cold air with them and generating

Charge separation in storm clouds

A lightning flash is an electric spark and, like any flow of electric current, it travels between two regions of opposite charge. These regions form inside big cumulonimbus storm clouds—and also in the clouds of material ejected by volcanic eruptions.

In a storm cloud, positive charge usually accumulates near the top of the cloud and negative charge near the bottom. There is also a small area of positive charge, of uncertain origin, at the base of the cloud.

Scientists are uncertain just how this separation of charge occurs, but probably several processes are involved. Some separation may be due to the fact that the ionosphere, in the upper atmosphere (above about 37 miles; 60 km), is positively charged and in fine weather the surface of the Earth is negatively charged, with a steady, gentle, downward flow of current. This means it is possible that the negative charge below induces a positive charge on the underside of cloud droplets and a negative charge on their upper surfaces. If the droplets then collide in such a way as to split them, the charges may separate. It is also possible that falling cloud particles may capture negative ions (atoms that have gained one or more electrons).

The most important mechanism is believed to occur when water freezes to form hail pellets. A hailstone forms when a supercooled water droplet freezes. This happens from the outside inward. Hydrogen ions (H^+) then move toward the colder outer region, so the hailstone contains a preponderance of H^+ in its outer, icy shell and of hydroxyl (OH^-) in its liquid interior. As freezing progresses, the interior of the hailstone expands, bursting the outer shell. This releases tiny splinters of ice carrying positive charge (because of the H^+). Being so small and light, these splinters are carried to the top of the cloud by updrafts. The heavier hailstone center, with its negative charge (OH^-), sinks to a lower level.

downcurrents. As they fall, the raindrops merge with more and more cloud droplets, so they are large by the time they fall from the base of the cloud. The cloud is now delivering a heavy rainstorm. It dies when the cold downcurrents fall into the upcurrents, cooling the rising air and eventually preventing it from rising. The cloud may then release all of the water it still holds in a brief but intense *cloudburst.*

Before it dies, a big cumulonimbus often produces thunder and lightning. Lightning is an electric spark that flashes between areas of electric charge inside a cloud, between two adjacent clouds, or between a cloud and the ground. The flash heats the air around it so strongly and so fast—by up to 54,000°F (30,000°C) in less than a second—that the air explodes. Thunder is the sound of the exploding air. Over the world as a whole, about 1,500 thunderstorms are happening at any one time. Many of these are in the Tropics.

Scientists are still working to discover how one part of a storm cloud can acquire a positive charge while another acquires a negative charge. There are several possible ways this *charge separation* may occur (see the sidebar).

Monsoons

Over most of the Tropics, outside the area that lies permanently within the Intertropical Convergence Zone, climates are more or less seasonal. The seasons are not distinguished by changes in temperature, however, but by the distribution of rainfall. Instead of a warm summer and cold winter, there is a dry season and a rainy season. This type of seasonality is most extreme in those parts of the world that have a *monsoon* climate.

Monsoon means "season." The English word is derived from the Dutch *monssoen,* which in turn comes from the Portuguese *monção,* from *mausim,* the Arabic word for "season." It is a season bringing weather dramatically different from that of the preceding season. In fact, there are two seasons, or monsoons, one dry and the other wet, marked by a change in the direction of the wind.

The climate on the western coast of India illustrates just how dramatic the seasonal contrast can be. An average of four inches (104 mm) of rain falls on the city of Mumbai (Bombay) between October and May. The summer monsoon begins in June, and from then until the end of September the average rainfall is 67 inches (1,707 mm). Cherrapunji, in the foothills of the Himalayas, is one of the rainiest places on Earth—but for only part of the year. It receives about 33 inches (838 mm) of rain between October and March, but 392 inches (9,957 mm) between April and September. If the water did not drain away, the summer monsoon would deliver enough to flood Cherrapunji to a depth of about 33 feet (10 m). Between May and August it rains almost every day.

In winter the land in central Asia loses the heat it absorbed in summer and, as the temperature drops, the cold ground chills the air above it. The cool air settles, producing a large area of high atmospheric pressure. Air flows outward from the region of high pressure and to the south it rises over the Himalaya Mountains. As the air subsides on the southern side of the mountains, its temperature increases (see the sidebar "Adiabatic cooling and warming" on page 57). Warm air is able to hold more water vapor than cold air, and so the *relative humidity* of the air—the amount of water vapor as a percentage of the amount needed to saturate the air at that temperature—decreases. Subsidence makes the air extremely dry. Subsiding air also produces high pressure at the surface. Consequently the air sinking on the southern side of the mountains produces a wind blowing from the northeast, bringing warm, extremely dry weather to the Indian subcontinent.

Water in the Indian Ocean is warmer than the land in central Asia because the ocean cools more slowly than land. Warm air rises over the sea, producing a region of low surface pressure that draws in air from the region of higher pressure over India. At the same time, the rising air moves in a northeasterly direction over the continent and subsides into the high-pressure area in central Asia. The circulation therefore consists of dry air moving across India at low level in a southwesterly direction and air moving in the opposite direction at high level.

In summer the land warms more rapidly than the sea, and the situation reverses. Air rises over central Asia, producing low surface pressure, and it is replaced by moist air drawn in

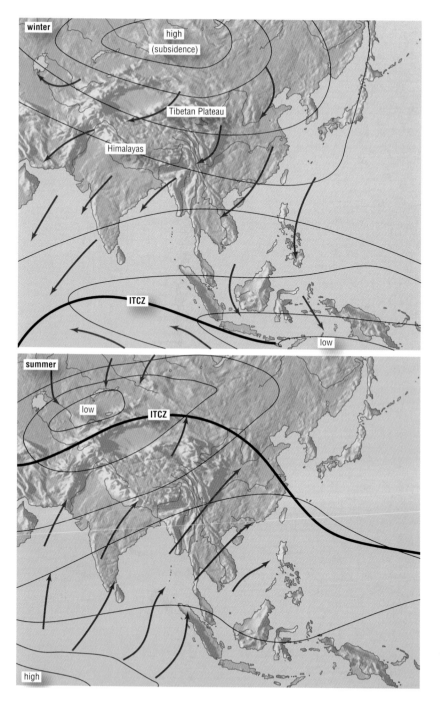

The Asian monsoons. In winter the Intertropical Convergence Zone (ITCZ) is far to the south, and a dry, southeasterly airstream flows across southern Asia from the high pressure over central Asia. This is the dry, southeasterly, or winter monsoon. In summer the ITCZ is to the north, low pressure is centered over central Asia, and a southwesterly airstream brings rain to southern Asia. This is the wet, southwesterly, or summer monsoon.

from over the Indian Ocean. The effect is exaggerated by the Himalayas. They form a barrier that prevents the summer monsoon winds moving farther north, but at the same time

Lapse rates and stability

Air temperature decreases (or lapses) with increasing height. The rate at which it does so is called the *lapse rate.* Although all air contains some water vapor, air that is not saturated with moisture—all of its moisture is present as vapor rather than liquid droplets or ice crystals—is said to be *dry.* When dry air cools adiabatically, it does so at 5.4°F for every 1,000 feet (9.8°C/km) that it rises. This is known as the *dry adiabatic lapse rate* (DALR).

When the temperature of the rising air has fallen sufficiently, its water vapor will start to condense into droplets. Condensation commences at the *dew-point temperature* and the height at which this temperature is reached is called the *lifting condensation level.* Condensation releases *latent heat,* which warms the air. Latent heat is the energy that allows water molecules to break free from each other when liquid water vaporizes or ice melts. It does not change the temperature of the water or ice, which is why it is called *latent,* meaning "hidden." The same amount of latent heat is released, warming the surroundings, when water vapor condenses and when liquid water freezes. Consequently, the rising air then cools at a slower rate, known as the *saturated adiabatic lapse rate* (SALR). The SALR varies, depending on the rate of condensation, but it averages 3°F per 1,000 feet (6°C/km).

The actual rate at which the temperature decreases with height in air that is not rising is called the *environmental lapse rate* (ELR). It is calculated by comparing the surface temperature, the temperature at the tropopause (it is about −85°F; −65°C at the equator), and the height of the tropopause (about 10 miles; 16 km over the equator).

If the ELR is less than both the DALR and SALR, rising air will cool faster than the surrounding air, so it will always be cooler and will tend to subside to a lower height. Such air is said to be *absolutely stable.*

If the ELR is greater than the SALR, air that is rising and cooling at the DALR and later at the SALR will always be warmer than the surrounding air. Consequently, it will continue to rise. The air is then *absolutely unstable.*

If the ELR is less than the DALR but greater than the SALR, rising air will cool faster than the surrounding air while it remains dry but more slowly once it rises above the lifting condensation level. At first it is stable, but above the lifting condensation level it becomes unstable. This air is said to be *conditionally unstable.* It is stable unless a condition (rising above its lifting condensation level) is met, whereupon it becomes unstable.

Stable air brings settled weather. Unstable air produces heaped clouds of the *cumulus* type. The base of these clouds is at the lifting condensation level, and the cloud tops are at the altitude where the rising air has lost enough water vapor to make it dry once more, so it is cooling at the DALR. If the air is sufficiently unstable, however, the clouds can grow into towering *cumulonimbus* storm clouds. Equatorial air is usually unstable.

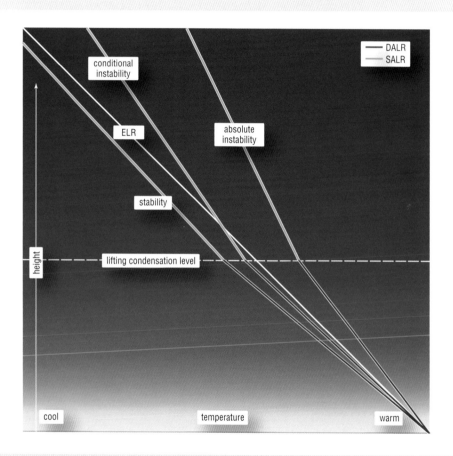

Stability of air. If the environmental lapse rate (ELR) is less than both the dry (DALR) and saturated (SALR) lapse rates, the air is stable. If the ELR is less than both the DALR and SALR, the air is absolutely unstable. If the ELR is less than the DALR but greater than the SALR, the air is conditionally unstable.

air is being heated strongly over the Tibetan Plateau, driving the circulation.

The ITCZ moves northward in summer to between 25°N and 30°N. The pressure distribution produced by the combination of the ITCZ and the Himalayan barrier generates a high-level wind—the easterly jet stream—blowing from east to west. The easterly jet stream intensifies the rainfall over southeastern Asia, the Arabian Sea, and the Horn of Africa. The maps illustrate the differences between the summer and winter monsoons over Asia.

Moist air, moving northeastward from the Indian Ocean, rises as it reaches the high ground inland from the Indian coast. It becomes highly unstable—that is, once it starts to rise it continues to do so (see the sidebar "Lapse rates and stability")—producing the towering storm clouds that bring the rains of the summer monsoon.

Less extreme monsoon seasons also affect tropical Africa and the eastern part of the Amazon Basin in South America—where the summer monsoon occurs in November, December, and January. The southwestern United States and parts of Europe also experience mild monsoon seasons.

El Niño

At intervals of between two and seven years, the weather over large parts of the Tropics changes radically. Drought afflicts places that are ordinarily wet, and dry regions are deluged with rain.

Changes of this kind were first recorded along the coast of Peru. Weather there is usually very dry, but the change brought heavy rains that meant farmers could look forward to a bumper harvest, followed by a year when everyone had plenty to eat. It brought what was truly a year of plenty, *año de abundancia,* and it became apparent in the middle of summer—December in the Southern Hemisphere. People thought it was a gift from God, given at Christmastime, and they called it *El Niño,* the (boy) child.

El Niño events are caused by a change in the distribution of atmospheric pressure. Scientists watch for signs of it developing in the measurements they receive from weather stations in Darwin, Australia, and Tahiti, an island in the central South Pacific. Usually, pressure is low at Darwin and high at Tahiti. This drives the Walker circulation (see the sidebar on page 52), and winds blowing offshore from the South American coast strengthen the trade winds (see "Trade winds" on page 50) across the tropical South Pacific Ocean. The trade winds drive the South Equatorial Current, an ocean current carrying warm water away from South America and toward Indonesia. Warm water forms a deep layer around Indonesia, but the layer is shallow near South America. At the same time, air converges into the area of low pressure around Indonesia; this low-pressure zone is generated by the heat in the region. The air rises, carrying with it the moisture evaporated from the warm ocean. Tall clouds develop in the rising air, bringing heavy rain. The South American coastal belt, on the other hand, experiences dry weather because air is cooled by contact with the cold water and it settles, so there is little convection to bring moisture over the land. This is the normal pattern of weather in the lands on either side of the equatorial South Pacific.

The change, called a *southern oscillation* because it takes place south of the equator, begins with the pressure distribution. Pressure rises at Darwin and falls at Tahiti, and the Walker circulation weakens or reverses direction. In response, the trade winds and the South Equatorial Current weaken or change direction. Warm surface water is no longer driven away from South America and toward Indonesia, and a strong southern oscillation may make it flow the other way. The layer of warm water becomes thinner around Indonesia and deeper off the South American coast. Towering clouds then form in the east, bringing heavy rain to South America, and subsiding air brings clear skies—and drought—to Indonesia. This is an El Niño.

When it ends, the pattern may swing past the usual state and into one where the pressures intensify, causing the trade winds to blow harder than normal and the ocean current to flow more strongly toward Indonesia. This is called *La Niña* and it makes the usual weather even more extreme— Indonesia is inundated with rain and the South American coastal belt is even drier than normal. The complete cycle of

El Niño and La Niña is known as an *El Niño–Southern Oscillation* (ENSO) event.

The heavy rains and flooding generated by El Niño extend into the Gulf states of the United States, and the droughts, often with wildfires, affect southern Africa, southern India and Sri Lanka, the Philippines, Australia, and Central America, as well as Indonesia.

Mountain climates

New Guinea is a large island lying just to the south of the equator. It has one of the world's largest swamps. The average annual rainfall in the lowlands is 145 inches (3,700 mm) and the average temperature is about 86°F (30°C). It is a land of lowland rain forest punctuated by land where snow covers the ground all year.

The snow lies at the top of high mountains and, as the map shows, a range of high mountains runs along the center of New Guinea for its entire length. The tallest of these mountains is Mount Jaya, also called Puncak Jaya.

Mount Jaya has three peaks: Jayakesuma (or Carstensz) Pyramid (16,024 feet; 4,884 m), Ngga Pulu (15,952 feet; 4,862 m), and Meren (15,775 feet; 4,808 m). Until recently, all three were covered permanently by ice, but this has been disappearing steadily over the past century, probably because of a reduction in the amount of snow falling onto the snowfields that feed the glaciers. Mount Jaya is the tallest, but several other mountains rise to more than 13,000 feet (4,000 m), and snow often lies on all of them early in the morning, although it melts later in the day.

Air temperature decreases with height from the surface to the *tropopause,* which is the boundary marking the top of the lower region of the atmosphere, called the *troposphere.* At the equator the tropopause is at a height of about 52,500 feet (16 km), and the temperature there is about –85°F (–65°C). If the daytime temperature at sea level is 86°F (30°C), then it will decrease by about 3.26°F with every 1,000 feet of elevation (5.9°C/km). At 13,000 feet (4,000 m) the daytime temperature will be about 44°F (6.4°C), and it will fall below freezing at night.

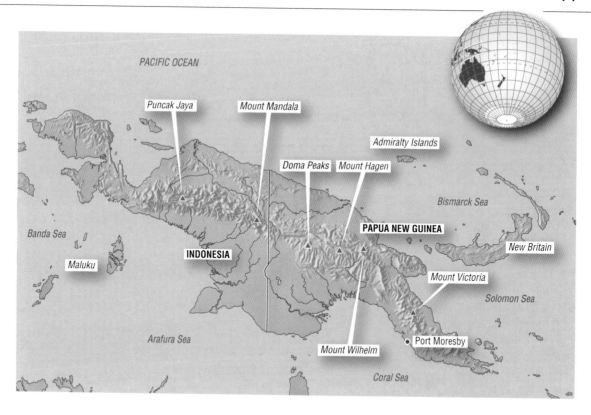

The mountains of New Guinea

Moist air will cool if it is forced to rise as it crosses the mountains (see the sidebar "Adiabatic cooling and warming" on page 57), and its water vapor is likely to condense. Thus clouds will form and the climate will be generally wetter, because of low cloud and increased rainfall, than that of the lowlands. The average annual rainfall in parts of the mountains of New Guinea reaches 197 inches (5,000 mm).

The daily temperature range is greater than the seasonal range throughout the equatorial region (see "Dry seasons and rainy seasons" on page 53), and the daily range is much bigger high in the mountains than it is at sea level. Guayaquil, Ecuador, at latitude 2.2°S, is 20 feet (6 m) above sea level. Its average temperature ranges between a daytime maximum of 89°F (32°C) and a nighttime minimum of 65°F (18°C). This is a range of 24°F (14°C). Quito, Ecuador, at latitude 0.2°S, is 9,446 feet (2,879 m) above sea level. There the temperature ranges between 73°F (23°C) and 44°F (7°C), a range of 29°F (16°C).

Temperatures range more widely at Quito than they do at Guayaquil because of the difference in the density of air at the two places. Air is compressed by the weight of air above it, all the way to the top of the atmosphere. Consequently, air at sea level is subjected to a greater weight of air than air at a higher level, which is closer to the top of the atmosphere. At sea level, the density of air is about 0.08 pounds per cubic foot (1.23 kg/m³). The air density at Quito is about 0.06 pounds per cubic foot (1.0 kg/m³). During the day, the surface warms at the same rate in the mountains as it does at sea level, but at night the lower air density allows heat to escape faster, and so temperatures fall lower.

Low air pressure also allows water to evaporate more easily. At Quito, water boils at 196°F (91°C) rather than 212°F (100°C). When the cloud clears, the ground will dry more quickly than it would at sea level.

Anyone who has walked in the hills knows that the air temperature decreases as elevation increases. Mountain climates are cooler than lowland climates. This is only the most obvious of the differences, however. Temperatures fall at night much farther from the daytime maximum than they do in the lowlands. Plants and animals living in the mountains must survive cold nights. The mountain climate is also wetter, especially due to fog—in fact low cloud—that coats every surface with moisture. Bearing this out, lowland Guayaquil has an average annual rainfall of about 39 inches (991 mm), while the average at Quito, high in the mountains, is 44 inches (1,118 mm). When the fog clears, however, the ground dries faster than it does at lower levels.

Snow lines

Jayakesuma Pyramid, on the island of New Guinea, is 16,024 feet (4,884 m) above sea level, and patches of permanent ice and snow cover parts of it. The patches are small, but this is not surprising: The peak is not quite high enough to be covered with snow all year round.

Many mountains, though not those in New Guinea, do have permanent caps of snow. The lower edge of the snow in the middle of summer is called the *snow line.* Its height above sea level varies with latitude; there are also differences between the Northern and Southern Hemispheres. In the latitude of

New Guinea (0°–10°S), the snow line is at about 17,400 feet (5,310 m)—only a little higher than Jayakesuma Pyramid. In Antarctica the snow line is at sea level all year round.

Air temperature decreases with height and, regardless of the temperature of the surrounding air, rising air cools at a steady rate. This is called *adiabatic cooling* (see the sidebar on page 57). Subsiding air warms at the same rate.

Air temperature decreases with height at approximately the same rate throughout the world, but air at sea level close to the equator is warmer than the air is in, say, Canada. So although the air cools at the same rate everywhere, it cools from a different starting temperature.

The rate at which the air temperature decreases with increasing height is called the *lapse rate* (see the sidebar "Lapse rates and stability" on page 66). It is calculated by comparing the actual temperatures at sea level and at the top of the lower atmosphere. Its average value is 3.5°F per 1,000 feet (6.5°C/km), but this varies locally due to the nature of the surface and to seasonal atmospheric changes. At the equator it is approximately 3.8°F per 1,000 feet (6.9°C/km) in January and 3.7°F per 1,000 feet (6.7°C/km) in July. At the North Pole, the rate is 5.2°F per 1,000 feet (9.4°C/km) in January and 2.5°F per 1,000 feet (4.5°C/km) in July. There is much more land in the Northern Hemisphere than there is in the Southern Hemisphere and this also affects the lapse rate.

Average heights for the snow line in the Tropics of both hemispheres are given in the table. Close to the equator, the snow line is higher in the Southern Hemisphere than it is in the Northern Hemisphere, but everywhere outside the Tropics it is higher in the Northern Hemisphere.

Mean snow line

Latitude	Height	
	(feet)	(meters)
0–10°N	15,500	4,727
10–20°N	15,500	4,727
20–30°N	17,400	5,310
0–10°S	17,400	5,310
10–20°S	18,400	5,610
20–30°S	16,800	5,125

Hurricanes

A hurricane is the biggest and most violent storm the Earth's atmosphere can produce. It brings sustained winds of more than 75 MPH (121 km/h) and winds of more than 155 MPH (249 km/h) in the fiercest hurricanes, with much stronger gusts. The rain is torrential and causes flooding, landslides, and mudslides. Tornadoes produce stronger winds, but hurricanes affect a very much larger area and, in any case, they often trigger tornadoes.

These storms are known as hurricanes if they develop in the Atlantic Ocean and Caribbean. In the Pacific they are called typhoons, in the northern Indian Ocean and Bay of Bengal they are cyclones, and they have several more local names elsewhere. Scientists call all of them *tropical cyclones*. They occur only in the Tropics.

Tropical cyclones can be up to 600 miles (965 km) across, which means a cyclone affects an area larger than Texas. The strongest winds are found around the central eye, but the gales that blow around the edge of the cyclone are also capable of causing damage.

When one of these storms strikes a tropical forest, trees are often uprooted over a wide area. The winds can leave plant debris littering hundreds of square miles. Near coasts, the combination of low pressure in the eye of the cyclone and onshore hurricane-force winds causes a *storm surge,* in which the tide rises much higher than usual. This can flood low-lying land, and the force of the water can uproot coastal trees, such as mangroves.

The effect of these storms is dramatic, but tropical forests have endured tropical cyclones throughout their history. Big, mature trees are uprooted, but this creates gaps in the forest canopy that allow sunlight to reach the forest floor. Tree seedlings, sheltered from the wind by the fully grown trees around them, grow rapidly. At the same time, plant material that is swept to the ground decomposes rapidly (see "Tropical soils" on page 35), making nutrients available to stimulate the growth of young plants. The gap in the forest fills within a few years. The proportions of the different plant species may change because of the storm, but the forest as a whole recovers.

A tropical cyclone begins as an atmospheric disturbance far out at sea. An area of low air pressure develops, with air circulating around it counterclockwise in the Northern Hemisphere and clockwise in the Southern Hemisphere. Air converging toward the center rises and cools, producing clouds. At this stage it is known as a *tropical disturbance* and may last for no more than a few hours. If it survives longer, however, the pressure at its center may fall lower and the winds increase; it is then a *tropical depression.* If it continues intensifying until the wind speed exceeds 38 MPH (61 km/h), it becomes a *tropical storm* and is given a name. It becomes a tropical cyclone, keeping the same name, when the sustained wind speed exceeds 74 MPH (119 km/h).

Water evaporates readily from the warm sea, so the rising air is warm and moist. The converging air swings to the right in the Northern Hemisphere (and to the left in the Southern Hemisphere) due to the rotation of the Earth. This is called the *Coriolis effect,* and it is what sets the entire cyclone turning. As the air rises, the water vapor it carries condenses, releasing heat and causing the air to continue rising. The air is highly unstable (see the sidebar "Lapse rates and stability" on page 66).

Seen from above, a mature tropical cyclone comprises a spiral of clouds that tower sometimes to 59,000 feet (18 km), inside of which warm air is rising. At the center there is an open *eye* where the air is subsiding. Inside the eye the air is warmer than the air in the surrounding clouds, the wind is gentle, and the sky is clear. That is also where the air pressure is lowest. In the fiercest storms, generating sustained winds of more than 155 MPH (250 km/h), the surface atmospheric pressure in the eye is more than 10 percent below the average sea-level pressure. Around the eye, the *eyewall* contains the biggest clouds. That is where the strongest winds are found. The air pressure rises and wind speeds decrease with increasing distance from the eye.

Tropical cyclones derive their energy from the condensation of water vapor. Consequently, they need a warm sea to supply them with abundant moisture and are able to develop only when the temperature over a large area of the sea surface is at least 80°F (27°C). The sea is never warm enough

The Coriolis effect

Any object moving over the surface of the Earth, but that is not firmly attached to it, does not travel in a straight line. As the diagram illustrates, it is deflected to the right in the Northern Hemisphere and to the left in the Southern Hemisphere. As a consequence of

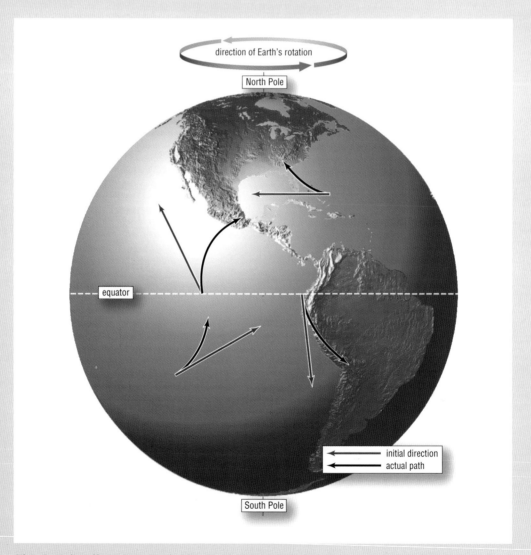

The Coriolis effect. Moving bodies, including air and water masses, are deflected to the right in the Northern Hemisphere and to the left in the Southern Hemisphere. The broken line shows the initial path, the black line the deflected (actual) path.

Consequences of the Coriolis effect. An airplane heading for New York and flying due north will be deflected to the right on a path taking it out over the Atlantic.

this, moving air and water tend to follow a clockwise path in the Northern Hemisphere and a counterclockwise path in the Southern Hemisphere.

The French physicist Gaspard-Gustave de Coriolis (1792–1843) discovered the reason for this in 1835 and it is called the *Coriolis effect*. It happens because the Earth is a rotating sphere, and as an object moves above the surface, the Earth below it is also moving. The effect used to be called the Coriolis "force" and it is still abbreviates as CorF, but it is not a force—there is nothing pushing or pulling the moving object sideways.

(continues)

(continued)

The Earth makes one complete turn on its axis every 24 hours. This means every point on the surface is constantly moving and returns to its original position (relative to the Sun) every 24 hours. Because the Earth is a sphere, however, different points on the surface travel different distances to do so. If you find it difficult to imagine that New York and Bogotá— or any other two places in different latitudes—are moving through space at different speeds, consider what would happen if this were not so: The world would tear itself apart.

Consider two points on the surface, one at the equator and the other at 40°N, which is the approximate latitude of New York City and Madrid. The equator, latitude 0°, is about 24,881 miles (40,033 km) long. That is how far a point on the equator must travel in 24 hours, which means it moves at about 1,037 MPH (1,668 km/h). At 40°N, the circumference parallel to the equator is about 19,057 miles (30,663 km). The point there has a shorter distance to travel and so it moves at about 794 MPH (1,277 km/h).

Suppose you planned to fly an aircraft to New York from the point on the equator due south of New York (and could ignore the winds). If you headed due north you would not reach New York. At the equator, sitting on the runway prior to takeoff, you are already traveling eastward at 1,037 MPH (1,668 km/h), carried by the Earth itself. As you fly north, the surface beneath you is also traveling east, but at a slower speed the farther you travel. If the journey from 0° to 40°N takes 6 hours, in that time you will also move about 6,000 miles (9,654 km) to the east, relative to the position of the surface beneath you. The surface itself would also move, however, at New York by about 4,700 miles (7,562 km). Consequently, you would end not at New York, but (6,000–4,700 =) 1,300 miles (2,092 km) to the east of New York, way out over the Atlantic. The diagram illustrates this.

The size of the Coriolis effect is directly proportional to the speed at which the body moves and to the sine of its latitude. The effect on a body moving at 100 MPH (160 km/h) is 10 times greater than that on one moving at 10 MPH (16 km/h). Since sin 0° = 0 (the equator) and sin 90° = 1 (the poles), the Coriolis effect is greatest at the poles and zero at the equator.

more than 20° from the equator. Between the equator and 20°N and 20°S, the sea warms through the summer, but it is late in the summer before it is warm enough for tropical cyclones to develop. Thus the season for tropical cyclones lasts from late summer until late autumn.

Cyclones must rotate. The Coriolis effect sets them turning, but this does not exist at the equator. Hence the initial depression must be no closer to the equator than 5°. These requirements mean that tropical cyclones develop only between 5° and 20°N and S, and only when the sea-surface temperature is 80°F (27°C) or higher. The necessary conditions are met in all the tropical oceans, with the exception of the South Atlantic, where until 2004 no tropical cyclone had ever developed because the Intertropical Convergence Zone (see "Trade winds" on page 50) never moves far enough to the south over the Atlantic. In March 2004, however, a hurricane producing winds of about 90 MPH (145 km/h) developed in the South Atlantic, crossing the coast of Santa Catarina State, Brazil, on March 28. This was highly unusual, and South American tropical forests are at risk of hurricane damage only in the far north of the continent—northern Colombia, Venezuela, and Guyana, and all of Suriname and French Guiana. Tropical cyclones never reach the Amazon Basin.

Once they have formed, tropical cyclones move westward at 10–15 MPH (16–24 km/h). They then turn away from the equator and accelerate, sometimes to as much as 30 MPH (48 km/h). As they move farther from the equator they experience a stronger Coriolis effect. This swings them still more. A tropical cyclone starts to weaken as soon as it crosses a coast because it loses contact with the warm sea that supplies its energy.

CHAPTER 4

TYPES OF TROPICAL FORESTS

Lowland wet forest

Seen from the air, a tropical forest appears as a vast, unbroken carpet of dark green. Beneath this canopy of treetops it is easy to picture a riotous tangle of vegetation, with shrubs, climbers, seedlings and saplings, and the lower part of the full-grown trees filling every corner. Anyone walking through the forest has to hack a path through the obstructing plants with a machete.

Not every tropical forest is like this, but many are. Forest of this type occurs close to the equator where the rain falls heavily throughout the year, from sea level to an elevation of about 4,000 feet (1,200 m). It is called *lowland wet forest,* and it is the most widespread type over much of the Asian Tropics. It also occurs in South America, most extensively near the mouth of the Amazon, and to a smaller extent in Africa. When people talk about tropical rain forest, this is the forest they have in mind. It is especially common on well-drained soils along broad river valleys and in the foothills of mountain ranges. Swamp forest takes the place of the lowland wet forest wherever the ground is covered by water for all or most of the year. There are large areas of swamp forest in the Congo River Basin in tropical Africa, where wide, slow-moving rivers feed water into the Zaire River (also known as the Congo River).

More plant species grow in lowland wet forest than in any other environment. A study of one 2.5-acre (1-ha) plot of lowland forest in Costa Rica found that it contained 223 trees belonging to 70 different species. Of this total, 66 species were represented by only one individual, and in many lowland wet forests the most abundant tree species contributes no more than about one in every 100 of the trees present. The lowland wet forest of Sarawak and Brunei, in Borneo, is believed to

Lowland rain forest supports a bewildering variety of plants, yet walking through the forest is not difficult. The floor is quite open. (Courtesy of Chad Truemper)

contain 1,800–2,300 species of trees. In contrast, the adjacent swamp forest supports only 234 species.

Mature trees often grow to a great height. On the best soils in New Guinea the crowns of the trees meet to form a complete canopy more than 100 feet (30 m) above the ground. Some trees, called *emergents* (see "Emergents" on pages 172–176), rise above the canopy to a height of more than 165 feet (50 m).

The tall trees are broad-leaved evergreens—trees that bear leaves at all times of year (see "Broad-leaved evergreen trees" on page 100). In Malaysia and Borneo many of the trees belong to the family Dipterocarpaceae. Dipterocarps have a characteristic shape. The lower part of the trunk is buttressed; that is, the lower part of the trunk has projections that help support the tree (see "Drip tips, buttress roots, and stilt roots" on pages 100–102). Above the buttresses, the trunk is smooth, cylindrical, and up to 15 feet (4.5 m) in circumference, with no branches below the crown. Until steps were taken to conserve stocks, their growth habit and pale, light-weight wood made dipterocarps the principal source of tropical hardwood, used to some extent in construction but mainly to make plywood and veneers. Krabak (*Anisoptera curtisii*), mersawa (*A. laevis*), Brunei teak (*Dryobalanops* species), lauan (*Parashorea malaanonan*), and red balan (several *Shorea* species) are typical dipterocarp timbers. *Dipterocarpus* species produce timbers known as *keruing* in Malaysia, *gurjun* in Indonesia, and *yang* in Burma. It is common to find many dipterocarp species growing side by side, which makes harvesting particular timbers difficult and destructive (see "Logging" on pages 216–220).

Elsewhere, other trees predominate. Dipterocarps grow in New Guinea, for example, but they do not form forests. Among the many species found in the New Guinea forests, there is one that produces the tallest of all tropical trees. Klinki pine (*Araucaria hunsteinii*) grows to a height of almost 295 feet (90 m), and its unseasoned timber is used to make plywood.

Tropical South America has the world's largest continuous area of lowland rain forest, known simply as *selva*, the Spanish word for "forest." The forest canopy is up to 120 feet (37 m) above the ground, and many of the emergent trees rise to 200 feet (61 m).

Many of the trees yield familiar, everyday products. Natural or Para rubber, for example, is obtained from *Hevea brasiliensis*, a tree belonging to the spurge family (Euphorbiaceae), and Brazil nuts are from *Bertholletia excelsa*. Brazil nuts are harvested from trees growing wild in the natural forest, and they have become so popular that there is a shortage of seedlings in some areas due to the removal of too many seeds. Kapok, which was used to stuff cushions until it was replaced by synthetic fibers, comes from the silk-cotton tree (*Ceiba pentandra*), and a hard timber called sucupira is obtained from two species of *Bowdichia* trees. Sapucaia nuts, also known as paradise nuts, are used to flavor chocolates. They are the fruits of *Lecythis zabucajo,* but nuts from the closely related trees *L. minor* and *L. ollaria* are poisonous. Anyone eating them will feel nauseous and may temporarily lose her or his hair and nails.

The Amazon forest contains many tree species. There may be 16–120 different species growing in a single acre of forest (40–300 species per hectare). This is not the most diverse forest, however. Scientists have found that the composition of Central American forests varies much more over short distances. An area of South American forest may contain many species, but unlike Central America, where the landscape is more varied, the same species are likely to occur in almost the same proportions over hundreds of square miles.

Seasonal forest

Even at the equator, the noonday Sun is directly overhead on only two days each year—the March and September equinoxes (see "Dry seasons and rainy seasons" on pages 53–56). Consequently, there are small variations in climate through the year, although over much of the equatorial region these are too small to be significant.

With increasing distance from the equator, however, the climate becomes more seasonal. Rain falls predominantly during one part of the year, and there is a dry season lasting for at least a few weeks and in some places for six months or even longer. The most extreme contrasts between the wet and dry seasons produce a *monsoon* climate, with its own type of forest (see "Monsoon forest" on pages 94–96). The monsoon contrast is greatest in Asia, but strongly seasonal climates occur even in the interior of South America. Cuiabá, Brazil, for example, is at latitude 15.5°S and close to the western edge of the Mato Grosso Plateau in the center of Brazil. It has an average annual rainfall of 54 inches (1,376 mm), of which 49 inches (1,253 mm) falls between October and April. During the dry season, from May to September, the area receives only five inches (123 mm). The Caribbean islands also experience seasonal variations in rainfall, as does most of tropical Africa.

Temperature remains high throughout the year, with a greater difference between day and night temperatures than between seasonal temperatures. June is the coolest month at Cuiabá, with an average temperature of 74.8°F (23.8°C), and the warmest months are September, October, and November, when the temperature averages 81.9°F (27.7°C), giving an annual temperature range of only 7.1°F (3.9°C). The warm temperature means that the rate of evaporation is high at all times of year, and during the dry season it may exceed the rainfall. If more water evaporates than falls as rain, the ground will dry out and there may be drought.

Vegetation adapts to the climate, and the character of tropical forest changes. Where the dry season is short, the trees are evergreen and the forest closely resembles lowland wet forest (see pages 80–83). Where the dry season is rather longer, the composition begins to change. The evergreen trees are smaller and form an understory. The dominant trees forming the upper canopy are deciduous, shedding their leaves during the dry season as a means of conserving moisture. In semi-evergreen rain forest, up to one-third of the trees are deciduous, although not all of them shed their leaves at the same time.

This is seasonal forest, and it covers a bigger area than any other type of tropical forest, occupying the central part of the Amazon Basin, the moister parts of tropical Africa, and parts of many Caribbean islands. It contains many tree species but fewer than are found in a comparable area of lowland wet forest, and extensive stands of a single species are common. Forest of this type is known in Africa as *miombo,* and *Brachystegia, Julbernardia,* or *Isoberlinia* species dominate large areas of it. Elsewhere in Africa and Asia the forest consists mainly of teak—*Tectona grandis* in Asia and *Oldfieldia africana* in Africa—and mountain ebony (*Bauhinia* species). Beneath these deciduous trees the understory contains evergreens, such as *Eucalyptus* species in parts of New Guinea and the banyan tree (*Ficus benghalensis*) in Asia.

The banyan is one of more than 800 species of figs, and like several others it begins life as an *epiphyte* growing in the crown of another tree (see "Stranglers" on pages 187–189), which is where its seeds germinate. Its roots grow downward all around the host tree, and once they have reached the ground and developed side roots, the upper parts thicken into trunks. In Portuguese a *banyan* or *banian* (originally from a Gujarati word) is a trader, and the tree is said to have acquired its name from the traders often seen resting in its shade. Legend has it that the army of Alexander the Great sheltered among the trunk roots of a banyan. In addition to the banyan, epiphytic ferns and orchids are common in some places.

Many of both the deciduous and evergreen trees have buttresses, and their bark tends to be thicker and rougher than that of the trees in lowland wet forest. The thicker bark may be an adaptation to more frequent forest fires. When the leaves of deciduous trees dry out on the forest floor during the dry season, they provide fuel that can be ignited by lightning. Fires are fairly common. The trees are more widely spaced than in the lowland wet forest, allowing more light to reach the forest floor. This also accelerates the drying of litter.

Still farther from the equator, between the seasonal forest and the open savanna grasslands, there are areas that receive less than one inch (25 mm) of rain per month during two months of the dry season. Forest trees can survive in this climate, but they consist of broad-leaved deciduous species and this is sometimes known as dry forest. Dry forests occur in South America and Asia, but not in Africa. The canopy is at a height of 60–80 feet (18–24 m), and emergents—the tallest trees—are widely scattered. The understory trees are 10–30 feet (3–10 m) tall. There are few climbers or epiphytes and, although sunlight reaches the forest floor, herbs are sparse. Typical shrubs include *Mimosa* and *Acacia* species. Bamboos are common, and there are bamboo thickets in some places.

Montane forest

Mountaineers wear warm clothes even though they are engaged in a strenuous sport. Without their gloves, sweaters, thick trousers, woolen hats, and thick socks, climbers might well succumb to the cold because the higher they climb the colder the air becomes. The rate at which the temperature decreases with height varies depending on the amount of moisture in the air, but it averages 3.6°F for every 1,000 feet (6.5°C per kilometer). Even at the equator, it is possible for the peak of a high mountain to be permanently covered in snow. If the temperature at sea level, in the lowland wet forest, is 80°F (27°C), at 15,000 feet (4,575 m) it will be 26°F (–3°C). And that is not the only change: Winds usually blow more strongly on mountainsides. This is because the wind reaching a mountainside travels a shorter distance through the trees that slow it down than the wind blowing over more level ground, as shown in the illustration, and wind has a chilling effect.

The plants that grow in a tropical forest are adapted to the high temperature. Not surprisingly, lowland plants fail to thrive at high elevations. Tropical mountainsides are blanketed in forest, but the forest is different from the lowland forest. It is called *montane forest,* the forest of mountains, and because air temperature decreases with elevation, the composition of the forest also changes. There are several types of montane forest.

In a lowland wet forest, the majority of trees are broadleaved evergreens. The forest canopy is about 80–145 feet (24–44 m) above ground level, and emergent trees, towering above the canopy, grow to a height of 200–260 feet (61–79 m).

Wind on a mountainside. Wind blowing along the level ground at the foot of the mountain is slowed by friction with the trees. On the steep mountainside it passes through fewer trees, experiences less friction, and therefore blows more strongly.

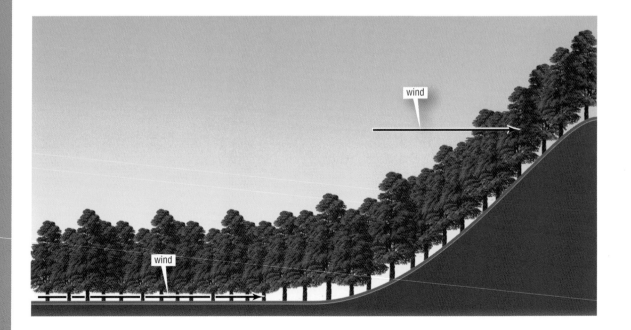

The trees have large leaves and many of them have trunks with large buttresses (see "Drip tips, buttress roots, and stilt roots" on pages 104–108). Lowland trees often produce their flowers directly on their branches and trunks—a feature called *cauliflory*. There are big, woody climbers everywhere, many of them firmly attached to the trunks of the forest trees, and epiphytes (plants growing on the bark of the trees) are common, but there are few lichens, mosses, or other non-vascular plants.

The change with height begins slowly, and the plants growing 1,000 feet (300 m) above sea level are often indistinguishable from those of the lowlands. But some of the lowland trees are absent above this elevation, and others, less tolerant of the lowland climate, take their place. By about 2,500 feet (760 m) the change is more obvious as the forest becomes *lower montane forest*. The trees are related to those of the lowland forest, but they belong to different species and are not so tall. The canopy is at about 50–100 feet (15–30 m). There are few emergents, with none at all over large areas. Those that do occur grow only to about 120 feet (37 m). Fewer of the trees bear buttresses, and the buttresses themselves are smaller. Cauliflory is uncommon. The big woody climbers have disappeared, but there are more of the climbers that cling to tree trunks. There are more epiphytes than in the lowland forest and some are nonvascular.

Above about 4,000 feet (1,200 m) the character of the forest changes radically. The trees of the lowland forest disappear entirely and their place taken by oak and laurel—species more typical of temperate climates. If the average sea-level temperature is 80°F (27°C), at 4,000 feet (1,200 m) it is 66°F (19°C).

The *upper montane forest* occurs above about 5,000 feet (1,500 m). No lowland trees grow at this altitude. Instead there are coniferous trees, heaths and heathers—some of them the size of small trees—and myrtles. Most of the woody plants have small or needle-shaped leaves, which help the plant conserve moisture. This is necessary because the wind has a strong drying effect. The forest canopy is lower than about 60 feet (18 m). Emergents are rare, but those that do rise above the canopy are no more than about 85 feet (26 m) tall. Few of the trees have buttresses, and none is cauliflorous. There are few climbers of any kind, but there are many epiphytes. Ferns, lichens, and nonvascular epiphytes are especially common.

At this height the forest growing on the mountainside is very different from the forest growing on the lowlands at the foot of the mountain.

Cloud forest

Mountain peaks are often shrouded in mist. In fact, the mist is really low cloud, although it feels like very wet fog to anyone walking through it. The tiny water droplets cling to everything, and so everything is wet—the ground, exposed rocks, and plants. It is a thoroughly sodden environment and one that supports its own distinctive communities of plants.

The low cloud that envelops tropical mountainsides provides abundant moisture for mosses, ferns, and many other plants, making the vegetation of cloud forest especially exuberant. These plants are growing in the Monteverde Cloud Forest Reserve, Costa Rica. (Courtesy of Michael and Patricia Fogden/ Minden Pictures)

Why it rains more on mountainsides

When air rises, its temperature falls. Warm air can hold more water vapor than cold air can, so reducing the temperature of the air raises its relative humidity (RH), which is the amount of water vapor present in the air measured as a percentage of the amount needed to saturate the air at that temperature.

The *lifting condensation level* is an altitude at which the RH in rising air reaches 100 percent and the air becomes saturated. When air rises above the lifting condensation level, its water vapor starts condensing to form clouds. When the clouds are big enough, their droplets or ice crystals merge until they are heavy enough to fall as rain or snow.

Air is forced to rise as it approaches a mountain. The air is dry until it is lifted above the lifting condensation level; that is, all of the moisture it carries is present as water vapor (a gas) rather than liquid droplets, so the RH is less than 100 percent. Cloud starts to form at the lifting condensation level, and precipitation begins to fall on the mountainside. The air continues to rise, and more cloud forms at higher elevations. This intensifies the precipitation on the mountainside.

When the rising air reaches the top of the mountain it may continue to rise or it may subside down the opposite (lee) side of the mountain. If it continues rising, eventually it will lose enough water for precipitation to end, although cloud may extend some distance downwind. If the air subsides, it will sink below the lifting condensation level once more. Precipitation will then cease and the cloud will dissipate as its droplets evaporate.

The overall result is that mountainsides receive more precipitation than the low ground surrounding the mountain.

Mountainsides are wet places because air is forced to rise as it crosses a mountain and as it rises its temperature falls (see the sidebar "Adiabatic cooling and warming" on page 57). The amount of moisture air can hold is proportional to the air temperature, so rising air is likely to become saturated. When air is saturated, its water vapor starts to condense into liquid droplets, forming cloud, and as the droplets merge with one another and grow the moisture may fall as rain. On the upper slopes of high mountains, where the air temperature is below freezing, water vapor condenses into ice crystals that join together to form snowflakes, and the moisture falls as snow (see the sidebar).

Cloud envelops parts of the upper montane forest (see "Montane forest" on pages 85–88) for much of the time. This alters the character of the forest, transforming it into *cloud forest,* also known as *mossy forest.*

Abundant moisture provides ideal growing conditions for mosses, liverworts, and hornworts, the nonvascular plants that together are known informally as *bryophytes,* and also for ferns, which are vascular plants that reproduce by means of spores rather than seeds. Instead of producing pollen that can be dispersed by the wind or by animals, male bryophytes and ferns release sperm that swim through water to find and fertilize the eggs of female plants. Consequently, the plants are able to grow only where there is a film of water through which their sperm can travel.

In tropical cloud forests the warm temperatures combine with the moisture to produce luxuriant growths of bryophytes and ferns. This type of forest grows especially well in high valleys and the saddle-shaped depressions between areas of high ground, where the moist air tends to be funneled. In these places the mosses, including *Sphagnum* bog moss, which can absorb and hold several times its own weight of water, form a thick carpet on the ground. Mosses are not confined to the ground, however. Other species coat the trunks and branches of trees. Ferns grow on tree branches as well as on the ground, and some of those on the ground are tree ferns. Even the crowns of the trees are encased in bryophytes.

As well as the ferns and bryophytes, bromeliads grow in the American tropical forests. These are epiphytes—"air plants" that use forest trees only for support, drawing all their nutrients from the air and from water that collects in the hollows where large branches join the main trunk. One of the most characteristic plants of the American cloud forests is known as Spanish moss, Florida moss, and old man's beard. It occurs from Florida to Argentina—a range of 5,000 miles (8,000 km) from north to south—and hangs in great festoons from the cloud-forest trees. It is not a moss at all, however, but a bromeliad (*Tillandsia usneoides*). Many orchids grow as epiphytes, and they are also abundant in the cloud forest.

Elfin forest

On really high mountains, the upper part of the cloud forest takes on a strange, unreal appearance. The trees are smaller. In places the canopy is no more than about five feet (1.5 m) above ground level, and the trees themselves are twisted into curious shapes. The trunks and branches are covered in mosses and lichens (see the sidebar). Long festoons of lichens also hang down from tree branches. Ferns grow upright on the upper sides of branches, and there are many filmy ferns, with leaves that are only one cell thick and almost transparent. The ground is littered with fallen branches that decompose much more slowly than surface litter in the warmer lowland forest. Fallen branches make the surface uneven, but they are not visible. A thick carpet of moss covers them.

This otherworldly environment is called *elfin forest.* Elfin forest is very remote. It develops in the Tropics only on mountains that are more than about 10,000 feet (3,000 m) high, so reaching it involves a trek through the lowland forest followed by a long climb. Its remoteness adds to its eerie quality. Sometimes dry and sunlit, but often quiet and shrouded in mist, elfin forest is a place that is easy to imagine inhabited by fairy folk.

Elfin forest grows close to the uppermost margin for trees. Trees rarely grow where the mean summer temperature is lower than 50°F (10°C). The boundary above which there are no trees is known as the *tree line.* In the Tropics the tree line is at about 12,500 feet (3,800 m).

The name *tree line* is a little misleading because the boundary is not abrupt. With increasing elevation, the forest becomes more open. Shrubs grow among the trees where daylight reaches the ground, and eventually the forest gives way to scrub dominated by scattered shrubs that are no more than knee-high, with the occasional small tree rising above them. Then there are no more trees. The tree line has been crossed, but it is impossible to mark its precise location: It is not clearly defined, like the boundary separating a temperate forest from a cultivated field.

If the mountain is tall enough, grasses and flowering herbs cover the ground above the tree line, with occasional shrubs in sheltered places. This is *alpine meadow.* Higher still, the climate

What are lichens?

Some look like tiny shrubs, others resemble flattened leaves, and there are those that look like a smear of paint. All of them are lichens. They grow on rocks, the roofs of buildings, and the trunks and branches of trees. In some forests they festoon tree branches.

People often suppose that lichens are a type of moss, but they are not. Strictly speaking they are not plants at all. A patch of lichen consists of millions of single-celled organisms living inside a fungus. This kind of close relationship, from which both partners benefit, is known as *mutualism.*

Mushrooms, toadstools, and molds are all fungi, but the part of the fungus that you see is the *fruiting body*—the structure the fungus produces when it is time for it to release spores for reproduction. The main part of the fungus exists as minute threads called *hyphae* (singular *hypha*) that form a network called a *mycelium.* The fungus absorbs nutrients through its hyphae.

In a lichen, photosynthesizing cells are lodged among the hyphae, just below the lichen's upper surface. Depending on the species of lichen, these cells are either algae or cyanobacteria, and they may live as separate cells or be joined to form fine filaments. The fungus is the main part of the lichen, and the scientific name of the lichen is taken from that of the fungal partner.

The fungus protects its photosynthesizing partner. Its hyphae retain water and dissolved minerals and produce pigments that shade the photosynthesizing cells from intense sunlight. The hyphae also secrete acids that assist in the uptake of minerals, and in some species the hyphae secrete poisons that prevent the lichen from being eaten. The algal or cyanobacterial partner produces sugars by photosynthesis, some of which are used by the fungus. As well as reproducing by means of fungal fruiting bodies, lichens also release *soredia,* structures comprising a few fungal cells together with a few algal or cyanobacterial cells that will grow if they fall onto a suitable surface. Releasing soredia is a type of asexual reproduction, meaning that it does not involve the fertilization of an egg by sperm.

Lichens are extremely tough organisms. They can survive prolonged drought, and when water becomes available they can absorb more than 10 times their own weight and resume their growth immediately. Some individual lichens are thousands of years old. Most species of lichens cannot tolerate sulfur dioxide, however, and disappear in areas where the air is polluted. This sensitivity makes them useful indicators of polluted air.

There are more than 25,000 species of lichens. These can be divided into three groups on the basis of their appearance. *Foliose* lichens are loosely attached to the tree or rock surface and have a flattened, leaflike appearance. *Fruticose* lichens are attached to the surface at only one point; some are upright and shrublike, others hang down like tassels. *Crustose* lichens are firmly attached to the surface and look as though they have been smeared onto it.

is too cold and the soil too thin for meadow. Scattered clumps of grass and patches of herbs grow among the bare rocks. Finally there is a region where no plants grow, and above that, at 15,500–17,400 feet (4,727–5,310 m) in the Northern Hemisphere Tropics and 16,800–17,400 feet (5,125–5,310 m) in the Southern Hemisphere Tropics, lies the *snow line*. The snow line marks the boundary above which the mountain is covered with snow throughout the year. It is lower where cold air clings in shaded gullies and higher on exposed surfaces facing the equator, but the line is clear.

Bamboo forest

Where tropical forest has been cleared and the site left to such plants as may chance to arrive and colonize it, the resulting vegetation tends to form an almost impenetrable thicket. Roads are often lined by thickets of this kind, composed of plants that have grown up on the land that was disturbed when the roads were built. This is the vegetation that visitors see when they drive through the forest. People sometimes call lowland tropical forest *jungle,* but this dense vegetation on disturbed ground is the true jungle, and it is quite different from the mature forest lying behind it.

In places the jungle is dominated not by trees or shrubs but by thickets of bamboo. Bamboo thickets also occur naturally in undisturbed cloud forests. In Africa, for example, the bamboo zone occurs between about 7,875 feet and 9,200 feet (2,400–2,800 m), where the forest is dominated by dense stands of montane bamboo (*Arundinaria alpina*) that are 40–50 feet (12–15 m) tall. Bamboos grow naturally in the tropical forests of America and Africa, but the greatest number of species occurs in Asia. The most famous animal inhabitants of the bamboo forests are the giant panda (*Ailuropoda melanoleuca*) of central China and the red panda (*Ailurus fulgens*) which lives in the mountains from southwestern China through western Burma to Nepal. Both pandas eat bamboo shoots, and these are the main food for the giant panda.

Although extensive bamboo thickets are called "forests," and the plants are sometimes as much as 130 feet (40 m) tall, bamboo is not a tree but a member of the grass family (Poaceae). There are about 480 species of bamboos, but despite the number of species, all of them are instantly recognizable as bamboos. A bamboo has a hollow, woody stem, called a *culm,* with solid partitions, called *nodes,* at intervals along it. The regions between nodes are *internodes.* The culms are green because the cells immediately beneath the surface contain chlorophyll (see the sidebar "Photosynthesis" on page 171), but after bamboo has been cut the chlorophyll breaks down and the culms turn brown. Branches, leaves, and flowers develop from the nodes. After it has flowered and set seed, a bamboo plant dies. In most species the plant grows from nodes occurring at intervals along underground stems called *rhizomes,* which is why bamboos often form dense clumps. Their ability to spread by extending their rhizomes and to grow rapidly allows bamboos to spread into disturbed ground. It also makes bamboos a nuisance when they colonize places where they are not wanted.

Throughout much of the Tropics, but especially in Asia, bamboos are possibly the most useful of all plants. Bamboo shoots are eaten as a vegetable and the seeds are also edible. Smaller bamboos can be cultivated to make hedges. The culms of the bigger bamboos can be up to 12 inches (30 cm) in diameter. They are waterproof and extremely strong. Bamboo of this type is used to make scaffolding, to build bridges, and to construct the framework for buildings. Split and flattened culms are used as flooring. Hollowed culms are used as pipes to carry water, and internodes sealed at one end by their node partitions make useful containers. Smaller bamboos are made into musical instruments, walking sticks, umbrellas, and chopsticks, and are woven to make fish traps and baskets, mats, window blinds, hats, and fans. Bamboo is also pulped to make high-quality paper.

Monsoon forest

Despite their proximity to the equator, most parts of the Tropics have a seasonal climate. Temperatures change little through the year, but the rainfall is not spread evenly. There are, at least to some extent, two seasons, one dry and the other rainy, and the plants growing in tropical forests are adapted to them (see "Seasonal forest" on pages 83–85). This contrast is most extreme in those regions with a monsoon climate (see "Monsoons" on pages 63–68). There the rainfall is very intense during the rainy season, and the dry season is a time of severe drought.

Plants must adapt to these seasonal changes, and forests that grow in a monsoon climate—the *monsoon forests*—are therefore different from the lowland wet forests in composition and appearance. Monsoon forests occur in eastern Brazil, the southern part of central Africa, and northern Australia, but they are most extensive in southern Asia. This is not surprising because the contrast between monsoon seasons is strongest in southern Asia and the monsoons affect a much bigger area of Asia than of any other continent.

Drought during the dry winter monsoon is the condition the forest plants must tolerate, and some species are more successful than others. The severity of the winter drought varies considerably from place to place, however, and soils also vary: Some retain water for longer than others or supply more plant nutrients. Consequently there are many different types of monsoon forest, and since the variations in rainfall and soils occur fairly locally—on opposite sides of a range of hills, for example—the monsoon forest is usually an intricate patchwork of slightly different forest types.

Lowland wet forest also occurs in monsoon areas. It penetrates the monsoon forests along river valleys, where soils are moist even through the dry season. These long, narrow strips of rain forest are known as *gallery forest*. Elsewhere, patches of monsoon forest and rain forest occur side by side. In some places, for example, including eastern Java and the Lesser Sunda Islands to the east of Java and south of Sulawesi, the forest is mainly of the monsoon type, with isolated patches of rain forest on south-facing mountainsides exposed to onshore winds that bring rain. In the Molucca Islands to the north of the Sundas, the pattern is reversed. There the rain forest predominates but with patches of monsoon forest among it. At about the Isthmus of Kra (10.42°N, 99.33°E) in southern Thailand, there is a sharply defined boundary between the monsoon forest to the north and the evergreen rain forest to the south and continuing into Malaysia.

Many of the trees in monsoon forest and most of the trees in some forests are broad-leaved and deciduous, shedding their leaves during the dry season. An exception to this is found in Australia, where monsoon forests are dominated by evergreen *Eucalyptus* species. Pine trees (*Pinus* species) also grow in the Asian monsoon forests, and bamboo thickets are common. The trees tend to be shorter than those of the lowland wet forest, and the forest canopy is more open.

During the dry season the fallen leaves and other forest-floor litter dry out and become highly flammable. Natural fires, ignited by lightning, are common in some areas. In other areas fires are set deliberately by people wishing to clear land for conversion to farmland, to drive game into the open where it can be killed, and for a number of other reasons— even to annoy people in neighboring villages. Grasses quickly establish themselves on land that has been cleared by fire, and little by little the monsoon forest is transformed into savanna grassland. Some ecologists suspect that most or even all tropical grasslands, except for those in obviously swampy areas, were once monsoon forest and that repeated burning by local people transformed the forest into grassland. Monsoon forests and the grasslands derived from them are the principal vegetation types in Thailand, Myanmar, Cambodia, India, and Sri Lanka.

Whether or not all tropical grasslands are derived from monsoon forest, the two vegetation types merge, with the forest becoming more open and grasses occupying the ground between them, until there are only scattered trees and shrubs among the grass. In contrast, the boundary between monsoon forest and rain forest is often sharp— because rain forests are too wet to burn readily.

Mangrove forest

A tree that is able to grow where no other tree can survive has no competitors for nutrients or light, and there is one group of trees that thrive at the edge of the sea. They grow in shallow salt water, with their roots immersed deep in black, waterlogged—and therefore airless—mud. The trees are *mangroves,* a general name that describes any tree or shrub that grows with its roots in salt water. Scientists disagree about just how many species of mangroves there are, but depending on how they are defined, there are between about 54 and 75 species belonging to 16–24 plant families.

The greatest number of species occurs in the Indo-Malayan region, which is where mangroves likely originated. Mangroves produce seeds that float and also floating fruits with seeds that germinate inside them. Most generate new plants not far from where they enter the water, but ocean currents carried some of these seeds and fruits westward to India and East Africa and eastward to Central and South America. Later, mangroves spread by similar means through the Caribbean and seeds drifted crossed the Atlantic Ocean to West Africa. Eventually they reached as far as New Zealand.

Mangroves now grow along sheltered coasts between latitudes 32°N and 38°S. This includes the coasts of Baja California and the Gulf of Mexico, where the most widespread species are red mangrove (*Rhizophora mangle*), black mangrove (*Avicennia germinans*), white mangrove (*Laguncularia racemosa*), and sweet mangrove (*Maytenus phyllanthoides*). Species of *Sonneratia* and *Bruguiera* are especially common among the mangroves found along Asian coasts.

As well as their floating *propagules*—structures such as seeds and fruits that allow a plant to propagate itself some distance from the parent—certain mangroves, including *Rhizophora* and *Avicennia* species, are *viviparous,* which means they produce live offspring. Seeds germinate inside the fruit, which remains on the tree until the young plant has grown into a small seedling. The young plant then falls from the tree, and it stands a much better chance of surviving in the mud below than a seed would have of germinating and reaching the same stage of development.

Many species also spread *vegetatively*—without the help of seeds. These mangroves constantly produce *adventitious roots*—roots that grow from an unusual part of the plant—from their trunks and branches. The roots arch downward until they reach the mud, where they produce side roots and shoots that grow upward to become new trunks. In this way a single tree grows into a clump of trees with a dense tangle of aerial roots and trunks.

Mangroves must also thrive with their roots in airless mud and in salt water. All plant roots need to absorb air for respiration. To solve this problem, mangrove trees have roots that project above the mud (see "Growing in mud: peg roots" on pages 108–111). The parts of the root above the surface have small pores, called *lenticels,* that open to allow air to enter the root, where it spreads throughout the root through *aerenchyma*—plant tissue containing air spaces. The lenticels open at low tide, when the roots are exposed, and close as the tide rises and immerses them.

There are two ways in which different mangrove species deal with excess salt. All plants absorb water through their roots, and some mangrove roots are able to exclude salt, so they absorb only freshwater. Other species take in salt water but then remove the salt and excrete it as concentrated brine from *salt-secreting trichomes*—specialized glands in their leaves. The brine is either washed from the leaves by rain or a rising tide, or it dries to a powder and is blown away by the wind.

Mangroves grow only in calm, sheltered water, although they can withstand occasional storms. If the water moved vigorously all the time, the seeds, fruits, and seedlings would be swept away before they were able to establish themselves. Leaves and dead branches from the mangroves remain where they fall, and particles of silt and sand, carried by the tides, are trapped among the mangrove roots and settle. Accumulating mud around the tree roots makes the water shallower, and this allows the trees to grow a little farther from the shore. Little by little the mangroves advance, and in doing so they extend the land outward from the shore and form mangrove forests. The forests comprise plants ranging in size from low shrubs to trees up to 130 feet (40 m) tall.

Today mangrove forests grow along most sheltered tropical and subtropical coasts and estuaries. (An estuary is a body of coastal water in which outflowing river water meets saltwater at a boundary that moves back and forth with the tides.) They begin in mud but will expand onto sand and even onto the surface of coral. Provided tides regularly immerse their roots in saltwater, mangroves growing in estuaries will spread far upstream, taking them a long way inland. Altogether, mangrove forests cover an area of about 85,000 square miles (220,000 km^2), but they are being cleared, partly through logging for timber and partly to provide land for other uses, especially artificial ponds for raising shrimps.

Mangrove trees provide useful timber and edible fruit for local communities, and they are also ecologically important. By trapping sediment they also protect offshore beds of sea grass and coral reefs from being buried in silt. In addition, the forests provide an environment that supports a wide diversity of species, such as young fish, crabs, shrimps, and mollusks, as well as manatees and dugongs, crab-eating monkeys, fishing cats, lizards, sea turtles, and many others. The trees offer nesting sites to many species of migratory birds. Without mangrove forests—"rain forests by the sea"—many tropical coasts would quickly deteriorate.

CHAPTER 5

LIFE IN TROPICAL FORESTS

Broad-leaved evergreen trees

Plants that grow in a seasonal climate must be able to survive drought lasting weeks or months. This is true everywhere, not only in the Tropics. Summer droughts happen only occasionally in temperate regions, but the cold winters of high latitudes have a similar effect. Roots absorb liquid water. Frozen water cannot cross cell membranes to enter root tissue, so it is useless to them. Consequently, a period when water in the soil is frozen down to the level of plant roots is effectively a drought, even though the ground is deeply covered by snow and will become sodden when the snow and ice thaw.

Coniferous trees grow well in strongly seasonal climates. They form the vast forests stretching across northern Canada and Eurasia where winters are harsh, and they also thrive in lower latitudes, where almost no rain falls during a dry season lasting several months. The leaves of coniferous trees are reduced to needles or small scales, most of them with a tough, waxy outer coat. Each leaf bears very few *stomata*—the pores through which gases are exchanged and water evaporates. Consequently, individual leaves retain moisture well. Many flowering plants solve the problem differently. They avoid the loss of water from leaf stomata by shedding their leaves at the commencement of the dry season. Because their leaves need to last for only a few months and must be replaced each year, the plants economize on the resources used to grow them by making the leaves thin and no more rigid than is necessary for them to expose their upper surfaces to the light.

Trees that shed their leaves prepare to do so in response to the shortening days and falling temperatures of early autumn. They withdraw useful substances from the leaves into the main body of the tree before detaching the leaves.

Conditions in a tropical forest are rather different. Temperatures change more between day and night than they do from one season to another, and although the day length changes, except very close to the equator the seasonal change is small. The result is that within the same patch of forest there are often trees that retain their leaves throughout the year, others that shed their leaves during the dry season, and trees that retain their leaves through the dry season and shed them during the rainy season. In lowland wet forests, however, where there is no dry season, most of the trees are broad-leaved and bear leaves at all times of the year—they are evergreen.

Evergreen broad-leaved trees must produce leaves that last longer than those of deciduous trees. The leaves must be tougher to resist damage from battering by the wind, from rubbing against each other, or from attacks by leaf-eating insects. Evergreen trees pay a price for this: The tree must devote more resources to producing its leaves, and tough, relatively thick leaves are less efficient at photosynthesis than the flimsier leaves of deciduous trees, so the tree may need more of them.

Some broad-leaved evergreen trees and shrubs grow in temperate regions, in places where they can find water throughout the year. These include holly (*Ilex aquifolium*), rhododendrons (*Rhododendron* species), and laurel (*Laurus* species). Leaves of these plants are very similar in structure and texture to those of the broad-leaved evergreen trees of the tropical forests.

Leaves do not last forever, of course, no matter how tough they are, and so evergreen trees replace their leaves from time to time. Some tropical trees even shed all of their leaves at the same time and grow new ones within a matter of days. Cyp or cypre trees (*Cordia alliodora*) of the Central and South American forests sometimes stand leafless for weeks on end in the middle of the rainy season. No one knows why evergreen trees do this, but it may be to rid themselves of plant-eating insects.

Trees do not waste resources, and shading is the most common reason for shedding leaves. If higher leaves shade those below, the shaded leaves photosynthesize less efficiently than the illuminated ones and the tree discards them. Many leaves are shed in this way as trees compete with one another high in the forest canopy to expose as many leaves as possible to the bright sunlight. With some species, even the slightest shadow on a leaf may be enough to make it fall, but other species are more tolerant of shade, allowing the crowns of different species to overlap. Adjacent trees of the same species do not overlap their crowns because both are equally intolerant of shading. Generally, the competition for light produces a closed canopy in which tree crowns fit together to maximize exposure to sunlight. The different shades of green that are clearly visible when the forest canopy is viewed from the air probably reflect differences in shade tolerance among the dominant species. Once the crowns are established, evergreen trees replace leaves only when they are damaged, and individual leaves can last for several years.

Dominant trees have few branches below the crown. As the trees grow taller they shed their lower leaves and branches. These are no longer of much use for photosynthesis, they are vulnerable to attack by insects and other plant eaters, and they provide points of attachment for climbers, factors that combine to make the lower leaves a liability to the tree.

Shrubs growing beneath the canopy, as well as tree seedlings and saplings (see "Forest layers" on pages 166–167), have leaves that tolerate shade and are tougher than those in the canopy. Being closer to ground level, they are more likely to be damaged by animals that brush past them or try to eat them.

How plants are adapted to the climate

Tropical sunlight is intensely bright, and the trees of tropical forests compete vigorously with each other to expose as much leaf surface to it as they can. This produces a closed canopy, and once adjacent tree crowns meet, there is not much an individual tree can do to win a bigger share of the sunshine.

There is one possible strategy, however, and many of the forest trees exploit it. They have long roots that run horizontally just below the ground surface, and new shoots are able to grow from nodes at intervals along them. If the new shoots, called *suckers,* appear beneath a gap in the canopy, they produce root systems of their own and are capable of growing into full-size trees. In effect the tree is spreading its crown. This is not a form of reproduction, because the new trees are really part of the older tree and share its root system. Even if the root connection is severed, the young and old trees are genetically identical and so are clones of each other, rather than parent and offspring. There are tree species that spread in this way in temperate forests, but suckering is much more common in tropical forests, where the climate allows roots to continue growing throughout the year.

There are clear advantages to the tree that spreads in this way. Seeds may or may not germinate and seedlings will survive only if they emerge where there is space for them to obtain the nutrients they need. In contrast, the root sucker has unrestricted access to the resources of the established tree until it is able to rely on its own roots. In seasonal climates a sucker can continue to grow leaves well into the dry season and long after tree seedlings have had to shed their leaves. Once the sucker matures, it is able to reproduce sexually, allowing the tree to disperse seeds and spread still farther.

The ability to spread by means of root suckers can make species invasive. Indian plum (*Flacourtia rukam*) is an example. A tree up to 65 feet (20 m) tall, Indian plum is native to Malesia (the region comprising Malaysia, Indonesia, Papua New Guinea, and the Philippines). Cultivated in gardens, it has escaped from cultivation and become naturalized on other Pacific islands, and in some of them it is invading the habitat of native species.

Many climbing plants (see "Lianas and other climbers" on pages 176–177) also spread by root suckering, and climbers have the added advantage of using trees for support. With no need to grow strong trunks, they can gain height much faster than a tree and reach the sunlight by opening their leaves in the crowns of dominant trees.

Out on open grasslands, where it is often windy, many plants are pollinated by the wind. This is not suitable for the plants growing in tropical forest, however, where the dense vegetation blocks the wind and usually the air is still. Instead, insects pollinate most forest plants, some plants are pollinated by birds, and some by bats. Even close relatives of plants that are wind-pollinated in open environments rely on animals for pollination in the forest. There are insect-pollinated grasses, palm trees, bananas, and many others.

Thousands of species of plants in the American tropical forests rely exclusively on hummingbirds for pollination. Honeyeaters—169 species of birds belonging to the family Meliphagidae—pollinate plants of the African, Asian, and Australian forests. There is a risk to the plants in relying on birds and bats for pollination. Birds probing for nectar sometimes damage flowers, and bats sometimes eat the entire flower. On the whole, however, the strategy is successful and the plants thrive.

Plants that rely on animals for pollination must attract their pollinators. They do this by producing conspicuous flowers, and that is why there are so many flowers in tropical forests: Flowers are the plants' adaptation to the lack of wind. The pollinators also thrive, of course, and the flowers of tropical forests support countless thousands of species of insects.

Just as the plants cannot rely on the wind for pollination, neither can they rely on wind to disperse their seeds. Some of the trees forming the canopy produce wind-dispersed seeds, because the wind is more reliable above the forest, but those growing at lower levels use animals to carry their seeds to new locations. Most do this by producing edible and attractive fruit. Animals eat the fruit and either drop the seeds onto the ground or swallow them and excrete them later, unaltered by their passage through the digestive system. The fruits attract particular consumers that will not destroy the seeds or take them to places where they cannot germinate. Fruits intended for birds are often brightly colored; those that attract bats are usually green or yellow; very sweet fruits are eaten by animals that also eat insects or leaves; and oily fruits attract species that feed mainly on fruits. Fruits with similar flavors are eaten by the same animal species.

Drip tips, buttress roots, and stilt roots

Too much rain can be as harmful as too little, especially for the leaves of evergreen plants. Water clings to surfaces, coating them with a thin film. Most of the moisture that reaches a tropical forest arrives as rain. Approximately 25 percent of the rain falls onto leaves in the forest canopy and evaporates from them, and approximately 40 percent runs down the bark of tree trunks. Some of the water running down trunks soaks into dry bark and some evaporates before it reaches the ground. Of the remaining rain, some falls onto leaves in the understory (see "Forest layers" on pages 166–167) and evaporates from there. Less than 30 percent of the total rainfall reaches the ground.

Most of the moisture arrives as rain, but not all of it. There is usually heavy dew on clear nights. Clouds envelop montane forests at high level (see "Cloud forest" on pages 88–91), and mist and fog often form along river valleys and near the coast. Dew, clouds, mists, and fogs all deliver water to the forest plants.

Water that coats leaves blocks their stomata—the pores through which they absorb carbon dioxide and release oxygen. When their stomata are blocked, the plants cannot manufacture sugars by photosynthesis (see the sidebar "Photosynthesis" on page 168) and cannot lose water by transpiration. Transpiration is the evaporation, through the stomata, of water from inside leaves that has traveled through the plant from the roots.

Leaves with drip tips. Drip tips help the leaf shed water. Many plants of the tropical forests have leaves with drip tips.

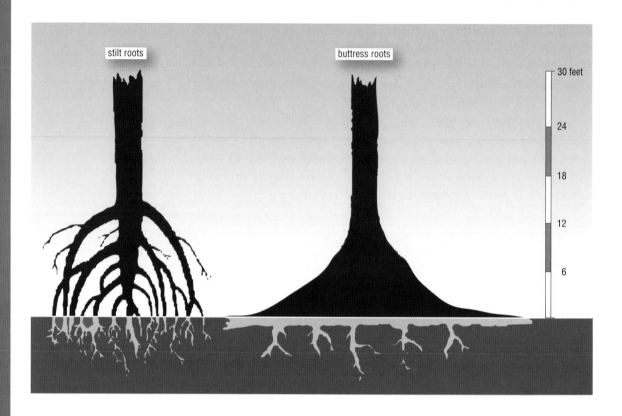

		30 feet
		24
		18
		12
		6

Stilt roots and buttress roots. These help support the tree and also increase the soil area from which the tree can absorb water and mineral nutrients.

Fog and dew often form around dawn, and at the start of the day, leaves tend to be coated with water. If they remain coated for more than about two hours, the reduction in transpiration can upset the balance of water in the plant for the rest of the day. It is therefore important for the plant to rid itself of surplus moisture as quickly as possible. Tropical plants achieve this by having leaves that end in a sharp and often long point, called a *drip tip*. The drawing shows several quite different leaves, each of which has a prominent drip tip. Water runs along the leaf, collects at the tip, and drips from there. Drip tips help the leaves to dry much faster than they would if they had rounded shapes.

Little of the rain may reach the ground directly, but along coasts and low-lying river valleys the forest floor is often sodden. It is difficult for a tree more than 100 feet (30 m) tall to anchor itself securely in soft ground. Many species solve the problem by standing on stilts.

Stilt roots begin as adventitious roots—roots that emerge from an unusual part of the plant, in this case from the trunk of the tree some distance above the ground. Many tropical trees produce roots like these. In some species the roots do not develop fully but simply hang beside the trunk, but in others the roots grow outward and then downward until they reach the ground, where they produce secondary roots. The aerial roots then grow thicker until eventually, as shown in the illustration, the stilt roots may support the entire weight of the tree. Once it is rooted in this way the tree is very secure and unlikely to fall. All flowering plants produce *tension wood*, comprising fibers on the upper sides of branches that pull the branch upright if it bends. Like the guy ropes holding a tent or flagpole, stilt roots support the trunk by pulling on it.

Other trees stabilize themselves by means of buttresses—supports that look like extensions of the trunk and in fact are partly trunk and partly root. These structures, called *buttress roots,* vary in shape from one tree species to another. They are valuable aids to identifying species because the

These trees have buttressed roots. The buttresses emerging from the trunk help support the tree. (Courtesy of Ben Ryan)

height, thickness, and general form of buttresses are fairly constant for a particular species. Although the drawing shows buttress roots emerging like triangular planks from the lower trunk, not all buttress roots are like this. There are wide variations in size and thickness of the "planks," and some are attached to the trunk only where they emerge, so that they form flying buttresses.

Forest trees are not always symmetrical. In some, the crown is bigger and denser on one side of the tree than on the other, and climbers sometimes attach themselves to one side of a tree, making this side much heavier than the opposite side. Roots buttressing trees that have more weight on one side than on the other are bigger and stronger on the lighter side, so they help prop up the tree. On windy sites buttress roots grow on the upwind side of the tree and on slopes they grow on the uphill side. This shows that buttress roots serve mainly as mechanical support. Additional evidence comes from the observation that buttress roots are less common with increasing elevation above sea level (see "Montane forest" on pages 85–88), and where they do occur they are smaller. Trees also become smaller with increasing elevation and therefore require less support.

Both buttress and stilt roots are sometimes called *prop roots* because they give support to the tree, but they also have a second function. Nutrients are recycled rapidly in tropical forests. Like all roots, stilt and prop roots produce side roots and root hairs where they are established in the soil, so they gather nutrients for the tree at some distance from trunk.

Growing in mud: peg roots

A swamp is an area that lies beneath shallow water for most of the time. It may be dry occasionally, but the ground remains covered by water through most or all of the dry season. Saltwater swamps occur on low-lying ground along tropical coasts and estuaries. Freshwater swamps occur inland, on level ground close to major rivers. There are extensive freshwater swamps throughout tropical Asia—they are widespread along the valleys of the Mekong and Irrawaddy Rivers, for example—and they are also common in Africa. In South

America, the Amazon River is bordered along its entire length by permanent swamp, known as *igapó,* and seasonal swamp forest, called *várzea,* in which the water level rises and falls with changes in the water level in the river. Tropical coastal swamps are noted for their mangrove forests (see "Mangrove forest" on pages 96–99).

Swamp soils are sometimes rich in nutrients, but their fertility varies widely. There is one feature they share in common: They are waterlogged and consequently airless, and this makes them very inhospitable for most plants. All plant cells, including root cells, need to be in contact with air because they obtain the energy they need by respiration—the oxidation of carbon transported to them in sugars made by photosynthesis in the leaves. Roots absorb the water and minerals that the plant needs, so they are highly active and require a good air supply, which they find in the tiny spaces between soil particles. In a waterlogged soil, however, all of those spaces are filled with water, so the soil is airless. Roots cannot survive in this environment yet tropical swamps are as crowded with plants as any other type of forest because the trees and other plants that grow there are not troubled by the lack of air below ground. They absorb air above ground and transport it down to the roots, where it is needed.

Ordinarily, roots grow downward. They are said to be *geotropic*—growing downward in response to gravity. If a root is in any position other than vertical, it grows faster on the upper side than on the lower side and bends over until it points downward. Swamp plants have roots with sections that are *negatively geotropic*—instead of growing downward when they find themselves lying horizontally, they turn the other way and grow upward. When they emerge above the surface these roots are known as *pneumatophores,* or *breathing roots.*

The structure of a pneumatophore is different from that of the remainder of the root. At the center of every root there is a structure called the *stele,* containing the *xylem vessels* through which water and minerals move upward to the main body of the plant and the *phloem vessels* that transport sugars produced in the leaves downward to the root. The stele inside a pneumatophore is thinner than the stele in the main root and is surrounded by tissue called *aerenchyma* containing a large air space. Outside the aerenchyma there is a layer of cork with many small pores called *lenticels*. Air passes through the lenticels into the aerenchyma and diffuses from there into the main part of the root. *Phellogen,* also known as *cork cambium,* is the actively dividing tissue that gives rise to aerenchyma tissue. The *pericycle* is the outermost layer of the stele and the *epidermis* is the outer covering, or "skin" of the root. The *endodermis* is a layer of tissue surrounding the stele. The tissue between the endodermis and epidermis is known as the *cortex.*

All pneumatophores work in the same way, but they take various forms, illustrated in the diagram. Some plants, such as *Symphonia globulifera,* a tropical South American tree known as the hog plum or hog gum, produce a lateral root that emerges growing upward—it is negatively geotropic— from the upper side of a horizontal main root. The lateral rises above the surface, then changes its direction of growth and returns to the ground, so that part of the root projects as a loop above the surface. This is a *knee root* of the type shown in the top left drawing. Mangrove trees belonging to *Ceriops* and *Bruguiera* species also produce knee roots, as loops of root rising above the surface, but their knee roots are made from

Knee roots and peg roots. Plants adapted to growing in ground that is permanently waterlogged have roots that project above the surface to allow them to absorb air.

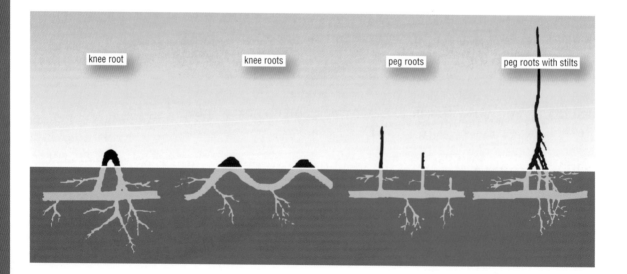

knee root   knee roots   peg roots   peg roots with stilts

undulations in the main root, as shown in the top right drawing.

Peg roots perform the same function, but, as shown in the lower left drawing, they emerge approximately vertically from the horizontal root and project above the soil. As their name suggests, they look like pegs. They are up to 12 inches (30 cm) tall and about the thickness of a pencil. Pneumatophores of this type are produced by *Avicennia* species of mangrove trees and also by several palm trees, including *Raphia* species—the source of the raffia used in handicrafts. *Sonneratia* mangrove trees have conical peg roots.

There is a second type of peg root, illustrated in the drawing, that grows much taller than an ordinary peg root in some *Xylopia* species of African trees reaching a height of more than six feet (1.8 m). These tall peg roots produce lateral roots of their own that arch downward and secure themselves in the soil, where they branch out like any other root. Their lateral roots, emerging above ground, look like stilt roots, and so these are known as *peg roots with stilts* or *stilted peg roots*.

Beetles and butterflies

Jewel beetles have wing cases—the scientific name is *elytra*—with bright metallic colors that are so beautiful that the elytra from dead beetles are often used in jewelry. The family of jewel beetles (Buprestidae) contains approximately 15,000 species, and most of them live in tropical forests.

No one knows how many insect species there are in the world, for the simple reasons that they are small, they often live in inaccessible places, and counting them is difficult. Scientists have so far identified almost 1 million insect species, and the latest estimates suggest that in the world as a whole there are 4 million–6 million species. Approximately 40 percent of these species are beetles (order Coleoptera). This means that in the world as a whole there are 1.6 million–2.4 million species of beetles. One scientific study counted 18,000 species of beetles in 2.5 acres (1 ha) of forest in Panama. That is 7,285 species per acre. There are possibly as many as 10 quintillion (that is, 10 followed by 18 zeros) individual insects in the world, equal to about 1.6 billion for every person alive.

Tropical forests, with their wide variety of luxuriant vegetation, support more insect species than any other environment, but most of the insects stay out of sight. Many live up in the forest canopy; most are active only at night; and even when they are active, insects tend to keep under cover, safe from the keen eyes of the many animals that would eat them given a chance.

Insects are small because they are encased in a hard case forming a skeleton on the outside of their soft bodies. An external skeleton, or *exoskeleton,* works well for a small animal but becomes too heavy and cumbersome to house a large animal. In order to provide the necessary strength for a big animal, the exoskeleton would have to be so thick that its owner would have great difficulty moving its limb joints, and most of the insect's body would have to consist of the muscles it needed simply to move around.

Small though insects are, however, the insect world does have its giants. A male rhinoceros or Hercules beetle (*Dynastes hercules*) grows up to 6.3 inches (16 cm) long, almost half of its length accounted for by its pair of spiny, hair-fringed horns. He uses these to fight rival males, trying to seize his opponent and throw him onto his back. He also has another trick. The color of his elytra changes naturally, depending on the humidity of the air, because the elytra absorb water. At night, when it is very humid, the elytra are black, and during the day, when the air is drier, they are greenish-yellow. When he is threatened or angry, however, the male rhinoceros beetle can change the color from black to greenish-yellow and back again to reflect his mood. Rhinoceros beetles live in the South American forests.

Rhinoceros beetles are huge, but Goliath beetles (four species of *Goliathus*) are heavier and only slightly shorter. Goliath larvae grow up to six inches (15 cm) in length and weigh up to 3.5 ounces (100 grams). Measuring from the tips of their extended front and rear legs—the normal position for this beetle—the adults are 4.7–5.0 inches (11.8–12.8 cm) long and weigh up to 8.75 ounces (250 grams). One species of Goliath beetle lives in temperate southeastern Africa, but the other three live in African tropical forests.

Both of these giants are scarabs: They belong to the family Scarabaeidae, which also includes chafer beetles. This is one of several beetle families all of whose members feed on dung. Most dung beetles are quite small, and there are many of them living on the forest floor. Dung beetles collect animal dung, rolling it into balls that they bury. They lay their eggs in the dung balls, and both adults and larvae feed on the dung. Dung beetles play an important part in the recycling of nutrients.

Beetles have strong elytra that protect them, but other insects lack this armor. Most avoid the insect eaters by means of camouflage. Leaf and stick insects are the most extreme examples. There are about 50 species of leaf insects, many of them *Phyllium* species, found in the forests of Asia, New Guinea, and Australia. They have leaf-shaped bodies complete with a central "rib" and "veins," and they often swing slightly from side to side, as though moving in a light breeze. Some look like the living leaves of the plants on which they feed, sometimes complete with blotches of "diseased tissue" or indentations in their edges where they seem to have been eaten by insects. Others look like dead, slightly shriveled leaves. Stick insects—of which there are about 2,500 species—are more widely distributed, but most are tropical. They look like twigs and are colored to match their background, and some even have outgrowths that look like the lichens on the tree bark on which they sit.

Camouflage can be used for attack as well as defense, however, and the fiercely predatory mantids are well disguised as they wait patiently to ambush their prey. Orchid mantises (*Hymenopus* species) look so like flowers that they attract—and catch—butterflies in search of nectar.

Butterflies and many moths want to be seen. They are big and brightly colored, and the biggest and gaudiest of them all live in the tropical forests.

Papilio antimachus is one of the largest of all butterflies and certainly the biggest in Africa. Its long, narrow wings have a span of up to 10 inches (25 cm) in males and rather less in females. Males are quite common in some areas, but females are very rarely seen. Like many butterflies, *Papilio antimachus* is poisonous, probably because its body accumulates poisons from the plants it eats as a larva. Because it is so big, this butterfly is said to have enough poison in it to kill six cats.

Not all tropical butterflies are huge, however. *Cymothoe sangaris,* found throughout the African tropical forests, has a wingspan of less than two inches (5 cm). Its wings are a deep blood-red color, making it one of the most eye-catching of insects.

Hestia species, found in tropical Asia, have big, broad, delicate wings about six inches (15 cm) across with black, white, and pale yellow markings and almost float in the air like kites. Perhaps the most beautiful of all butterflies are those known as birdwings, which live in the forests of New Guinea. *Ornithoptera paradisea,* with gold and green wings that end in curved tails, is one of the most splendid of all birdwings. Females of another birdwing, *O. alexandrae,* are as big as *Papilio antimachus,* with wings 10 inches (25 cm) across. The females of this species have brown wings, but those of the smaller males are colored green, yellow, pink, blue, and black.

The tropical forests of Central and South America have more species of butterflies than any other part of the world, and many of the butterflies have reflective, iridescent colors that change when seen from different directions. There are owl butterflies (*Caligo* species) with huge eyespots on their wings, swallowtails (family Papilionidae), and skippers (family Hesperiidae) with tails.

Most moths fly only at night, so they are seen less often, but there are even more moths in tropical forests than there are butterflies, and some of the moths are giants. The biggest is the atlas moth (*Attacus atlas*) with a wingspan of 12 inches (30 cm). Atlas moths live in Asia, where there are several species, all of them very large. The Hercules moth (*Coscinocera hercules*) of Papua New Guinea and northern Queensland, Australia, is almost as big, with a wingspan of 10.6 inches (27 cm).

The Indian moon moth (*Actias selene*) is one of the most beautiful of all moths. Its body is pure white, its legs maroon, and its wings are a delicate pale green, with long tails. It is closely related to the American moon moth, or luna, but the

Indian moon moth is larger and lives among the shrubs and understory of the forests of India.

Tropical ants

Bees, wasps, and ants are related and all belong to the order Hymenoptera, comprising at least 280,000 species, making them the second most numerous order of insects after beetles (order Coleoptera). Bees play a vital role in pollinating flowering plants, and many wasps are parasites of other insects. Most wasps eat meat—other insects—but a few feed only on plants. Bees, which eat pollen and nectar, are wasps that became vegetarian about 100 million years ago, soon after flowering plants first appeared.

Some bees and wasps are social, living in colonies, but by no means all species do so. Ants, on the other hand, are invariably social and their societies are so highly developed that some scientists liken them to a "superorganism," in which groups of specialized individuals called *workers* perform particular tasks, almost like the organs of a body.

Ant societies have developed in many different ways, and many ants have close relationships with the plants on which they depend for food, or on other insects that they manage in much the same way that farmers manage their cattle or sheep.

There are also slave societies—35 species of ants that raid the nests of other ant species in order to capture workers which they take back to their own nest to perform all the heavy work. *Polyergus* ants of the Amazon forests are among the most advanced slave-owners. Their workers are warriors, equipped with jaws that can pierce the body of another insect but are useless for anything else. From time to time *Polyergus* workers stream out of their nest to attack the nest of a slave species, where they kill the defenders and seize the pupae containing developing workers. The ants carry the pupae back to their own nest, and when they hatch, the emerging workers regard the *Polyergus* workers as their sisters and immediately begin to carry out the tasks involved in maintaining the nest and feeding the *Polyergus* workers. All worker ants are females that have lost the ability to reproduce, so when the slaves grow old the *Polyergus* ants have to send out another raiding party to capture replacements.

Not all ants make their nests on the ground. Weaving ants (*Oecophylla* species), found in the tropical forests of Asia and Australia, bind together the edges of leaves to make a secure space in which to build their nest. *Oecophylla* larvae produce silk, but the adult ants do not. The adults hold the larvae like tools and use the silk they emit to stick the leaf edges together.

In tropical Central and South America and the islands of the Caribbean, many *Cecropia* trees have hollow twigs inhabited by colonies of *Azteca* ants. At the bases of the leaf stems the tree produces structures called *Müllerian bodies* containing starch, fats, and protein as food for the ants. The ants attack any other ants that climb the tree, thus protecting the tree from leaf-eating species, especially leaf-cutting ants.

Army ants (Eciton species) making a bridge from their own bodies to allow other ants to cross. These ants are in a rain forest in Panama. (Courtesy of Norbert Wu/ Minden Pictures)

There are approximately 200 species of leaf-cutting ants, all of them found only in American tropical forests. Columns of worker ants march up the tree and along a branch and cut pieces from the edges of leaves. Long processions of ants march back to the nest carrying these pieces held above their heads—they are sometimes called parasol ants. Leaf-cutting ants attack one tree at a time, and they can strip it bare. Back in the nest, the workers make the leaves into a pulp on which they grow a fungus. The fungus is the only food the ants eat, and without the ants to tend it, the fungus dies.

Army or driver ants, in contrast, have no permanent homes. While they are on the move they rest in temporary nests called *bivouacs,* which are shelters for the queen made from the bodies of living ants, and every evening they move to a new location. Their colonies are huge. Even the smallest comprises at least 100,000 ants, and those of some *Dorylus* species, found in Africa, consist of more than 20 million individuals. Approximately 150 species of army ants live in America and 100 species in Africa, Asia, and Australia, the great majority inhabiting the Tropics.

While they are raising larvae and tending pupae, the armies stay in one place and send out only small foraging parties to find food. These *statary* periods last for about three weeks, but once the new workers, called *callows,* emerge from their pupae the ants start to emigrate, and for approximately the next two weeks they follow a regular routine. At dawn several columns of ants leave the bivouac. At some distance from the bivouac, the columns divide, each contingent running along trails with the foraging workers guarded by soldiers. Soldiers are worker ants that are bigger than the other workers and have long, curved, very sharp jaws that can deliver a powerful bite—it can pierce human skin. When the workers find food, they tear it into pieces that they carry back to the bivouac so that before long the column consists of ants moving in both directions. At sunset all the ants return to the bivouac, and then the entire colony, surrounding the queen for protection, moves to a new location.

The ants feed almost entirely on meat, mostly other insects, although they sometimes eat other small animals such as lizards and snakes. It is not true that they will devour pythons, elephants, gorillas, and people. It is true, however, that so many ants require a large amount of food, and after they have passed through an area, the population of invertebrate animals is greatly depleted—and that, of course, is why they must move.

Many species of ants forage for food as individuals. The workers may be numerous close to the nest, but some distance away each worker operates alone. Army ants are different. They work together in tightly controlled groups. They are almost completely blind and communicate by touch and by chemical signals. As they run along their trails each ant deposits a chemical substance that other ants detect and follow.

Tree frogs and frog poisons

Frogs and toads are found on all continents except Antarctica and on most islands, but about 80 percent of all frog and toad species live in the Tropics and subtropics. Frogs usually have smooth skin and long legs and live in water, while toads usually have stout bodies and warty skin and live away from water. The distinction is not important, however, because these features reflect their ways of life, and there are many groups of closely related species that include both frog and toad types.

They are amphibians (Amphibia), the class of animals that also includes newts and salamanders. Most amphibians, but not all of them, spend part of their lives in water and part on land. Some frogs live entirely in the water and others live entirely on land, but those that live on land must keep their skins moist. This is because amphibian skin is not watertight, and if it becomes very dry the animal may die. The need to keep moist presents no difficulty for the inhabitants of tropical forests, where there are frogs that spend all or most of their time in the trees, high above the ground.

Amphibians lay eggs in water and the eggs hatch into tadpoles, or pollywogs. At least, that is how most of them reproduce, but there are exceptions. There are more than 500 species of rain frogs (*Eleutherodactylus* species) found in Florida, Arizona, Texas, and throughout the American tropical forests. They lay eggs on land, and the eggs hatch into

The barred tree frog (Phyllomedusa tomopterna) *has long legs and suction pads on its fingertips to help it climb about in the trees of the Amazon rain forest.* (Courtesy of Claus Meyer/Minden Pictures)

tiny frogs without going through a tadpole stage. The eggs of the Puerto Rican live-bearing frog (*E. jasperi*), which is now believed to be extinct, developed inside their mother's body and were born alive.

Other species reproduce in even more unusual ways. Female gastric-brooding frogs (*Rheobatrachus silus*) of tropical Australia swallow 20 or more of their own fertilized eggs. These develop in her stomach, during which time she does not eat and her digestive system shuts down. When the young are ready, she "vomits" them out as tadpoles and froglets—baby frogs.

Darwin's frog (*Rhinoderma darwinii*) lives in tropical South America. The female lays 20–30 eggs on land. Male frogs gather around the clusters of eggs and, when they are about to hatch, the males snap up the emerging tadpoles, each male gathering up to 15 hatchlings with his tongue and placing them in his vocal sac. This is very large, forming a pouch that covers most of the underside of his body. The tadpoles complete their development in the vocal sac and emerge from his mouth as froglets.

There are even marsupial frogs (*Amphignathodon* and *Gastrotheca* species)—tree frogs in which the female has a large pouch, or *marsupium,* on her back. After she has laid eggs and a male has fertilized them, the pair transfer the eggs to the pouch, where they remain until they emerge as either tadpoles or froglets, depending on the species.

Glass frogs (family Centrolenidae) live in Central and South America. Their name refers to the fact that their bright green skin is almost transparent—their muscles, internal organs, and bones can be seen through it. They are small animals, 0.8–2.4 inches (2–6 cm) long. The adults live in the trees, and most of the 64 species lay their eggs on leaves that overhang running water. When the eggs hatch, the tadpoles drop into the water below.

Like other tree frogs, glass frogs have adhesive disks on the tips of their fingers and toes that help them when climbing up smooth surfaces. The approximately 600 species of true tree frogs belong to a different family (Hylidae), however. They have flattened bodies that distribute their weight evenly and help them to balance. This feature combined with their adhesion disks allows them to move quickly and confidently along branches and across leaves.

Many tree frogs have webbed feet. In the fringe-limbed tree frog (*Hyla miliaria*), a canopy dweller of Central America, the webbing is so extensive that this small frog—males are up to 2.2–4.2 inches (57–106 mm) long—is able to use it like wings to glide between trees with its toes spread wide. Leaf frogs, most of them big and brightly colored, live in the lowland wet forests and montane forests of Central and South America. The female lays her eggs in leaves that overhang water and keeps them moist by repeatedly emptying her bladder over them.

All frogs and toads have skin glands that secrete poisons. Most are strong enough to cause nothing worse than eye and nose irritation in animals that come into close contact with them and nausea in any animal that swallows them; they also stimulate the heart. In South America, though, there are more than 100 species of frogs, 0.8–2.0 inches (2–5 cm) long, that secrete much more deadly poisons. These are the poison-arrow frogs (family Dendrobatidae). The deadliest of all is the kokoi poison-arrow frog (*Phyllobates bicolor*) of Colombia. Like many poison-arrow frogs, it is brightly colored, in this case orange and black, and one ounce of its poison could kill about 100,000 average-size men (one gram could kill 3,500 men). Local people tip their arrows and blowpipe darts with poison from poison-arrow frogs. Members of the Chaco tribe can tip 50 arrows or darts with the poison carefully wiped from the back of a single kokoi frog.

The poison is not meant to be used in this way, of course. It exists to protect the tiny frog from the many reptiles, birds, and mammals that might consider it a tasty snack. Such predators quickly learn to leave small, vividly colored frogs strictly alone, although any animal that ate a frog as deadly as the kokoi would certainly die and so would learn no lesson from the encounter.

Tree snakes and snakes that live on the ground

Many animals of the forest live high above the ground. Insects feed on leaves in the crowns of the trees, and that is where insect-eating birds and lizards hunt for them. Birds and lizards have enemies of their own that also live in the trees. The treetop hunters include several species of well-camouflaged snakes that wait patiently for prey to come within their reach.

Snakes are masters of disguise, and their camouflage is not only based on skin colors that are difficult to see against the background: Some have a highly modified body shape. The most extreme example is found in the two groups of vine snakes, one group found in Central and South America and the other in Asia from India to Indonesia.

The American vine snakes comprise four species of *Oxybelis*. *O. fulgidus* is typical. This pencil-thin snake is no more than 0.5 inch (1.25 cm) wide, but it is 5–6.5 feet (1.5–2 m) long, and its head is long and narrow with a pointed snout. Greenish-brown in color, *O. fulgidus* blends perfectly with the climbers that entwine the trunks and branches of forest trees. It moves slowly in pursuit of its prey and feeds mainly on young birds, which it steals from their nests, and lizards. The Asian vine snakes—eight *Ahaetulla* species (until recently called *Dryophis*, which is the name used in many books)—are very similar. Their green and greenish-yellow skins keep them well hidden as they hunt for lizards, which are their principal food. Both groups of vine snakes are mildly venomous.

Not all tree snakes are thin and delicate. Tree boas (*Corallus* species) are heavy, thick-bodied snakes. There are eight species, all of them found in the forests of South America. The best known, and the only member of the species that very rarely visits the ground, is the emerald tree boa (*C. caninus*). Bright emerald green with white markings, the emerald tree boa lies with its coils draped over a branch and its head at the center of the coils, gripping the branch with its tail. The emerald tree boa is about four feet (1.2 m) long and preys mainly on birds and bats, which it kills with a bite from its powerful front teeth.

The green tree python (*Chondropython viridis*) is almost identical to the emerald tree boa in appearance, but it lives in the forests of Papua New Guinea and northern Australia and the two species are not closely related. Their similarity is an instance of *parallel evolution*—the way unrelated species come to look alike and behave in the same way as a result of adopting similar ways of life in similar environments (see also the sidebar "Parallel evolution and convergent evolution" on page 156).

Much bigger snakes live on the forest floor, and these include the biggest of them all, the anaconda, also called the green anaconda (*Eunectes murinus*), the boa constrictor (*Boa constrictor*), and pythons (*Python* species). Anacondas live in swampy river valleys and along riverbanks in tropical South America, inhabiting remote areas that few people have visited, and they spend much of their time in the water. The biggest anaconda ever recorded was about 29.5 feet (9 m) long and probably weighed more than 330 pounds (150 kg), but there may well be much larger ones. The boas and pythons (family Boidae) are nonvenomous, killing their prey by biting or crushing it, and there are African and Asian pythons almost as long as the anaconda, but these are of lighter build. A reticulated python (*P. reticularis*) 33 feet (10 m) long was once reported from Indonesia. A rock or African python (*P. sebae*) grows to about 29.5 feet (9 m), an Indian python (*P. molurus*) to 21 feet (6.5 m), and a boa constrictor to 20 feet (6 m). These are the largest ever recorded, however, and most individuals are much smaller. There are many unconfirmed accounts of anacondas measuring 100 feet (30 m) or more, but none of these is based on actual measurements. The anaconda is undoubtedly a very large snake and people tend to exaggerate its size to make it seem even bigger.

There are also venomous snakes in the forests, including the largest of all venomous snakes, the king cobra (*Ophiophagus hannah*), which can be up to 16 feet (5 m) long. It lives in Asia, from India eastward to Indonesia, and prefers cool, wet places in dense undergrowth and swamps. It sometimes crosses the ground with one-third of its body raised, giving it a better view, and this is also the posture it adopts when threatened. Despite its size, however, the king cobra is not aggressive toward people. Generally it keeps out of their way and, if confronted, it usually retreats. Its diet consists almost wholly of snakes. The female king cobra constructs a nest for her eggs by coiling her body to gather twigs and other plant material and then making a hollow at the center. She lies in the top layer of her nest for about two months after she has mated, then lays up to 40 eggs, which she guards for two months more. She departs just before her eggs hatch, perhaps to avoid the risk of eating her young by mistake. King cobras may be the only snakes to make nests.

The gaboon viper (*Bitis gabonica*) of the African forests is also large, growing up to 6.5 feet (2 m) long and with a thick, heavy body. Its fangs are up to two inches (5 cm) long—the longest of any venomous snake. Its skin is marked with geometrical patterns that hide it very effectively as it lies among the dead leaves on the forest floor. It hunts only at night for frogs, toads, and small mammals.

The Gaboon viper (Bitis gabonica) *is a large snake that lives in African forests. It hunts frogs and small mammals and is active only at night.* (Courtesy of Kevin Tate)

The longest of all vipers lives in the forests of Central and South America. This is the bushmaster (*Lachesis muta*), which can be up to 11.5 feet (3.5 m) long. The bushmaster spends the day in a hollow tree or cave, emerging at night to hunt prey up to the size of a small deer. It lives on the ground. Its large size means that it produces copious quantities of venom, and the fangs with which it injects it are very long. It is a rare snake, but one of the most dangerous in the world.

Cats, civets, and the tayra

Snakes are not the only hunters in the forest. There are also the cats, and these include the tiger (*Panthera tigris*), which is the largest cat living today. An adult male tiger weighs up to 440 pounds (200 kg). At one time tigers were distributed widely, from the eastern shores of the Black Sea to western China, and throughout India, Southeast Asia, eastern China, and eastern Siberia. Today they are rare and in danger of extinction, mainly due to the destruction of their habitat. Tigers hunt large mammals, such as deer, that live amid fairly dense vegetation. They stalk their prey rather than ambushing or chasing it, their coat colors and markings providing good camouflage as they take full advantage of the cover. If the forest is cleared, however, both prey animals and cover for stalking them are lost and the tiger cannot survive.

Leopards (*P. pardis*) also hunt in African and Asian tropical forests, mainly at night. They catch small mammals and birds and often carry their food into trees, where they can eat without risk of interruption and where they sometimes leave the remains of a meal and return to it later. Leopards with very dark coats, found mainly in Asia, were once thought to be a different species and called "black panthers."

The leopard cat (*Felis bengalensis*) looks like a tiny leopard: It is only 15–24 inches (38–60 cm) long, not counting its tail, and lives in the Asian forests. It swims and climbs well, often catching its prey of small mammals and birds by leaping onto them from above. It is one of several small cats living in the forests of Asia. The marbled cat (*F. marmorata*), about the same size as the leopard cat but with a longer tail, spends most of its time up in the trees. It eats insects, lizards, and snakes as well as small mammals. The jungle cat (*F. chaus*), up to 30 inches (75 cm) long not counting the tail, hunts rodents, frogs, and birds in lowland forests. Unlike most cats, the jungle cat is active by day. The fishing cat (*F. viverrina*) lives in swampy areas and catches fish and crabs as well as small mammals, birds, and insects. It is 22–33 inches (57–85 cm) long with a tail up to 12 inches (30 cm) long. Most small cats have patterned coats. The golden cats are the exceptions. There are two species, found in the forests of Africa (*F. aurata*) and Asia (*F. temmincki*). They are very similar, but the African cat is much bigger than the Asian golden cat. Golden cats hunt by night, the African species catching animals up to the size of a small deer.

The South American forests are home to the jaguar (*Panthera onca*), a cat about the same size as a leopard, but more heavily built. Some jaguars are black. Jaguars climb and swim well but usually hunt on the ground, catching fish, turtles, and caimans (a type of alligator) as well as mammals up to the size of capybaras, tapirs, and peccaries, which are their favorite food.

Ocelots (*F. pardalis*) spend much of their time in the trees, but hunt mainly on the ground in open forest, where they chase their prey rather than stalking or ambushing it. An ocelot is two to three feet (60–90 cm) long not counting the tail, making it the largest of three species of South American spotted cats. The margay cat (*F. wiedi*), up to 30 inches (75 cm) long, is a shy nocturnal hunter also called the tigrillo, and the tiger cat (*F. tigrinus*), also called the little spotted cat or ocelot

The jaguar (Panthera onca) *lives in South American forests. Peccaries are its favorite food, but jaguars swim well and sometimes attack caimans.* (Courtesy of Claudia Meythaler)

cat or oricilla, is up to 22 inches (55 cm) long. Both these cats live deep inside the forest.

The jaguarundi (*F. yagouaroundi*), is approximately the same size as the margay cat but rather heavier. It is known in Mexico as the otter cat, probably because of its unmarked black, gray, or chestnut coat, although it is not related to the otter. Jaguarundis live on the edge of the forest and are found as far north as Arizona.

Civets, palm civets, linsangs, and genets (family Viverridae) are about 35 species of small animals related to the mongooses. Animals of this family (viverrids) are found throughout tropical Africa and Asia, with one species, the common genet (*Genetta genetta*) occurring in parts of southern Europe. They resemble cats but have long muzzles, and their tails are as long as their bodies or longer. Some viverrids live on the ground, but most spend their time in the trees, sleeping by day and foraging for food at night. Their diet consists mainly of fruit, supplemented with small rodents, birds, scorpions, and snails. The binturong (*Arctictis binturong*), measuring about 30 inches (76 cm) from its nose to the base of its 30-inch (76-cm) tail, is the largest of the palm civets. Also known as the bear cat, it lives in the Asian forests. Palm civets, a subfamily (Paradoxurinae) of the civets, love bananas and steal them from plantations.

Martens belong to the weasel family (Mustelidae) and are animals of temperate climates, but there is one exception—the tayra (*Eira barbata*), found in American forests from Mexico to Argentina and also in Trinidad. It is 35–45 inches (90–115 cm) long with a tail 14–18 inches (35–45 cm) long and has a dark brown or black coat. The tayra is very agile and can leap from branch to branch when moving above ground. Its diet contains some plant material, but it also hunts insects, birds, and small mammals.

Plant-eating mammals

Sir Harry Hamilton Johnston (1858–1927) was an explorer, a painter, and the first commissioner of the British protectorate of Nyasaland (1891–97), and the British government appointed him special commissioner in Uganda from 1899 until 1901. Many public servants have held important offices, but Johnston has another claim to fame. He listened to stories of a horselike animal living deep in the central African forests that local tribes hunted for food. Their name for it was *okapi.* Johnston set off in search of the animal and in 1901 he found it. It is named for him—*Okapia johnstoni.* Its striped legs led Johnston to believe it was a kind of zebra, but in fact the okapi closely resembles some of the ancestors of the giraffe, known only from fossils. Hence the okapi is a close relative of the giraffe. Although it stands only five to six feet (1.5–1.8 m) tall and its color and overall body shape are not suggestive of a giraffe, its head is distinctly giraffe-like.

The okapi lives in the densest part of the forests in the east of the Democratic Republic of the Congo. It prefers secondary forest—forest that is growing back after clearance and is rich in young shrubs and saplings—as well as clearings and riversides, where sunlight penetrates and there are low-growing shrubs. It feeds mainly on the leaves and shoots of young trees.

African tropical forests are also home to 16 species of small antelope (*Cephalophus* species) that vanish into the undergrowth if disturbed. Afrikaans speakers refer to them as "divers" because of the way they dive for cover. The Afrikaans word for diver is *duiker,* so that is what these animals are called. Duikers are 22–29 inches (55–72 cm) long, with short tails, and live alone or in pairs. They eat grass, leaves, and fruit, but they are so secretive and inhabit such inaccessible places that not a great deal is known about their way of life.

Chevrotains or mouse deer are even smaller. The water chevrotain (*Hyemoschus aquaticus*) is the biggest, standing up to 16 inches (40 cm) tall, and the smallest of the four species is the lesser mouse deer (*Tragulus javanicus*), which is only eight inches (20 cm) tall—no bigger than a rabbit. Chevrotains are *ruminants;* like cattle and sheep they have four-chambered stomachs, although one chamber is poorly developed. They live in the tropical forests of Africa and Asia and feed on fallen fruit and leaves.

Anoas, found only in the forests of Sulawesi, Indonesia, and the tamaraw, found only on the island of Mindoro, Philippines, are tiny cattle, resembling miniature water buffalo. The resemblance is no coincidence because they are closely related to the much bigger water buffalo (*Bubalus arnee*). There are two species of anoa, the lowland (*B. depressicornis*) and mountain anoa (*B. quarlesi*). The mountain anoa is approximately 27 inches (70 cm) tall and the lowland anoa about 34 inches (86 cm) tall. The tamaraw (*B. mindorensis*) is slightly larger, standing about 39 inches (100 cm) tall. They live near water and feed on water plants and will attack fiercely if disturbed.

The plant eaters of the South American forests include the world's biggest rodent, the capybara (*Hydrochaerus hydrochaeris*). An adult weighs up to 145 pounds (66 kg) and stands up to 24 inches (60 cm) tall at the shoulder. Capybaras live as groups and are never far from water. They feed on grasses that grow near water and are strong swimmers with webbed toes.

Guinea pigs, or cavies, originated in South America, and several of the forest rodents are related to guinea pigs. The pacarana (*Dinomys branickii*) is a gentle, slow-moving rodent about 30 inches (76 cm) long and weighing up to 30 pounds (14 kg). It eats leaves, fruit, and plant stems, sitting on its haunches and holding the food in its front paws. The pacas (two *Agouti* species) live beside rivers, spending the day in burrows in the riverbank and feeding at night. Pacas are about the same size as pacaranas. There are 10 species of agoutis (*Dasyprocta* species). They are social, agile animals about two feet (60 cm) long that are active during the day. They also live beside rivers.

Rhinoceroses of Africa and Asia

Grazing and browsing mammals that have hoofs at the tips of their toes are called *ungulates,* and there are two types, or orders. Those with an even number of toes make up the order Artiodactyla, and those with an odd number of toes compose the Perissodactyla. Cattle, antelope, sheep, goats, deer, camels, pigs, peccaries, giraffes, and hippopotamuses are artiodactyls. There are far fewer perissodactyls; although there were once many species, almost all of them are now extinct. The only survivors are the horses, asses, and zebras, the tapirs (see "Tapirs" on pages 132–133), and the rhinoceroses.

Rhinos look ancient, as though they belong to another age. Their bare, wrinkled skin, tiny eyes, massive build, and especially their nose horns seem out of place in a world filled with more modern-looking animals. There is a sense in which it is true that the rhinos are relics of the past: The five species living today are all that remain of a much greater number that lived about 40 million years ago.

It is the horns that give them their name, from the Greek *rhinos,* meaning "nostril," and *keros,* meaning "horn." They are "nostril-horns" and belong to the family Rhinocerotidae. The horns are made from tightly packed *keratin,* the fibrous protein from which hair and fingernails are also made and, unlike the horns of artiodactyls, they have no bone at the center. The size and number of horns varies from species to species.

Two rhinoceros species live in Africa, one species in India, and two in Southeast Asia. The white rhino (*Ceratotherium simum*) grazes on the African savanna grasslands, and the Indian rhino (*Rhinoceros unicornis*) lives on floodplain grasslands. The remaining species dwell in tropical forests.

All rhinos are vegetarians with huge appetites. Their diet is not especially nutritious, and they need to eat a large amount of food to maintain their massive bodies. They will eat grass but prefer the leaves of trees and shrubs, which are more nourishing, and they eat fruit. Both African rhinos lack front teeth. Instead they have large, tough, and very mobile lips with which they can take large mouthfuls. The Asian species possess front teeth, but they use them only for fighting. For eating they also rely on their lips. Rhinos drink on most days, although when water is scarce the African species can go for several days without drinking.

Rhinos have a keen sense of smell and excellent hearing. They can swivel their ears to pick up sounds. Their eyesight is poor, however, and in order to see what is directly in front of it, a rhino has to turn its head to look out of first one eye and then the other. It cannot distinguish objects more than about 100 feet (30 m) away unless they move.

It is partly their poor eyesight that accounts for their reputation for attacking without provocation. If a rhino is taken by surprise, suddenly discovering an intruder in its feeding area, it is likely to charge in order to drive the trespasser away—the exception being the white rhino, which often runs away from intruders. If the intruder fails to leave, a charging rhino can inflict terrible injuries.

The black rhino (*Diceros bicornis*), also called the hooked-lip rhinoceros, occurs throughout much of Africa in montane forests (see "Montane forest" on pages 85–88) and scrubland. It has two horns, stands 4.7–5.2 feet (1.4–1.6 m) tall at the shoulder, and weighs up to 1.4 tons (1.3 tonnes). The black rhino is the most numerous and widespread of all the rhinos, but hunting has greatly reduced its numbers, so today there are probably fewer than 3,000 black rhinos. They were killed for sport in the 19th and early 20th centuries and more recently for their horns, used to make handles for the daggers worn by young Yemeni men. Rhino horn is also used as an ingredient in traditional Asian medicines. All rhinoceros species are now protected, and it is illegal under international law (CITES—the Convention on International Trade in Endangered Species) to trade in any part of a rhino or product made from one, including rhino horn. Despite the ban and severe penalties for offenders, the trade has not been entirely stamped out, and rhinos continue to be killed.

The white rhino (*Ceratotherium simum*), also called the square-lipped rhinoceros, stands 5.6–6.1 feet (1.7–1.9 m), tall at the shoulder and weighs up to 1.87 tons (1.7 tonnes). As its name suggests, it has very broad lips that give it the huge bite it needs to take in enough of the short grass on which it feeds for much of the year.

The Indian rhinoceros (*Rhinoceros unicornis*) has one horn and is sometimes called the greater one-horned rhinoceros. It is approximately the same size as the white rhino but heavier, and both are larger than the forest rhinos. The Indian rhino stands 5.6–6.1 feet (1.7–1.9 m) tall and weighs 2.4 tons (2.2 tonnes).

The Javan rhinoceros (*Rhinoceros sondaicus*), or lesser one-horned rhinoceros, is closely related to the Indian rhino and also has only one horn. Smaller than the Indian rhino, it stands up to 5.6 feet (1.7 m) tall and weighs up to 1.5 tons (1.4 tonnes). It inhabits lowland wet forests (see pages 80–83).

The Sumatran rhinoceros (*Dicerorhinus sumatrensis*), or Asian two-horned rhinoceros, has two horns. It is the smallest of all the rhinos, standing up to 4.5 feet (1.4 m) tall and weighing up to 0.9 ton (0.8 tonne). It differs from other rhinos in being thinly covered with long hair. It lives in montane forests.

Tapirs

A tapir looks like a large pig with a long, mobile nose to which its upper lip is attached. It looks as though it could be a kind of pig or, because of its trunk, perhaps a kind of elephant. In fact, it is neither. Its closest relatives are the horses and rhinoceroses. It is a perissodactyl—an odd-toed ungulate with hoofs on all of its toes.

There are four species of tapirs, all in the same genus, *Tapirus.* Three species live in South America, one of which is found as far north as Mexico, and the fourth lives in Asia, from Myanmar and Thailand through the Malay Peninsula to Sumatra, Indonesia. Modern tapirs closely resemble *Tapirus* species that lived 20 million years ago, and their disjunct distribution, in South America and southern Asia but nowhere else, is evidence that these regions were once joined together in a single supercontinent (see "Continental drift and plate tectonics" on pages 25–30).

The Asian species is the Malayan tapir (*T. indicus*), an inhabitant of dense lowland wet forests (see pages 80–83). Its head, shoulders, rump, and legs are black, and the middle part of its body is white. It is up to about 40 inches (1 m) tall at the shoulder, approximately 40 inches (1 m) long from its nose to the root of its short tail, and it weighs up to 660 pounds (300 kg).

The three American species are the Brazilian tapir (*T. terrestris*), mountain tapir (*T. pinchaque*), and Baird's tapir (*T. bairdii*)—the national animal of Belize. The Brazilian tapir lives in open forests with grassy areas, the mountain tapir in montane forests (see pages 85–88), and Baird's tapir in montane forests and also in swampy areas in other types of forest. Baird's tapir is the species found through Central America. All are of approximately similar size to the Malayan tapir. The Brazilian and mountain tapirs have reddish brown coats; adult Baird's tapirs have dark brown or red, almost black coats. Young of all species are born with a reddish brown coat marked with white spots and stripes. The markings soon fade, and the animal has its adult coat by the time it is six months old. All tapirs have very thick skin. In the Malayan, Brazilian, and Baird's tapirs the body is sparsely covered with hair, and the skin is gray. The mountain tapir has a thick coat.

Tapirs have stocky bodies, wider at the rear than at the front; short, sturdy legs; short necks; and tapering heads. This is an excellent shape for pushing through dense vegetation. At night, while feeding, they are constantly on the move, taking just a few bites before turning their attention to the next plant, but often following a regular route.

Tapirs live deep in the tropical forest, resting hidden during the day and emerging at night to feed in clearings and along riverbanks. They eat grass, leaves, fruit, and water plants—and farm crops if any are within their reach—using their trunks both to locate food by its scent and to pull food items toward their mouths. They swim well, spending much of their time in water, and will climb steep banks.

Except when they are mating or when females are caring for their young, tapirs are solitary animals. Females usually give birth to single offspring, rarely twins, and the youngster stays with its mother until it is about seven months old. Their solitary way of life and nocturnal habits mean tapirs seldom encounter people. When they do, they are most likely to retreat into dense undergrowth, but if cornered they will bite.

Cats prey on them—jaguars in South America and tigers and leopards in Asia—and crocodiles and caimans will attack them in the water. People are not their natural enemies, but in modern times tapirs have been hunted for their skins, which make good leather, for food, and for sport.

Pigs and peccaries

Pigs and peccaries are animals of the world's forests and grasslands, and all but one species live in the Tropics. They are artiodactyls—hoofed mammals with an even number of toes—but they eat a much wider variety of foods than other artiodactyls and they are not ruminants. The pig has a simple stomach rather than one divided into chambers.

There are nine species of pigs (although some scientists recognize up to 16), six of which live in tropical forests, two in savanna grasslands, and one, the Eurasian wild boar (*Sus scrofa*), in temperate forests and grasslands. Pigs occur naturally in Europe, Africa, and southern Asia but not in North or South America or Australia.

Pigs are strong, highly intelligent animals. Some boars (adult males) live alone, but most pigs live in groups. There are groups of bachelor males, family groups led by a boar, and groups of one or more sows (adult females) with their young. These groups fragment as young pigs mature and leave their mothers. The sows among them then mate and produce young of their own, giving rise to fresh groups of mothers and young. Consequently, groups of pigs within an area are often related to each other and share resources, even sleeping in each other's dens, and pigs forage for food in family parties. Pigs do not hold territories that they defend against intruders.

Most species, although not all, eat a fairly wide range of food, and pigs are very adaptable. They will explore new areas, try new food items, and generally make the best of the circumstances in which they find themselves. Pigs like to dig into moist soil and litter on the forest floor in search of food. Years ago European farmers used to allow domesticated pigs to rid their fields of unwanted roots and weeds by digging their way across the land and at the same time fertilizing it with their dung. Domestic pigs are descended from the wild boar. The Vietnamese pot-bellied pig is a breed of domestic pig.

Domesticated pigs have lost them, but all wild pigs possess tusks. Boars are larger than sows and have bigger tusks. The tusks are the upper canine teeth. They curve as they grow until finally they protrude from the mouth, pointing upward. In some species the lower canines also grow outward and upward, giving the animal two sets of tusks. The babirusa (*Babyrousa babyrussa*) has the most extreme tusks of any pig. The upper tusks grow through the muzzle, piercing the skin, and curve backward toward the eyes. Babirusa boars also have large lower tusks that emerge from the mouth on either side of the upper tusks.

Some pigs have fleshy pads—warts—on their faces. These are more prominent in boars than in sows, and they protect the face when the pigs fight.

The bush pig or red river hog (*Potamochoerus porcus*) and giant forest hog (*Hylochoerus meinertzhageni*) inhabit the forests of tropical Africa. A bush pig weighs up to 260 pounds (118 kg). The giant forest hog is the largest of all pigs. It weighs up to 600 pounds (272 kg), and its head and body are up to seven feet (2.1 m) long. Both species have facial warts, but only bush pig boars possess them.

The four species of Asian forest pigs are the Javan warty pig (*Sus verrucosus*), bearded pig (*Sus barbatus*), Celebes wild pig (*Sus celebensis*), and babirusa. They occur in Indonesia—the Celebes wild pig only in Sulawesi (formerly called Celebes)—and the bearded pig is also found in Malaysia. Some scientists believe the Javan and Celebes pigs belong to the same species. Except for the babirusa, these pigs are close relatives of the Eurasian wild boar, but unlike the wild boar they have facial warts. The bearded pig is up to 5.5 feet (1.7 m) long and weighs up to 330 pounds (150 kg). The Javan pig is up to 6.3 feet (1.9 m) long and weighs up to 330 pounds (150 kg), and the Celebes pig is up to 4.3 feet (1.3 m) long and weighs up to 154 pounds (70 kg). The babirusa is much smaller, measuring up to 3.4 feet (1.05 m) in length and weighing up to 200 pounds (91 kg). It has no facial warts. Babirusas eat mainly fruit and grass.

Peccaries are the Central and South American equivalents of pigs. They look like pigs but are slightly smaller, measuring 2.5–3.5 feet (76–107 cm) in head and body length, and have longer, slimmer legs. Despite the resemblance, however, pigs and peccaries are not closely related, although peccaries are also artiodactyls. Peccaries have a more complex stomach than pigs, with two or three chambers, although they are not ruminants. There is a scent gland on their backs, about eight inches (20 cm) forward from the base of the tail. Peccaries rub against each other to spread secretions from this gland, so that every member of the group smells the same. Their canine tusks are shorter and sharper than those of pigs.

Peccaries use their tusks to cut roots, which are a favorite food. They also eat seeds and fruits and occasionally insects and other invertebrate animals.

They are very social animals, living in herds that vary in size according to the species. Chacoan peccary (*Catagonus wagneri*) herds number two to 10 individuals, those of the collared peccary (*Pecari tajacu*) 14–50, and those of the white-lipped peccary (*Tayassu pecari*) more than 100. Peccaries are highly vocal and make different calls to convey particular types of information, such as calling the group together, warning of danger, and expressing anger. Young peccaries that are separated from their mothers have a special call that prompts the mother to start looking for them.

Large cats, such as jaguars, hunt peccaries. When a hungry cat comes too close to a herd of peccaries on open ground, the animals give their alarm call and disperse in all directions. This confuses the cat, which hesitates while deciding which peccary to chase, allowing them to escape. If there are young to be protected, however, and there is dense vegetation nearby, the herd may take cover while one peccary stays behind to confront the cat—usually with fatal consequences for the peccary.

There are three species of peccaries. The collared peccary has dark fur with a distinct band of white hair around its neck like a collar. It is found from the southwestern United States to northern Argentina. The white-lipped peccary is dark with white lips and cheeks and occurs from Mexico to northern Argentina. The Chacoan peccary has both a white collar and white lips. It occurs in the Gran Chaco region of northern Argentina, eastern Bolivia, western Brazil, and western Paraguay.

Bats

Altogether there are in the world approximately 5,000 species of mammals. Of those, 925 species are bats—almost one species in five. Bats are found on every continent except Antarctica and on most islands, but there are more species in tropical forests than in any other type of environment. Despite being so abundant, however, bats are difficult to study. Most leave their roosts at dusk and return to them before dawn, and the roosts are usually in inaccessible places. It is highly probable that in the tropical forests there are bat species that have not yet been identified and classified.

Bats have adapted to a wide variety of diets. It is in acquiring the necessary skills and physical modifications needed to find and digest so many different foods that they have diverged into so many species. Most bats eat insects that they catch in flight, but there are also bats that eat vertebrate animals, including fish. Some eat fruit, others feed on nectar from flowers, and three species, the vampires, consume only blood.

All bats are able to fly and, although there are squirrels and other mammals that can glide from tree to tree, bats are the only mammals to have mastered powered flight. They have very long fingers, and their wings are made from skin stretched across the fingers and joined to the body at the shoulders, ankles, and tail, so that when the bat extends its legs it spreads its wings. The drawing shows how the bat's skeleton supports its wings. Not only are bats able to fly, they are superb aviators and more maneuverable than many birds. When it draws in its limbs, a bat's wings fold around its body like a cloak, with only its feet protruding. It sleeps in its roost hanging upside down, gripping with the curved claws on its feet.

Bat. The wings are made from skin stretched across the very long fingers and joined to the shoulders, ankles, and tail.

Bats (order Chiroptera) are of two general types, or suborders: Megachiroptera and Microchiroptera. The 166 species
of fruit bats or flying foxes (Megachiroptera) are found
throughout tropical Africa, Asia, and Australia, but not in the
Americas. Most fruit bats have doglike faces with huge eyes
that give them excellent vision in dim light. They rely on
their eyesight to find their way, although dog bats, also called
rousette fruit bats (*Rousettus* species), use echolocation to
help. Dog bats roost in caves, and a single colony can comprise several million individuals. They make an impressive
sight as they leave the roost at twilight, embarking on their
nightly search for the nectar and pollen that are their principal food.

The Samoan flying fox (*Pteropus samoensis*) is believed to be
the world's largest bat, with a wingspan of up to 6.5 feet (2
m) and weighing 3.3 pounds (1.5 kg). The common flying
fox or greater fruit bat (*Pteropus vampyrus*) of Indonesia is
almost as big. Its wingspan is up to five feet (1.5 m). It lives
almost entirely on fruit. Some fruit bats are small, however.
The long-tongued fruit bats (*Macroglossus* species) have a
wingspan of only 12 inches (30 cm). Some *Macroglossus* bats
may eat insects or leaves when food is short, but they prefer
nectar and pollen, which they extract with the bristles at the
tips of their very long tongues.

All other bats belong to the suborder Microchiroptera,
which comprises the approximately 759 species of microbats
found throughout the world. Microbats find their way, avoid
collisions, and locate their prey by echolocation, and the
apparatus they use gives them their bizarre faces and ears.

Their echolocation allows bats to fly in total darkness.
Echolocating bats emit high-pitched sounds either through
the open mouth or through the nose. Many bats have very
elaborately shaped noses. These modify and focus the sound
into a concentrated beam. When the sound strikes an object
it is reflected, and the bat's large, sensitive ears detect the volume, pitch, and direction of the reflected sound. By altering
the shape of their nose to vary the pitch of the sound they
emit and swinging their heads from side to side, bats can
identify objects and measure their direction and distance
very accurately.

The microbats include Kitti's hog-nosed bat (*Craseonycteris thonglongyai*), which lives in the bamboo forests and teak plantations of Thailand and is the smallest bat—indeed, the smallest mammal. Its wingspan is 5.9–6.7 inches (15–17 cm), and it weighs no more than 0.1 ounce (3 grams).

The fishing bulldog bat or fisherman bat (*Noctilio leporinus*) of Central and South America has long legs and big feet with extremely sharp claws. It apparently uses echolocation to detect ripples in the water made when a fish breaks the surface. It pulls its feet through the water, and when they strike the fish they seize it and transfer it immediately to the mouth. This bat also eats insects when it cannot find fish. A smaller member of the same genus, *N. albiventris*, eats only insects.

False vampire bats are four species of large bats that hunt larger animals. They include the Australian ghost bat (*Macroderma gigas*), named for its pale color, the yellow-winged bat (*Lavia frons*) of Africa, and the greater false vampire (*Megaderma lyra*) of Asia. These bats are not found in the Americas. False vampires hunt animals up to the size of small birds, rodents, and lizards—they will enter houses in search of wall lizards—and they also eat other bats. Their habit of swooping silently onto a bat and appearing to chew it for a time before finally eating it gave rise to the belief that they were drinking their victim's blood. This is now known to be untrue. Feathers and the remains of the wings and legs of their prey often litter the ground beneath the perches of false vampires.

The three species of true vampire bats, found only in Central and South America, feed only on blood. Two of the species, both of them rare, take blood from birds. The common vampire (*Desmodus rotundus*) feeds only from mammals—almost exclusively farm livestock, occasionally wild animals, but very rarely humans.

Vampire bats feed only on dark nights; on moonlit nights they remain in their roosts. A vampire that is looking for food alights on or close to the animal on which it will feed. Painlessly and without waking its sleeping host, it makes two tiny puncture wounds in the skin with the needle-sharp points of its upper incisor teeth. The bat's saliva contains a substance that prevents blood from clotting, and it feeds by lapping the blood that flows from the wounds. The bat itself is tiny, weighing up to about 1.5 ounces (43 grams), and in a single meal lasting nine to 18 minutes it can consume up to 0.4 ounce (11.4 grams) of blood. This is a large amount of blood in relation to its own body weight but an insignificant amount to its host, which weighs approximately 10,000 times more than the bat. The host may suffer if several bats feed from the same wound one after another, however, and bats sometimes transmit diseases, including rabies, to their hosts.

Monkeys and apes

At night in the African tropical forests, travelers are sometimes startled by what sounds like a baby crying. It is not a human baby, however, but a bush baby or galago. A nimble animal with long hind legs and a bushy tail, it can leap from branch to branch as it searches for food. Bush babies eat fruit and small animals, including insects that they sometimes snatch by hand as they fly past. They are active only at night. Their huge eyes are very good for seeing in dim light and their big ears detect the slightest sound. Bush babies are primates, the order of mammals that also includes the monkeys, apes, and humans.

Bush babies are social animals. Groups of them sleep together high in a tree, but they disperse at dusk to forage separately. Their cries keep them in touch with each other. A bush baby that encounters a dangerous animal utters a warning cry that alerts the others. Bush babies are small. The dwarf bush baby (*Galago demidoff*) measures only five inches (13 cm) from its head to the root of its seven-inch (18-inch) tail and weighs only two ounces (60 grams). The biggest is the thick-tailed bush baby also called the brown greater galago (*Otolemur crassicaudatus*), which weighs an average 2.4 pounds (1.1 kg) and measures 12.2 inches (31 cm) with a 16-inch (41-cm) tail. There are 11 species of bush babies.

Bush babies are closely related to the pottos of Africa and lorises of Asia, stocky animals weighing 10–40 ounces (285–1,135 grams) that climb rather than run and leap. They move slowly and smoothly, barely disturbing the vegetation as they travel along a branch. If disturbed by a strange sound or sight a potto or loris will "freeze" and remain motionless, sometimes for hours. There are two species of pottos, the potto (*Perodicticus potto*) and angwantibo or golden potto (*Arctocebus calabarensis*).

If threatened, a potto will turn to face its tormentor, burying its face beneath one arm and presenting its shoulders, which form a shield of thick skin over two projections from its spine that almost meet. In this position it will dodge attacks and then suddenly straighten its body and deliver either a heavy blow with its shield or a bite that can inflict terrible injury. An angwantibo is much smaller than a potto and has no shield. It curls into a ball with one arm covering its head and the other arm and just the tip of its tail protruding. The attacker is tempted to approach and sniff at the tail or to seize the angwantibo's rump. The angwantibo then pushes its head from beneath its arm and bites the attacker. This makes the attacker jump back, often throwing the angwantibo some distance away, whereupon it curls up into a ball once more.

Lorises are very similar to pottos. The slender loris (*Loris tardigradus*) inhabits the forests of India and Sri Lanka. The slow loris (*Nycticebus coucang*) lives in Bangladesh and in Southeast Asia from Malaysia to Borneo.

Africa, Madagascar, and India were once joined together. Madagascar and India were both on the same tectonic plate (see "Continental drift and plate tectonics" on pages 25–30), but the plate broke apart, leaving Madagascar isolated from both Africa and India. It has remained isolated for 50 million years, and during that time the animals present there at the time of the separation have continued to evolve independently. The most famous group comprises the lemurs (family Lemuridae), mouse and dwarf lemurs (Cheirogaleidae), indri and sifakas (Indriidae), and the aye-aye (Daubentoniidae). In all, there are approximately 22 species, ranging in size from mouse lemurs that are about four inches (10 cm) long with a six-inch (15-cm) tail to the indri (*Indri indri*), which is 22–27 inches (57–70 cm) long with a two-inch (5-cm) tail. The typical lemurs are intermediate in size—the smallest about the size of a squirrel and the largest about the size of a domestic cat. The smaller species are nocturnal, but the larger lemurs are active during the day.

The ring-tailed lemur (*Lemur catta*) spends some of its time on the ground, but the other lemurs live almost entirely in the trees. Sifakas and the indri visit the ground only to run across forest clearings. All lemurs are very agile, but the indri

New World and Old World primates

Lemurs, lorises, bush babies, and tarsiers are classified as *prosimians*. Marmosets, monkeys, apes, and humans are *anthropoids*. Together the prosimians and anthropoids comprise the order Primates.

The earliest primates lived about 60 million years ago. They were highly successful and spread throughout the Tropics. Approximately 58 million–50 million years ago (in reporting a range of dates in the distant past, it is customary to place the older date, and therefore larger number, first) the ancestors of the anthropoids became distinctly different from the ancestors of the prosimians. Prosimians and anthropoids thereafter became two separate groups.

Scientists are still debating when the next important split took place in the line leading to modern primates. Some believe it happened approximately 57.5 million years ago, others as recently as 30 million years ago. The true date is probably somewhere between these. That split separated the monkeys of the New World and those of the Old World. A further split in the Old World species about 25 million years ago produced one line leading to modern Old World monkeys and another line leading to apes and humans.

Since New World and Old World primates diverged, both groups have continued to evolve, but in isolation from each other. They live fairly similar lives in similar environments and so they continue to look broadly similar—it is easy to recognize a monkey—but there are now very profound differences between them. Many of the differences are internal, relating to the teeth and digestive system, for example, but others are external and visible.

New World monkeys are sometimes called *platyrrhines,* and Old World monkeys *catarrhines*. These names refer to their noses. In catarrhines the nostrils are close together and open downward. All the monkeys and apes of Africa and Asia have nostrils that open downward. Humans are primates that first appeared in Africa; we have nostrils that are close together and open downward. Platyrrhines, in contrast, have nostrils that are more widely separated and that open to the sides. All the monkeys of Central and South and sifakas especially so, leaping effortlessly from tree to tree. Lemurs are strict vegetarians that eat fruit and leaves; the mongoose lemur (*Eulemur mongoz*) also takes nectar from flowers.

There is one member of the group, the aye-aye (*Daubentonia madagascariensis*), that eats insect grubs as well

---

America are platyrrhines. The difference in nose reflects differences in the internal structure of the noses in platyrrhines and catarrhines.

All New World monkeys have tails, and most have long tails. In some New World monkeys, especially the larger ones, the tail is *prehensile,* or able to grasp. The monkey can grip a branch with it to steady itself, and some monkeys can hang by their tails. The prehensile tail may have a ridged pad near the tip. This pad is sensitive to touch, and nerves link it to a large area of the brain. Many Old World monkeys and all the great apes lack a tail entirely, and others have a very short tail, but no Old World monkey has a prehensile tail.

New World monkeys live in the trees. Many Old World monkeys spend a good deal of their time on the ground.

Many Old World monkeys have thumbs and great toes that can rotate so the pads at their tips can press against the pads of each of the other fingers or toes on the same hand or foot. Such thumbs and toes are said to be *opposable.* No New World monkey has fully opposable thumbs or toes.

Old World monkeys possess cheek pouches that they use to store food while they carry it to a safe place to eat. No New World monkey has cheek pouches.

New World monkeys have three molar teeth on each side of both jaws. Old World monkeys have two molars.

Old World monkeys possess *ischial callosities.* These are areas of hardened or thickened skin on the buttocks. They are often surrounded by brightly colored skin that becomes enlarged in females that are receptive to mating. No New World monkey has ischial callosities.

Monkeys of the New and Old Worlds share a common ancestor, but one that lived many millions of years ago at a time when the New and Old Worlds were joined together. Since the continents separated, each group has continued to evolve independently of the other. All monkeys look broadly similar, but that is mainly because they have similar lifestyles. There are many differences between New World and Old World monkeys, and the two groups are now only distantly related.

as fruit. Its teeth can rip through the shell of a coconut. It is a fairly large animal, up to 17 inches (43 cm) long and with a long tail, solitary, nocturnal in its habits, and of very strange appearance. It has large eyes, big ears with no fur on them, and extremely long fingers and toes with claws rather than nails on its fingers. Its middle finger is even longer than the others. The aye-aye uses it to pull out the flesh from hard-shelled fruits and to probe for insect larvae in holes in tree bark.

Lemurs have long muzzles, like dogs, but they are primates, related to the bush babies, lorises, and pottos. They are known as *prosimians* and retain characteristics more typical of the ancestors of the primates than of the monkeys and apes—the *anthropoids*. In the Philippines and Indonesia, however, there are three nocturnal species of prosimians that possess both prosimian and simian (apelike) features. These are the tarsiers, animals four to seven inches (10–18 cm)

The silvery or bare-ear marmoset (Callithrix argentata) *lives in the Amazon rain forest of Brazil. It is one of more than 20 species of these small primates, found only in the tropical forests of South America.* (Courtesy of Claus Meyer/ Minden Pictures)

long, with tails eight to 10 inches (20–25 cm) long, hind legs about twice the length of the body, big eyes, and very acute hearing. They leap from tree to tree with the body held vertically. Tarsiers feed on insects and other animals, and individual tarsiers have personal preferences. Some eat lizards, bats, birds, and even venomous snakes, but others ignore them.

There are no prosimians in the American tropical forests, and those in Africa and Asia are seldom seen because, with the exception of the lemurs found only in Madagascar, most are nocturnal. In daytime, in the tropical forests of all continents, the most abundant active primates are monkeys. These form two quite distinct groups. The monkeys of the New World are different in many ways from the monkeys and apes of the Old World (see the sidebar).

There are three families of New World monkeys. The family Cebidae contains marmosets and tamarins (subfamily Hapalinae) and capuchin monkeys in which the hair on the crown of the head is smooth and runs backward, resembling the cowl worn by Capuchin monks (subfamily Cebinae). Night monkeys and owl monkeys form the family Nyctipithecidae, with two subfamilies: Saki monkeys (Pitheciinae) and titi monkeys (Callicebinae). The family Atelidae comprises the howler monkeys (subfamily Mycetinae) and the spider monkeys and woolly monkeys (subfamily Atelinae).

Unlike the other monkeys, marmosets and tamarins have claws rather than nails except on the great toe, have two molar teeth rather than three, and tend to give birth to twins. Depending on the classification used, there are 20–30 species. Marmosets and tamarins are very similar. Marmosets belong to the genus *Callithrix,* tamarins to the genus *Saguinus,* and lion tamarins to the genus *Leontopithecus.* Goeldi's marmoset (*Callimico goeldii*) differs from other marmosets in having three molars and giving birth to single offspring.

Marmosets and tamarins are about the size of a squirrel. They have silky coats and long tails, and many have manes, crests, beards, or mustaches of long hair, often of a contrasting color. They feed on a wide variety of items, including fruit, flowers, leaf buds, nectar, insects, spiders, snails, frogs, lizards, and gum that exudes from injured trees.

Squirrel monkeys (Saimiri sciureus) *live in the lowland rain forests of South America.* (Courtesy of Kevin Tate)

There are approximately 30 species of monkeys. Apart from the night monkey (*Aotus trivirgatus*), also called the owl monkey because of its hooting call, which is found in dry forests and savanna forest, all these monkeys are active by day. Titi monkeys (*Callicebus* species) live mainly in the understory, up to 33 feet (10 m) above the forest floor. Squirrel monkeys (*Saimiri sciureus*) live in lowland wet forest (see pages 80–83) and mangrove forest (see pages 96–99), in groups of up to 40 individuals. Capuchin monkeys (*Cebus* species) inhabit tropical forests of all types and often visit the ground in search of food or to play. Saki monkeys

(*Pithecia* species) live in the lower and middle canopy of most forest types but are absent from swamp forest, and bearded sakis (*Chiropotes* species) live in the upper canopy. Uakaris (*Cacajao* species) live in lowland swamp forest. The noisiest monkeys are the howlers (six *Alouatta* species). They live at all levels and visit the forest floor, and they are found in forests of every type. Spider monkeys (*Ateles* species) and the muriqui or woolly spider monkey (*Brachyteles arachnoides*) live in wet forests, as do the wooly monkeys (*Lagothrix* species).

Old World monkeys belong to the family Cercopithecidae, with 80–85 species. They live in every type of habitat, not only in forests. Many climb well and spend most or all of their time in the trees, but some macaques and all baboons live on the ground.

There are two groups or subfamilies, the Cercopithecinae and Colobinae. The Cercopithecinae subfamily contains the mangabeys, guenons, macaques, and baboons. Mangabeys (*Cercocebus* and *Lophocebus* species) are closely related to baboons. They weigh 11–22 pounds (5–10 kg) and have tails longer than their bodies. All of them inhabit African tropical forests, most living near the west coast, although the Tana River mangabey (*C. galeritus*) lives only in Kenya. Agile mangabeys (*C. agilis*) are found only in rain forest; other species are more widespread. *Cercocebus* species, such as the golden-bellied (*C. chrysogaster*) and sooty (*C. atys*) mangabeys, feed and travel on the ground. *Lophocebus* species, such as the gray-cheeked (*L. albigena*) and black-crested (*L. aterrimus*) mangabeys spend most of their time in the trees.

Guenons (*Cercopithecus* species), also found only in Africa, have long tails and brightly colored coats. All but one of the approximately 22 species live in forests. They include the Diana monkey (*C. diana*), about 18 inches (45 cm) long with a tail about 24 inches (60 cm) long. It has a black face surrounded by a white beard and ruff, white chest, and gray-brown back and legs, with bright chestnut patches on its back and hind legs. Diana monkeys live high in the canopy and are one of the most widely distributed monkey species. De Brazza's monkey (*C. neglectus*) is of similar size to the

Diana monkey, but more heavily built and it lives partly on the ground.

Macaques (*Macaca* species) live in Asia. Most live partly in the trees and partly on the ground. The stump-tailed macaque (*M. arctoides*), found in forests, especially montane forests (see pages 85–88) from eastern India to southern China and Vietnam, is one of the most widely distributed species. It has a pink, mottled face, a yellowish to dark brown coat, and a very short tail. It eats leaves, roots, fruit, insects, and small animals and will invade gardens and fields to find them—and is fearless and aggressive if challenged. The stump-tailed macaque spends most of its time on the ground but climbs into trees in search of food and to sleep.

Baboons (*Papio* species) live in open country and desert, but two close relatives, the mandrill and drill, are ground-dwelling monkeys found in the wet forests of West Africa. Both are large, heavy animals. A female mandrill (*Mandrillus sphinx*) weighs approximately 25 pounds (11.5 kg) and a male 55 pounds (25 kg). The adult male has a brightly colored face, with a red stripe along the middle of the muzzle, blue, ridged "cheeks," and a yellow beard. Its naked rump is blue or purple. Females and juveniles are similarly colored, but duller. The drill (*M. leucophaeus*) is twice the size of the mandrill, with females half the size of males, and its face is black. Both species occur in troops of 20–50 individuals and sometimes more when two or more troops merge, led by a dominant male. They forage on the ground for fruit, seeds, fungi, roots, and small animals, and they sleep in trees.

The subfamily Colobinae comprises almost 40 species of Asian monkeys and the colobus monkeys of Africa. The colobine species of Asia include the proboscis monkey (*Nasalis larvatus*) of the Indonesian mangrove and lowland forests. The proboscis monkey has an elongated, bulbous nose, which is especially developed in the male. Ordinarily the nose hangs down, but it straightens out when the male makes his loud call. An agile monkey, it lives in the treetops but is able to swim.

Colobus monkeys eat leaves, and some species eat little else. Their diet is abundant but not very nutritious, so they have to eat a great deal. They have a stomach with three chambers to help them cope with the volume and to extract as much nutrition as possible from their food. All colobine monkeys have small thumbs, but in the colobus monkeys the thumb is completely absent or reduced to a small spur. There are three groups of colobus monkeys: the African, langur, and odd-nosed groups. All are long-legged tree dwellers that leap from branch to branch. Members of the African group lack thumbs and big toes, or if present they are very small. Preuss's red colobus (*Colobus preussi*) is typical. It lives in lowland wet forest in the Korup National Park, Cameroon, and has reddish-orange markings on its dark gray cheeks, flanks, and the outside of its limbs.

Langurs have brow ridges—a bony ridge along the forehead—resembling raised eyebrows, and newborn offspring have hair that is black, golden red, or white mixed with brown, black, or gray. Langurs are the most common monkeys in India and Pakistan. The hanuman, northern plains gray, or common langur (*Semnopithecus entellus*) lives in forest and scrub throughout most of Pakistan, India, and Bangladesh and is often seen on cultivated fields and even in the center of villages and towns.

Members of the odd-nosed group all have modifications to the nose. The group includes the douc (*Pygathrix* species) and snub-nosed (*Rhinopithecus* species) monkeys as well as the proboscis monkey (*Nasalis larvatus*) and pig-tailed langur (*Simias concolor*), which resembles the proboscis monkey but has a smaller nose.

Apes—gibbons, orangutans, gorillas, bonobos, and chimpanzees—live in Africa and Asia. They differ from monkeys in several ways. Apes do not possess cheek pouches; no ape has a tail; and all apes have opposable thumbs, although these are reduced in some species. Their teeth differ from those of monkeys, equipping them for a much more varied diet, and, unlike monkeys, apes have an appendix. They also have larger heads, longer limbs with the arms usually longer than the legs, and broader chests than monkeys.

Apes are classified as the superfamily Hominoidea, comprising two families: Hylobatidae and Hominidae. The Hylobatidae contains the gibbons. There are two subfamilies of the Hominidae: Ponginae and Homininae. The Ponginae contains only the two species of orangutan (*Pongo* species). The Homininae is the subfamily of African great apes: the gorilla (*Gorilla* species), chimpanzee and bonobo (*Pan* species), and humans (*Homo sapiens*).

Gibbons live in the forests of Southeast Asia and spend almost all of their time in the trees. They travel by moving hand-over-hand while hanging below tree branches. This form of locomotion is called *brachiation,* and gibbons have very strong arms and hands. Their posture is upright while they are hanging below branches and leaping from one tree to the next, giving gibbons a very humanlike appearance. They also walk upright along branches that are too thick for them to grip from below. Gibbons are much better than other apes at walking on two legs, and sometimes they walk this way on the ground. They are not big animals. When upright, most gibbons stand about 30 inches (76 cm) tall, but the siamang (*Hylobates syndactylus*) is taller. Gibbons weigh 12–13 pounds (5.5–6 kg), except for the siamang, which weighs about 23 pounds (10.5 kg).

Gibbons use vocal calls to keep in contact with each other and to warn other gibbons not to trespass on the territory of a family group. These calls, or songs, are often sung as a duet between a male and female pair, and some species have a throat sac that acts as a resonating chamber to amplify the sound and make it carry farther.

There are nine species. They are all placed in the same genus, *Hylobates,* but relationships among the species are complicated and they are usually divided into four groups.

The siamang lives in Malaysia and Sumatra and is the only gibbon to share its range with other gibbons—the lar and agile gibbons. The lar or white-handed gibbon (*Hylobates lar*) inhabits Thailand, Malaysia, and northern Sumatra. The agile gibbon (*H. agilis*) lives in Malaysia and Sumatra. The remaining gibbons have ranges that do not overlap. The concolor, black-crested, or white-cheeked gibbon (*H. concolor*) is found in Indochina and southern China. The hoolock or white-browed gibbon (*H. hoolock*) lives in Assam, Myanmar, and Bangladesh. The Kloss gibbon or beeloh (*H. klossii*) lives in western Sumatra and nearby islands. The pileated or capped gibbon (*H. pileatus*) lives

in southeastern Thailand and part of Kampuchea. Müller's Bornean gibbon (*H. muelleri*) lives in Borneo, except for the southwestern part of the island. The Moloch or silvery gibbon (*H. moloch*) lives in western Java.

The remaining apes are humans' closest living relatives. Orangutans live in Borneo and Sumatra. The Bornean orangutan (*Pongo pygmaeus*) is stouter and stockier than the Sumatran orangutan (*P. abelii*) and has shorter hair. Orangutans spend most of their time in the trees, but they do descend to the forest floor in search of food and to find the branches they use to construct the nests in which they sleep at night, usually making a fresh nest each evening. They use brachiation and are said to be able to move in this way faster than a human can walk across the ground below. Their diet

Orangutan (Pongo pygmaeus) *live in Borneo and Sumatra and spend most of their time in the trees. They are in danger of extinction because deforestation is destroying their habitat.* (Courtesy of Patrick Roherty)

consists mainly of fruit, together with leaves, shoots, insects, eggs, birds, and small mammals. Most orangutans are solitary, although young orangutans sometimes meet to play. When adults meet by chance at a rich source of food, they usually ignore each other, and when they have eaten their fill they go their separate ways.

The remaining apes live in Africa. The western gorilla (*Gorilla gorilla*) inhabits the forests of West Africa, and the eastern gorilla (*G. beringei*) lives farther to the east, its range extending into Rwanda and Uganda. The mountain (*G. b. beringei*) and eastern lowland (*G. b. graueri*) gorillas are subspecies of the eastern gorilla.

Gorillas are the biggest of all the apes. Adult males average 5.6 feet (1.7 m) in height and weigh an average 350 pounds (159 kg). Some individuals climb trees in search of food, but most gorillas, especially the huge adult males, live mainly on the ground. Their diet consists of leaves and stems. These foods are plentiful, so gorillas have no need to disperse in search of a meal. They live in fairly permanent groups, remaining in one place for a time and then moving on. They eat in the morning and afternoon, resting in the middle of the day. At night they sleep on platforms of branches and leaves that keep them off the ground.

The bonobo, sometimes called the pygmy chimpanzee (misleadingly, because it is no smaller than the common chimpanzee) or gracile chimpanzee (*Pan paniscus*), lives in central Africa. It is slender, with a small head, and its face is black from birth. The common chimpanzee (*P. troglodytes*) is more heavily built, and the young have pink faces that become black as they grow older. Both species of chimpanzees eat fruit and leaves, as well as ants, termites, and caterpillars. Chimpanzees regularly hunt, kill, and eat other mammals, including monkeys, antelope, and pigs, and occasionally they eat birds. They are highly social, living in communities of up to 100 individuals or sometimes even more.

Chimpanzees are humans' closest relatives. The line leading to chimpanzees and humans separated between 6 million and 4 million years ago. In evolutionary terms this split is very recent. Some scientists believe the chimpanzees should be classified with humans in the genus *Homo*. If people thought of them as relatives rather than regarding them as "just animals" people would have to think more carefully about the way they are treated.

Sloths

Animals have adapted in a wide variety of ways to life in the tropical forests, but sloths have developed what is possibly the most successful lifestyle of all. They are found only in the forests of Central and South America, where they live permanently in the trees and eat mainly leaves, with some buds, shoots, and fruit.

Leaves are not very nutritious, and sloths have very large, complex stomachs containing bacteria that break down their indigestible food. Digestion is a slow business. It takes a sloth a month or more to completely digest a meal.

Mammals expend a great deal of energy—derived from the food they eat—in maintaining a constant body temperature. Sloths economize by allowing their temperature to fluctuate between 86°F (30°C) and 93°F (34°C) so that they can remain healthy while eating far less food than most mammals of their size. Also, and most famously, they move about very slowly. Although it is not true that these animals remain almost permanently in one place, a sloth's top speed is about one MPH (1.6 km/h), and sloths move only with difficulty across the ground, although they swim well. Despite their generally slow movements, sloths will defend themselves with their claws if attacked, and they can inflict dreadful wounds.

Sloths spend most of their time hanging upside down from branches. They have very strong legs, and their hands and feet end in tough, curved claws that are three to four inches (7.6–10 cm) long. It is their claws that hamper movement on the ground. Sloths cannot walk normally, but must drag their bodies along by their claws.

A sloth's body is covered in fine fur beneath an outer coat of longer, coarser hairs. Grooves run along these hairs, and the hairs grow in such a way that they point toward the ground when the animal is hanging upside down, perhaps

Sloths live in the American tropical forests. They are famous for their slowness—they are truly "slothful"— but this is a superb adaptation to life in the forest, where food is plentiful but not very nutritious. (Courtesy of Keith Sirois)

to help shed water from the coat. Algae—single-celled plants—grow in the hair grooves, giving the animal a greenish color.

All sloths have three digits on the hind feet, but on the forefeet some species have two digits and others three. These are known as two-toed and three-toed sloths respectively, despite the fact that their "toes" are really "fingers." There are two species of two-toed sloths (*Choloepus* species) and three species of three-toed sloths (*Bradypus* species). Three-toed sloths average 22 inches (56 cm) in length and weigh nine pounds (4 kg). Two-toed sloths measure approximately 24 inches (60 cm) and weigh 13 pounds (6 kg).

Anteaters, armadillos, and pangolins

Modern sloths eat only plants, but their ancestors ate insects, and sloths are closely related to the anteaters and armadillos.

The giant anteater (*Myrmecophaga tridactyla*) is approximately four feet (1.2 m) long and has a bushy tail about 30 inches (76 cm) long. It has a very long snout and powerful front legs that end in sharp claws. When it walks the giant anteater turns its claws inward and moves awkwardly on the sides of its hands. It feeds on ground-dwelling ants, avoiding those that bite, and will sometimes eat termites. It locates its prey by scent and uses its claws to break open the ant or termite nest. Then it extends its tongue, covered in thick, sticky saliva, up to 24 inches (60 cm) from the end of its muzzle, moving it back and forth up to 150 times a minute, to collect insects. An anteater sleeps for more than 12 hours every day, covered by its tail, but it hears the approach of any predator. Its powerful hug and sharp claws can kill a dog or large cat.

There are two species of tree anteaters (*Tamandua* species), both about half the size of the giant anteater. A tree anteater has a long, prehensile tail that it uses as an extra limb, and it lives mainly above ground, feeding on tree-dwelling ants and termites that it gathers with its long, sticky tongue.

Little is known about the life of the silky or pygmy anteater (*Cyclopes didactylus*). Only six to seven inches (15–18 cm) long, with a tail of about the same length, it lives high in the trees and rarely visits the ground.

Armadillos are related to anteaters and, like them, they eat ants and termites. But they also eat other foods, and they collect insects on their long, sticky tongues. There are 20 species of armadillos. Most live in open country, but the giant armadillo (*Priodontes maximus*) dwells in South American forests. The biggest armadillo of all, it averages three feet (91 cm) in length, with a 20-inch (50-cm) tail, and weighs up to 132 pounds (60 kg).

Like all armadillos, the giant armadillo has hard plates covering the upper side of its body, which are made from bone covered with horn. Its plates are rigid but can slide over each other, giving the armadillo freedom of movement, and the giant armadillo is very agile. It can stand on its hind legs to rip open a termite mound with its big, sharp claws. In addition to termites, it eats small animals, including snakes, and the remains of animals killed by other species.

Pangolins live in Africa and tropical Asia. There are seven species, four in Africa and three in Asia. Some species live mainly on the ground, although they are agile climbers.

Parallel evolution and convergent evolution

When two species of animals resemble each other and behave in similar ways, it is natural to assume they are related. This is often the case. A domestic cat shares many features with a sand cat, for example, and a German shepherd dog bears a close resemblance to a wolf. Domestic cats and sand cats are closely related, and so are domestic dogs and wolves. Saying that two species are related implies that they are descended from a common ancestor.

Sometimes, though, appearances can be deceptive. Kangaroo rats (*Dipodomys* species) of the North American deserts and jerboas (*Jaculus* species) of the Sahara and Arabian Desert look similar and live in the same way, yet they are not closely related. They share a common ancestor, but the evolutionary lines leading to the modern animals diverged 57 million years ago. That ancestor probably had long hind legs and hopped, and both kangaroo rats and jerboas have retained these features because they live under similar conditions. Consequently, they are as alike as their remote ancestors were. This is an example of *parallel evolution*: If two species with a common ancestor separate, but both continue to live in the same way, they may continue to resemble one another.

The kowari (*Dasyuroides byrnei*) might pass for a kangaroo rat, except for being about half the size, and the pygmy planigale (*Planigale maculata*) looks very much like a house mouse (*Mus musculus*), but smaller. They look very similar, but kowaris and pygmy planigales inhabit the Australian deserts and are marsupials, the group of mammals that includes koalas and kangaroos. Mice and rats are *eutherian* mammals, along with cats, dogs, cattle, and most other mammals. Marsupials and eutherians diverged about 100 million years ago, so these apparently similar animals are very distant relations. They resemble one another because they live in almost identical environments, but the similarities are superficial. Desert rodents eat a mainly vegetarian diet, but marsupial "mice" are carnivores.

This is an example of *convergent evolution*: Over many generations, two or more unrelated species that live under similar environmental conditions may evolve to resemble one another.

Others spend most of their time in the trees and have prehensile tails. They feed on ants and termites. Ground-dwelling pangolins rip open ant and termite nests. Tree pangolins attack hanging ant and termite nests and columns of ants they find moving along branches. The giant pangolin (*Manis gigantea*) of Africa measures 30–33 inches (76–84 cm) from nose to the root of its 25–31-inch (64–79-cm) tail. The other species are smaller.

The body of a pangolin is covered with rigid, overlapping scales like roof shingles. The scales are made from bone covered with horn and move over each other. A pangolin could be mistaken for a cousin of the armadillos, although its scales are bigger than armadillo scales. Its muzzle, however, is more like that of an anteater—long, with a small mouth and a very long, sticky tongue—and its overall body shape is more like that of an anteater than an armadillo. Armadillos and anteaters are related. Perhaps, then, the pangolin is a cross between an armadillo and an anteater? In fact, the pangolins are not closely related to either armadillos or anteaters. The resemblance in appearance, behavior, and lifestyle arises from the fact that faced with a similar environment and similar diet, these species have adapted in similar ways with the result that they now look similar. It is an example of *convergent evolution* (see the sidebar).

Forest birds

Insects flying above the forest canopy have no cover to protect them from the birds that hunt them, and the birds have only bats for competition. Some of the birds that hunt insects above the canopy are tiny birds of prey. The Philippine falconet (*Microhierax erythrogonys*) is only six inches (15 cm) long—no bigger than a sparrow—but it is a falcon and hunts just like one. The African pygmy falcon (*Polihierax semitorquatus*) is only slightly bigger and it hunts birds as well as insects.

Swiftlets (20 *Collocalia* species) are even smaller than falconets and live entirely on the insects they catch in flight up to 900 feet (275 m) above the canopy. Swiftlets nest in caves in colonies that can number hundreds of thousands of birds and use echolocation to find their way around. They stick their nesting materials together with saliva, and the edible-nest swiftlet (*C. fuciphaga*) makes its nest entirely from dried saliva. These nests are collected to make bird's nest soup.

Any monkey that ventures to the top of the canopy in the Philippine forests may attract the attention of the monkey-eating eagle (*Pithecophaga jefferyi*), a bird that feeds principally on monkeys, though it also takes chickens and small pigs and dogs from villages. The South American equivalent of this eagle is the fearsome harpy eagle (*Harpia harpyja*). Both birds are about three feet (90 cm) long, making them the largest of all eagles. The monkey-eating eagle hunts above the forest and the harpy hunts below the canopy. Both birds are now rare and few people have ever seen either of them in the wild.

Most forest birds live below the canopy, feeding on insects and fruit, and different species hunt together in "armies" of approximately 40 birds belonging to about 10 different species. Each species keeps to a particular height, and the army advances steadily through the forest, flushing out insects that cannot escape by flying to a different level, because to do so would bring them within range of a battalion of other birds. In Asian forests, minivets (*Pericrocotus* species) and white-eyes (family Zosteropidae) move through the upper story. Below them, sultan tits (*Melanochlora sultanea*), flycatchers (subfamily Muscicapinae), scimitar babblers (*Pomatorhinus* species), and leafbirds (family Irenidae) move through the understory. Lower still, moving close to the ground, there are broadbills (family Eurylaimidae) and trogons (*Harpactes* species). Other bird species and even insect-eating mammals will occasionally join the bird army.

The bird army advances noisily because members of each species call to maintain contact with each other and must be heard above the cries of the other birds. It is also a colorful advance because the birds of the tropical forests are the most colorful in the world.

Trogons also live in Central and South America, where the cloud forests (see pages 88–91) stretching from southern Mexico to Panama are home to the resplendent quetzal (*Pharomachrus mocinno*), which some people believe is the most beautiful bird in the world. The short feathers on its

The resplendent quetzal (Pharomachrus mocino) *has iridescent feathers that make it one of the world's most brilliantly colored birds. It lives in the American rain forests.* (Courtesy of Michael and Patricia Fogden/ Minden Pictures)

head stand upright, forming a crest, its long wing feathers overhang its sides, and the feathers over its tail extend as a long train. The head and back are bright metallic green, and the breast, belly, and underside of the tail are bright red. There is a legend in Guatemala that prior to the Spanish conquest the quetzals were plain green, but after a particularly violent battle a flock of them flew down to watch over the dead Mayas, staining their breasts red. The birds are sacred to the plumed serpent god of the Mayas, Quetzalcoatl, and the quetzal is the national emblem of Guatemala. The Guatemalan unit of currency is the quetzal.

The hoatzin (*Opisthocomus hoazin*), a relative of the cuckoos, lives in the lowland forests farther south. It is a weak flier that glides from tree to tree and gains height by climbing up the tree to a higher branch. Despite this apparent drawback, hoatzins build their nests high in the canopy over water. They feed exclusively on leaves, and parents bring leaves to their chicks. As the parents approach, the naked and seemingly helpless chicks scramble through their tree, eager to seize their share of the meal, helped by small claws on the "elbows" of their wings. If danger threatens, the chicks have another trick. They simply drop from the nest into the water, swim to the shore, and scramble all the way back up the tree.

Many colorful birds live on the forest floor, and some are very familiar. The red jungle fowl (*Gallus gallus*) of Southeast Asia looks very like a barnyard chicken. This is no coincidence because it is the ancestor of all domestic chickens. Peafowl (males are *peacocks* and females are *peahens*) are so handsome that they are kept purely as ornaments in many large European and North American gardens and parks. All of them are Indian peafowl (*Pavo cristatus*), and their natural home is in the forests of India and Sri Lanka.

Parrots and macaws

Parrots are undoubtedly the most famous of all tropical birds. In about 328 B.C.E. Alexander the Great returned from India bringing parrots with him, and he gave some of them to his former teacher, Aristotle. The Greeks were amazed at the birds' ability to talk. On arrival the parrots spoke the language from the part of India where they were captured, and before long they also learned to speak Greek. Parrots have been popular pets ever since. Explorers returning from Africa to Rome presented Emperor Nero with African parrots in 54 B.C.E. and, when Europeans began exploring South America, Indonesia, Australia, and New Zealand, they found many new species.

Parrots occur naturally throughout tropical America, Africa, Madagascar, Asia, and Australia, and their range extends into temperate South America, Africa, Australia, and New Zealand. The Carolina parakeet (*Conuropsis carolinensis*) was the most northerly of all parrots. A green conure with a yellow head, it was a serious pest of fruit crops. The last member of the species died in 1918 in Cincinnati Zoo. Most parrots live in lowland tropical and subtropical forests, and even those that visit open country, such as budgerigars, seldom stray far from the forest edge.

Parrots are instantly recognizable by their bills, and many are brightly colored. All 328 species of parrots, lories, lorikeets, parakeets, macaws, cockatoos, conures, and budgerigars are related. Regardless of what they are called, they are all parrots. Different from other birds in several ways, they form the order Psittaciformes.

The upper section of a parrot's distinctive bill is attached to the skull by a kind of hinge that allows some movement, and the bill is a highly adaptable tool. It can be used to preen the plumage, to crush a tough nut such as a Brazil nut, or inflict a savage bite, and it functions as a third "foot" that the bird uses when climbing high above the ground. Two of its four toes point forward and two point backward. This very unusual arrangement, called *zygodactyly,* gives a parrot a very strong grip, and it also allows parrots that feed in trees to use their feet like hands to manipulate items; parrots that feed on the ground are unable to do this. Some parrots are left-footed and some are right-footed. The larger parrots are long-lived—individuals have been known to live for 80 years.

The great majority of parrots live in the trees, most commonly in lowland wet forests (see pages 80–83), building their nests high above the ground in holes in tree trunks or limbs. They will make nest holes for themselves, but they also steal holes made by other hole-nesting birds such as woodpeckers. Many species mate for life, with pairs remaining together all the time and often feeding and preening each other. Most species are very social, however, and parrots usually live in family groups or small flocks and roost together at night. Parrots are vegetarians, feeding on fruit and seeds, including nuts. Lories and lorikeets, found in the forests of

Indonesia, New Guinea, and Australia, feed mainly on pollen and nectar.

Flocks of parrots are noisy and quarrelsome while they are feeding, but if a large bird of prey comes near they fall silent, then fly screaming from the treetops, dispersing in all directions. This usually confuses the predator long enough for the parrots to make their escape.

Like other forest dwellers, many parrots are principally green as a useful camouflage, but some are among the gaudiest of birds. Male and female eclectus parrots (*Eclectus roratus*) have such different plumage that for a long time they were thought to be different species. Males are green, and females are red and blue.

Macaws, which are large South American parrots with long tails, are especially colorful. The hyacinth macaw (*Anodorhynchus hyacinthinus*) is purple and the scarlet macaw (*Ara macao*) has bright red, blue, yellow, and green plumage. The blue-and-yellow macaw (*Ara ararauna*), with its blue head and back and golden front, is also popular. Macaws come mainly from the Amazon Basin, and all of them are so attractive that they are becoming rare in the wild, partly because forest clearance is destroying their habitat, but also because so many birds have been captured for export as cage birds. Fortunately, it is now possible to breed macaws and other parrots in captivity, and birds offered for sale in reputable pet stores have not been taken from the wild.

Parrots are famously able to talk, and this ability has contributed greatly to their popularity. People used to think that the birds simply mimicked humans, repeating "parrot fashion" whatever they hear. Nowadays scientists are not so sure. Many birds mimic other species, but parrots have never been heard to do so in the wild, so they may not be natural mimics. It also seems possible that far from merely repeating what they hear, parrots may understand what they are saying and use human speech to communicate with humans. There have been several scientific studies of the use of language by parrots, the most advanced probably being the work of Dr. Irene Pepperberg with four African gray parrots (*Psittacus erithacus*), including one called Alex, that has continued for many years. Alex appears to use language purposefully and Dr. Pepperberg thinks it possible that one day he may learn to read.

Macaws, found only in South American forests, are the biggest and most brightly colored of all parrots. They are popular as pets and so many have been captured and exported for the pet trade that the populations of some species, especially the scarlet macaw (Ara macao) seen here, have been seriously depleted. (Courtesy of Kevin Tate/ Istockphoto)

Toucans and hornbills

Toucans are birds as characteristic of the American tropical forests as macaws. They are only slightly less colorful than macaws, and their appearance is much more extraordinary because of their huge bills.

The big bill is a useful tool and a weapon, and toucans are playful birds that use their bills in play fighting. A toucan is too heavy to venture along thin branches, but its bill allows it to sit safely in the hollow where a branch meets the trunk in the crown of a tree and reach out to pluck the fruits it could reach in no other way. Fruit is only part of its diet, however. Toucans also rob the nests of smaller birds of eggs and chicks. Its bill is so big, strong, and threatening that parent birds dare not attack the marauding toucan, and even as the robber flies away there is little they can do. If they pursue the toucan it is liable to perch on a branch and turn to face them.

Toucans spend most of their time high in the forest canopy, flying only short distances from one tree to another. They move around in flocks, but individuals within each flock are widely separated.

There are 38 species of toucans. The toco toucan (*Ramphastos toco*) is the one most often photographed. It is about 26 inches (66 cm) long and its yellow-and-black eight-inch (20-cm) bill is the longest of any toucan.

Toucans nest in holes in trees, and in Africa and Asia there are 45 species of very similar-looking birds, the hornbills, that also nest in hollows. Most hornbills live in forests and, although they prefer tree holes, they will also nest in holes in earth banks and rock faces.

In all but two species of hornbills that nest on the ground, once the female has made her nest she seals the entrance. Working from outside the nest, she blocks the entrance with mud, helped by her mate in some species, until all that remains is a hole just big enough for her to enter. She goes inside and finishes the job using her own droppings and remains of food, leaving only a narrow vertical slit high above the floor of the nest—its location ensures good circulation of air. There is often an escape tunnel above the nest hole for use in emergencies. While the female remains secure inside the hole, the male brings her food. Once the eggs have hatched, he also feeds the chicks, in some species for as long as four months. The female ejects droppings and food waste through the slit, keeping the nest clean. While inside she loses all of her feathers, which grow back in time for her to leave the nest.

Like toucans, hornbills have massive, slightly curved bills. In many species there is a large "helmet," or "casque," on top of the bill. Hornbills are bigger than toucans, averaging 15–63 inches (38–160 cm) in length, including the bill. The bigger species eat mainly fruit, but other species feed mainly on insects, and there are some meat eaters.

Despite their similarities, hornbills and toucans are not related, and it is possible that African hornbills are not closely related to the Asian species. The similarities are the results of species adapting in the same way to similar environmental conditions. This is an example of convergent evolution (see the sidebar "Parallel evolution and convergent evolution" on page 156).

Hornbills live in African and Asian forests. Despite their resemblance to South American toucans, toucans and hornbills are not closely related. (Courtesy of Goh Kheng Liang)

CHAPTER 6

ECOLOGY OF TROPICAL FORESTS

Forest layers

The mighty trees of the tropical forest tower high into the sky, and at ground level the tree seedlings, shrubs, and herbs form a tangled riot of vegetation, with plants growing to many different heights. Clearly the forest extends in three dimensions—vertically as well as horizontally.

Some forest plants are taller than others. This makes it possible to think of the forest as being arranged in a series of horizontal layers or strata, one lying above another like the layers of a layer cake. As the diagram shows, however, a real forest is not structured so neatly. Layers exist, and each layer supports particular plants and animals, but the layers are seldom defined clearly and it can be difficult to make them out.

The number of layers varies according to the type of forest (see "Types of tropical forest" on pages 80–99). Lowland wet forest—the typical tropical rain forest—is the richest. Other forests, including some lowland wet forests, may have fewer layers, but none has more. Since lowland wet forest is the type with the greatest number of layers, it is usually taken to represent an "ideal" tropical forest. The layers are as follows:

1. Emergent trees (see pages 172–176) form the uppermost layer. These giants of the forest typically reach to a height of 100 feet (30 m) or more, although they are not all the same height.
2. Below the emergents, the canopy or middle tree layer is composed of trees with crowns that are approximately 65 feet (20 m) above ground level.
3. An understory consists of smaller trees, some of them young saplings (see pages 171–172) of the canopy and

emergent species. These grow to an average height of about 30 feet (10 m).

4. Shrubs, smaller saplings, and small trees comprise a shrub layer of plants up to about 16 feet (5 m) tall.

5. At ground level, and growing to a height of 40 inches (1 m) or less, is the herb layer. It comprises tree and shrub seedlings, nonwoody herbs (called *forbs*), grasses, and ferns.

Layers in a lowland wet forest, showing the height of the layers and the horizontal spacing of trees

These five strata describe the forest above ground. As well as the trees and shrubs, each layer also contains climbers, parasites, and epiphytes, some of them found at one level but nowhere else. Plant roots then continue the layers below ground. Upper, middle, and lower root layers bring the total number of forest strata to eight.

Seeking the light

High above the forest canopy, leaves at the top of the crowns of the emergents (see pages 172–176) are exposed to full sunlight. Even inside the crowns, leaves receive up to 25 percent of the full sunlight, and because the tropical sunlight is so bright, this means they are well illuminated.

Obviously, bright sunlight benefits the trees, but other plants also take advantage of it. Epiphytes—plants that grow on the surface of other plants, using the host only for support—grow at various levels within the crowns, and climbers use the trees for support as they reach for the sunshine.

Photosynthesis

Green plants and some bacteria are able to use energy from sunlight (photo-) to assemble (synthesize) sugars. The process is called *photosynthesis* and it depends on a pigment called *chlorophyll*. Chlorophyll is green and it is what gives plants their green color.

Photosynthesis proceeds in two stages. The first stage depends on light, and it is called the *light-dependent* or *light* stage. The second stage does not use light energy, so it is called the *light-independent* or *dark* stage (although it also takes place in the light).

Light-dependent stage. When a photon (a unit of light) possessing precisely the right amount of energy strikes a chlorophyll molecule, the photon disappears and its energy is absorbed, allowing an electron (a particle carrying negative charge) in the molecule to break free. This leaves the chlorophyll molecule with a positive charge. The free electron immediately attaches to a neighboring molecule, thereby ejecting another electron that moves to a neighboring molecule. In this way electrons pass along an *electron-transport chain* of molecules. Each plant cell contains a number of chloroplasts and each chloroplast contains many molecules of chlorophyll, so while the plant is exposed to light there is a constant stream of photons being captured and electrons moving along the electron-transport chain.

Some of the transported energy is used to convert adenosine diphosphate (ADP) to adenosine triphosphate (ATP) by the addition of phosphate, after which the electron then returns to the chlorophyll. Converting ADP to ATP absorbs energy; converting ATP to ADP releases the energy. The ADP ↔ ATP reaction (the double arrow indicates the reaction can move in either direction) is used by all living organisms to transport energy and release it where it is needed.

The trees of the canopy layer fill most of the gaps below the emergents. Plants growing below the canopy are exposed only to dappled sunlight passing through gaps that appear and disappear as leaves move with the wind or rain or are disturbed by animals. Less than 1 percent of the sunlight above the emergents penetrates all the way to the plants on the forest floor. More than 99 percent of the light reaching the top of the forest—the *incident* light—falls on leaves. Some of the light is reflected, but as aerial photographs of tropical forest show, the forest is dark in color. This means that the forest absorbs more of the light falling on it than it reflects. In fact,

Energy that is not used to convert ADP to ATP is used to split a water molecule (H_2O) into a hydrogen ion, which bears a positive charge (H^+), and a hydroxyl ion, which has a negative charge (OH^-). (An *ion* is an atom that has gained or lost one or more electrons, so it bears a positive or negative charge.) The H^+ attaches to a molecule of nicotinamide adenine dinucleotide phosphate (NADP), converting it to reduced NADP (NADPH). The OH^- passes one electron to the chlorophyll molecule, restoring the neutrality of both chlorophyll and hydroxyl. Hydroxyls then combine to form water ($4OH \leftrightarrow 2H_2O + O_2\uparrow$). (The upward arrow in this chemical formula indicates that the oxygen is released into the air.) This completes the light-dependent stage.

Light-independent stage. Using ATP from the light-dependent stage as a source of energy, the first in a series of chemical reactions attaches molecules of carbon dioxide (CO_2) obtained from the air to molecules of ribulose biphosphate (RuBP), a substance present in the chloroplast. The enzyme RuBP carboxylase (the name is usually abbreviated to *rubisco*) catalyzes the reaction. In a cycle of reactions the carbon atoms, originally from the carbon dioxide, are combined with hydrogen obtained from NADPH; the NADP then returns to the light-dependent stage. The cycle ends with the synthesis of molecules of glucose and of RuBP. The RuBP is then available to commence the cycle again.

Glucose, a simple sugar, is the most common source of energy for living things; its energy is released by the process of *respiration*. Glucose is also used to synthesize complex sugars: starch and cellulose in plants and glycogen (also called animal starch) in animals. Plants use cellulose to build cell walls; starch and glycogen can be converted to glucose, releasing energy.

the leaves absorb at least 80 percent of the incident light. They use the energy of the absorbed light to manufacture sugars by the process of photosynthesis (see the sidebar).

Even on the forest floor the plants are not in total darkness, of course, and direct sunlight reaches ground level whenever movements in the canopy produce small and temporary gaps. The amount of sunlight reaching the ground also varies with the time of day. This is because when the Sun is low in the sky, sunlight passes through a greater thickness of trunks, branches, climbers and leaves than it does when the Sun is high. At noon, when the Sun is almost directly overhead, approximately 1 percent of the incident sunlight reaches the forest floor. At 3 P.M. sunlight approaches the surface at an angle of approximately 45°, so it arrives at the canopy with 67 percent of its noon intensity and 0.05 percent reaches the forest floor. At 4 P.M. the Sun is about 30°

Sunlight reaching the forest floor. The amount of sunlight penetrating the forest floor increases rapidly during the morning, reaches a maximum at noon, and decreases rapidly during the afternoon.

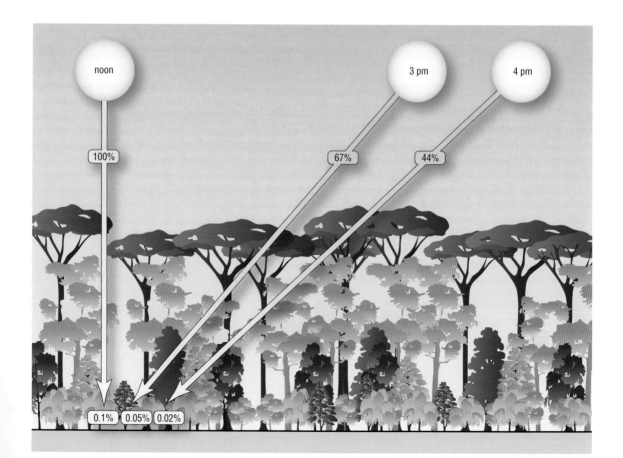

above the horizon. The sunlight reaching the canopy is 44 percent of the noon amount and only 0.02 percent reaches the floor. The diagram shows how sunlight penetrates a thicker layer of vegetation as the Sun moves lower in the sky.

Saplings: waiting for a chance to grow

The seeds of many tropical tree species start to sprout, or *germinate,* almost the moment they touch the ground. Seeds of some species cannot tolerate drying and must germinate quickly. Others have no *endosperm*—the food store that sustains most young plants until they are able to obtain their own nutrients—so they, too, cannot wait. Seeds of the Sumatra camphor tree (*Dryobalanops aromatica*) contain 44 percent water by weight and so are able to germinate quickly. There are seeds that can lie dormant in the ground, but in most cases even they do not wait long. Jelutong (*Dyera costulata*) is a massive tree, growing up to 200 feet (61 m) tall and up to eight feet (2.4 m) in diameter, found in Asian forests. Its seeds do not germinate immediately, but do so 24–130 days after reaching the ground. Seeds of the kempas tree (*Koompassia malaccensis*), another Asian species that is up to 180 feet (55 m) tall when fully grown and with massive buttresses, germinate 13–56 days after falling.

Many plants of temperate regions produce seeds that can remain dormant for months or even years, germinating as soon as conditions are favorable for them. This strategy is less common in the humid Tropics, where biological activity is so vigorous that a dormant seed is likely to be eaten or infected with fungi or bacteria. Seeds need to germinate quickly so the growing plant can produce thorns, bark, and poisons to defend itself from attack.

Even so, most seeds are lost. They fall in places where they fail to germinate or where the emerging plants fail to survive. Light levels are critical. Tropical tree seedlings demand varying depths of shade; they will fail if it is too light or too dark. Most tree roots work in close association with particular soil fungi. If the fungi are absent the young plant may fail. Overall, approximately 2 percent of all the seeds that fall from the forest trees germinate successfully and produce healthy young plants that survive past their first year of life.

Some trees, known as *pioneer species,* are quick to take advantage of gaps in the canopy. Their seeds germinate to produce a carpet of seedlings that die very quickly if they are shaded by taller plants. Where there is a gap, however, they grow fast to fill it. Other pioneers produce copious quantities of seeds that, in contrast to most species, remain dormant until a gap in the canopy exposes them to direct sunlight, when they germinate and grow rapidly. Pioneer trees die if they are shaded at any time during their growth.

Other trees tolerate shade. Their seeds often contain food to sustain the young seedling for some time as it slowly establishes itself. Then the tree continues to grow slowly, eventually joining the understory. Trees that prefer deep shade do not form part of the canopy.

Dominant species—those that form the forest canopy when fully grown—grow slowly for as long as they remain shaded. Kauri pine (*Agathis macrophylla*), for example, grows to a height of about three feet (90 cm) and then ceases to grow until a gap appears and the light intensity increases.

Once direct sunlight penetrates the canopy, competition to fill the gap becomes intense. Kauri pine requires a small gap that it can fill quickly. If the gap is too large, surrounding plants that grow faster soon shade the sapling, halting its growth. Other species, especially red meranti (*Shorea* species) and lauan (*Parashorea* species) in the Asian forests, grow fast enough to compete successfully, even with the climbers that are quick to invade large gaps. These trees often become emergents.

Emergents

Seen from above, a temperate forest forms a fairly even carpet across the landscape. Here and there a tree stands taller than its neighbors, but over most of the forest, all the trees are approximately the same height. A tropical forest is different. Its canopy is made up of tree crowns at so many different heights that the "carpet" is very lumpy.

The lumpiness arises mainly from the fact that a tropical forest is much more dynamic than a temperate forest. In a tropical forest there are trees at every stage of their growth

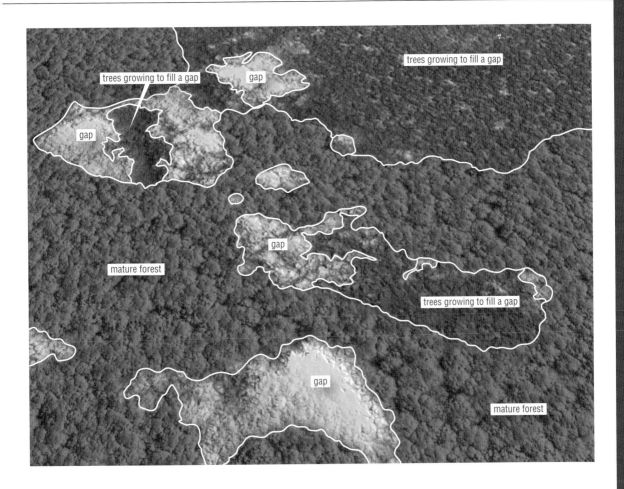

trees growing to fill a gap

trees growing to fill a gap

gap

gap

gap

gap

trees growing to fill a gap

mature forest

gap

mature forest

and most of them are growing rapidly. Trees fall because they die of old age or disease or because they are struck by lightning, and as one tree falls in the dense forest it often brings others down with it. A small group of trees crashes to the ground together and, before long, young trees are growing up to fill the gap in the canopy. The growing trees rise together, competing with each other for light and space for their roots, and their crowns approach the canopy together. Someone flying over the forest would see a patch where the canopy was lower than the surrounding canopy. Nearby, where the trees filling an earlier gap have almost attained their full size, the canopy is higher.

It is convenient to describe tropical forests in terms of layers, or strata (see pages 166–167), but this sounds static, as though the forest grew up into a series of layers and, once it

Canopy of a tropical forest, seen from above. The diagram shows the gaps in the forest and areas where trees are growing up to fill earlier gaps.

had attained its mature form, remained forever unchanged in structure. In reality, the forest is growing and dying constantly, and therefore it is in a constant state of change; this is seen most clearly at the canopy level. Rather than a smooth, even carpet, the canopy forms a patchwork, like that shown in the illustration.

The tallest trees, their crowns standing higher than the canopy around them, are called *emergents*—because they emerge above the canopy. All trees need sunlight, and an emergent is exposed to the full intensity of tropical sunshine. This gives the emergent a clear advantage over the other trees—but there is a price it must pay for its place in the sun. There is more to being a successful emergent than an ability to wait patiently until the appearance of a gap provides an opportunity to make a dramatic leap for the sun.

As well as greater light intensity, the emergent is exposed to higher temperatures. Air temperature decreases with height but in a tropical forest the closed canopy shades all the areas it covers, cooling the air. In clearings open to the sky and above the canopy there is no shading, and consequently the average temperature is a degree or two higher than it is in the shade. There is also a markedly greater difference between day and night temperatures, and that difference changes through the year. In a lowland forest in the Ivory Coast, at approximately latitude 7°N, the difference between day and night temperatures three feet (1 m) above ground level in December is about 8°F (4.4°C). At 150 feet (46 m) above the main part of the canopy, it is 19°F (10.8°C). The equivalent temperatures in June are 3°F (1.7°C) and 7°F (4°C).

It is also windier above the canopy. Trees slow the wind and deflect it so that the trees below the canopy are protected. Emergents, on the other hand, are exposed to the full force of the wind, and wind has a strong drying effect. This is because a thin layer of air covers all leaf surfaces and air in this layer retains moisture. Wind sweeps away the layer of moist air and replaces it with dry air. Water inside the leaf then evaporates through the leaf stomata, or pores, into the dry air, only to be swept away in its turn. The generally higher temperature above the canopy also contributes to the drying effect because water evaporates faster into warm air than it does into cool air. The combined drying effect of the wind and warm air can kill leaves that are not equipped to withstand it, and more leaves are lost as the death of the outermost leaves exposes the leaves they were sheltering. A tree that loses too many leaves from its crown cannot survive.

The crowns of emergent trees are also directly exposed to the torrential tropical rain. It may seem odd to suggest that the leaves suffer from both drying and soaking, but tropical weather alternates between bright sunshine and heavy rain. Leaves lose moisture through their stomata when it is hot, dry, and windy, but heavy rain can cover leaves, blocking the stomata and thereby preventing photosynthesis (see "Drip tips, buttress roots, and stilt roots" on pages 104–108). Heavy rain also subjects leaves to a severe battering.

Most emergent trees have much smaller leaves than do trees growing at lower levels, and their leaves often lack a distinct drip tip. Many trees have leaves that turn in response to the direction of the sunlight in a way that maximizes their exposure to light while minimizing their loss of moisture. Leaves that are exposed to full sunlight every day also tend to be a paler green than the shaded leaves below the canopy.

These leaf modifications are adaptations to conditions above the canopy that allow the emergents to thrive in the open air beneath an open sky—but a puzzle remains. Like all the forest trees, the emergents begin life down on the forest floor as seedlings that grow into saplings. In most cases they will have reached a certain height and then remained at that height until a gap appeared in the canopy, giving them an opportunity to grow. In other words, the trees spend the first years of their lives in shade, protected from the wind and rain, and in temperatures that vary little from day to night. When their crowns expand to fill the gap in the canopy and then rise above it, they find themselves in a quite different environment for which their previous adaptation is no longer appropriate. Trees of some species spend their entire lives in the understory in conditions that suit them. Emergents, however, move from one set of conditions to another and are well suited to conditions above the canopy that would kill an understory tree—and that would have killed them had they encountered it too abruptly during their early years. The emergents survive by altering the shape and structure of their leaves as they reach the canopy. In effect, they behave as two different kinds of tree, one adapted to conditions in the understory and the other adapted to conditions in the canopy.

Lianas and other climbers

When a tree falls, bringing others down with it, or an area of forest is cleared by felling, it is not long before young plants spring up in the clearing. These plants include tree seedlings, some of which one day will reach the canopy and close the gap. They will not grow alone, however. Climbers often attach themselves to these seedlings and grow with them. Climbers seek the light and allow their host trees to carry them aloft by matching their rates of growth. When the host reaches the canopy and grows branches to form its crown, the climber does the same, often producing a crown as large as that of its host.

There are other climbers that attach themselves to an established tree and then grow up its trunk. These are called *bole climbers—bole* is another word for trunk—and they have various techniques. Some twine themselves around the trunk and climb it in a spiral. Others produce tendrils that wind themselves around irregularities on the bark to support the weight of the plant as it grows. A third group consists of climbers that produce small roots, called *climbing roots,* to grip the bark for support by growing into small crevices.

Climbers do not restrict themselves to living trees. When a forest tree dies, it usually does so slowly. Dead branches fall to the ground, leaving the trunk standing alone. Then the bark falls from the trunk, bringing any climbers with it. Climbers then attach themselves to the dead, smooth trunk. They completely surround and hide it beneath their stems, roots, and leaves so that what was once a tree is transformed into a *climber tower*—a narrow column of vegetation.

A climber that allows itself to be transported aloft by its host is usually attached only to the host's crown. Its own trunk hangs free. The bole climbers are attached at many points, but tendrils and climbing roots sometimes break, and twining climbers may slip when they grow heavy. Fallen climbers lie on the ground in great loops and coils, their growing tips continuing to extend as they search for a new tree to climb.

Climbers are sun-seekers, so they spring up most prolifically in clearings and other openings in the forest, such as those made when a road is built. They contribute greatly to the tangled impenetrability of the jungle that is often the first part of the forest that a visitor sees.

Not all climbers reach the canopy. The smaller ones are more tolerant of shade and have fairly thin, nonwoody stems. These resemble ivy and are known as *vines*.

The most spectacular climbers are woody. Known as *lianas* or *lianes,* those are the ones that climb all the way to the forest canopy. Their stems average four to six inches (10–15 cm) in diameter and they often hang well clear of the trunk of their host. There are many species of woody climber, belonging to many plant families. Some of them are palm trees, including *Calamus* and *Daemonorops* species. The stems of these palms grow from particular regions called *nodes;* the stem between nodes is called an *internode,* and the plant grows by lengthening the internodes. At each node, the climbing palms have a circle of long, strong, and extremely sharp spikes to discourage any animal that might think of climbing the climber.

Climbing palms have commercial value. They are cut down, stripped of their bark, and then cut into long, narrow strips of cane, called rattan, that is woven into the seats and backs of wickerwork chairs. Thicker pieces of rattan are made into malacca cane walking sticks.

How rain reaches the forest inhabitants

Scientists use rain gauges to measure rainfall. A rain gauge is a cylindrical container with a funnel on top. Rain falls onto the funnel and flows from there into the cylinder. Covering the cylinder with the funnel prevents the water from evaporating. Rain gauges are accurate, but a rain gauge that is placed on the floor of a tropical forest will give very misleading measurements because it collects only the rainwater that reaches the ground—and on average that is approximately one-third of the water arriving at the top of the canopy.

Plants absorb moisture through their roots, taking it from water that is constantly moving through the soil (see "Movement of water through tropical soils" on page 42–45). Rain is what supplies water to the soil, and if only one-third of the rain enters the soil it is not difficult to see that from time to time plants are likely to be short of water, even in a rain forest.

Rain arriving at the top of the canopy wets the leaves in the crowns of the trees. Where the crowns of adjacent trees meet to form a closed canopy, the leaves intercept almost all of the falling rain. The leaves bend and the water runs off them (see "Drip tip, buttress roots, and stilt roots" on pages 104–108), but while it remains in the canopy some of the water evaporates. The forest loses approximately 25 percent of the incoming rainwater by evaporation in the canopy.

The remaining 75 percent of the rainwater flows down the limbs and trunks of the trees. As it does so, some soaks into dry bark and some evaporates. Approximately 40 percent of the total rainfall evaporates into the air between the underside of the canopy and the ground. Only about 35 percent—the remainder—of the water falling on the top of the canopy reaches the soil.

Although most of the rain fails to reach the ground, evaporation ensures that the air below the canopy remains moist. The amount of water vapor present in the air is known as the *humidity* of the air. There are several ways to measure humidity. The measure that is most often used is called the *relative humidity*, or RH. This is the amount of water vapor present in the air at a particular temperature as a percentage of the amount needed to saturate the air at that temperature; if the air is saturated, the RH is 100 percent (the "percent" is often omitted). At dawn the RH in the upper part of the canopy is about 90, but by noon it has often fallen to 70 or even lower. Close to the ground the RH remains fairly constant, at about 90, and the rate of evaporation is very low near ground level.

Rain is only one source of moisture, however. Dew very often forms on clear, still nights, and by dawn it can amount to the equivalent of 0.004–0.01 inch (0.1–0.3 mm) of rain. This is not very much, but it is significant. Dew forms on surfaces that are chilled because they have radiated away the warmth they absorbed during the day. When the sky is overcast, the warmth radiating from the surface is trapped by the clouds and warms the air, which in turn keeps the solid surfaces warm. Consequently, dew does not form on cloudy nights. A forest canopy behaves like a cloud, absorbing heat radiating from below. This means that dew forms on the ground in a tropical forest only in the clearings. Elsewhere the dew forms on leaves in the canopy. Some of the moisture drips from the leaves but very little moisture reaches the ground.

Dew is important for a different reason. Its fine droplets covering the leaves block leaf stomata for up to about three hours—the time it takes for the dew to evaporate. Blocking stomata greatly reduces the rate at which trees lose moisture by transpiration, and this in turn reduces the rate at which they draw water from the soil. Almost none of the dew reaches the ground, but it nevertheless helps to keep the ground a little moister than it would otherwise have been.

Fog and low cloud provide moisture on mountainsides and along coasts and river valleys (see "Cloud forest" on pages 88–91). The Atacama Desert in western South America is one of the driest deserts in the world, but there are places—sometimes called "fog oases"—in the mountains along the Peruvian coast where forests grow in the moisture the trees collect from clouds that roll in from the Pacific Ocean. There are similar fog oases in mountainous regions of Africa and Asia.

Not all of the water that trickles down the branches and trunks of trees is lost. It may not reach the ground, but this is important only for those plants that are rooted in the ground. Certain forest plants have no direct contact with the ground. These are the *epiphytes* (see pages 183–185), which absorb moisture from the air or from small pools of water that collect in the hollows where branches join bigger branches or the main trunk. Microorganisms and single-celled algae also live in these puddles, and some tree frogs lay their eggs in them. When the eggs hatch, the tadpoles remain in their puddles until they grow into frogs.

Food chains, food webs, and pyramids
Caterpillars eat leaves. Birds eat caterpillars. Snakes eat birds. Bigger snakes eat smaller snakes. In a tropical forest, or

indeed any other area where plants and animals live, the inhabitants are linked by relationships based on diet. These are known as *trophic* relationships, from the Greek word *trophe,* meaning "nourishment." Every animal must eat. *Herbivores* eat only plants, but they often specialize in the species of plants and parts of plants they prefer, eating roots, bark, leaves, buds, fruit, or seeds. *Carnivores* eat only other animals, but they also specialize, *insectivores* eating insects, for example. *Omnivores* eat both plant and animal foods.

Trophic relationships can be arranged in order of what organisms eat. In the example above, this gives the sequence: leaves → caterpillars → birds → snake → big snake. The arrows indicate where the members of each group go: Leaves go to the caterpillars that eat them, the caterpillars go to the birds, and so on. This type of sequence is called a *food chain.*

Food chains are useful because they show how nutrients move and also how certain environmental pollutants move. If a particular pollutant is present in the leaves, provided it is not broken down into harmless substances on the way, it may pass through all the organisms along the chain, and its concentration may increase as it does so. This is because caterpillars eat a lot of leaves, so their bodies contain the pollutant from all the leaves they have eaten. Birds eat a lot of caterpillars, and their bodies accumulate the pollutant from all of those; and snakes eat a lot of birds. Finally, the snake-eating snake consumes all the pollutant that has accumulated along the chain, and this may be enough to harm it.

Useful though they are, however, food chains are also misleading. They tell only a small part of the real story. It is true that birds eat caterpillars, but they also eat other foods. At certain times of the year, birds may eat spiders or fruit or seeds. Usually they eat whatever is abundant at the time. Snakes that eat birds also eat small rodents, and although snakes are a major part of the diet of many large snakes, a hungry snake will eat any suitable prey it can catch. A diagram that shows all of these relationships by lines linking organisms to the foods they eat does not look like a chain, but forms a much more complicated *food web.* A food web diagram provides a clear, broad picture of the way a particular area functions.

Even then, a food web diagram oversimplifies the trophic relationships that exist in the real world. No one knows precisely what every animal eats, and a diagram that shows all the known relationships is of little use. Such a diagram would be so big and so complicated as to be almost impossible to follow, and it would be so detailed that it applied to only the particular small area on which it was based. A few miles away the animal population might be a little different, so a fresh diagram would have to be drawn.

There is another way to show trophic relationships. All the organisms can be arranged as groups according to the way they feed. Green plants do not eat other organisms. They manufacture food by photosynthesis (see the sidebar on page 168) and from mineral nutrients they take from the soil. The food the plants manufacture is then available to the animals that eat the plants. Plants can therefore be described as *producers* (of food) and animals, which eat plants, as *consumers.* As the food chain illustrated, there are several levels of consumers. Herbivores, eating only plants, are *primary consumers.* The carnivores that eat herbivores are *secondary consumers,* and the carnivores that eat other carnivores are *tertiary consumers.*

These feeding groups can be arranged one above another as *trophic levels* and compared graphically, represented as rectangles that are all the same height but of varying widths. Let the widths represent the number of individual organisms at each level; this results in a wide producer rectangle, a much narrower primary consumer rectangle, a still narrower secondary consumer rectangle, and a very narrow tertiary consumer

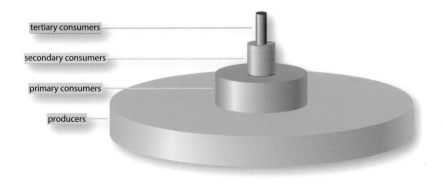

tertiary consumers

secondary consumers

primary consumers

producers

Ecological pyramid. The drawing is not to scale; each level in the pyramid should be approximately one-tenth the width of the layer below.

rectangle. Stacking these in order, with the producers at the bottom and the primary, secondary, and tertiary consumers above them, as shown in the illustration, forms a kind of pyramid. It is known as an *ecological pyramid* or an *Eltonian pyramid* after Charles Elton (1900–91), the British ecologist who devised it in 1927.

There are three kinds of ecological pyramids. One, which shows the number of organisms at each level, is known as a *pyramid of numbers*. Its disadvantage is that plants and animals come in many sizes, and including ants and gorillas in the same diagram makes the pyramid difficult to interpret. An alternative is to measure the total mass of all the organisms at each level, ignoring the number of individuals. The mass of organisms constitutes the biological mass, shortened to *biomass,* and the resulting diagram is a *pyramid of biomass.*

The most useful ecological pyramid, however, is the *pyramid of energy.* Green plants use the energy of sunlight to drive the chemical reactions in photosynthesis. Animals eating the plants and using the food they digest to power their own bodies are utilizing some of the solar energy absorbed by the plants, and carnivores also use energy that came originally from the Sun. The tigers and panthers that stalk the forests are powered by sunlight. A pyramid of energy shows the proportion of the energy of sunlight that is available to the organisms at each trophic level.

Perhaps surprisingly, all three pyramids look remarkably similar. They show that each trophic level is approximately one-tenth the size of the preceding level. If the producers use, say, 1,000 energy units of sunlight, the primary consumers use 100 units, the secondary consumers 10 units, and the tertiary consumers only one unit. At each level, about 90 percent of the energy the organisms absorb is used to drive their own bodies, and only 10 percent is used to build their own tissues, which provide food energy to the consumers that eat them.

Ecological pyramids show very clearly why there can never be very many large carnivores, such as tigers. Such a small proportion of the original energy is available to large predators that they need a very large area in which to find sufficient food. A female leopard (*Panthera pardus*) occupies a territory of four to 12 square miles (10–30 km²), and a tigress

(*Panthera tigris*) needs a similar area. Female ranges overlap slightly, but the forest cannot provide food for more leopards or tigers than this, so leopards and tigers must always be widely dispersed, even in the most productive forest. If the predators were bigger, they would require even larger ranges in which to hunt. But then they would encounter a physical limitation: They would expend more energy finding their food than their bodies would gain by eating it.

Epiphytes

Water is available at every level in a tropical forest, although only a small proportion of it reaches the ground. Most wets the branches, trunks, and leaves of trees. The water is never pure. It arrives after trickling across the bark, collecting particles of dust and organic matter. Spores of bacteria, fungi, and simple plants fall from the air onto the film of water and are held by it. Seeds of more complex plants, blown by the wind or dropped by birds, also land on the wet bark.

Some of the spores and seeds develop into plants. Plants that grow in this way are not confined to tropical forests. They also thrive in temperate forests, where many trees have ferns growing on the upper sides of horizontal branches, mosses clinging to the bark, and lichens growing as patches or hanging from branches. These plants have no direct contact with the ground. If they possess roots, their roots do not penetrate the soil. They grow upon (Greek *epi*) other plants (Greek *phyton*) and are known as *epiphytes*. Epiphytes are especially abundant in tropical forests.

Epiphytes are not parasites (see pages 185–187). They take nothing from the plant on which they grow, using it only for support. Their roots merely anchor them to crevices in the bark, and they obtain their nutrients and water from the air and from the water flowing across the branch or trunk on which they grow.

Many produce aerial roots—roots that hang below the plant and are not in contact with the host tree. Their aerial roots often form tangled nets that trap falling leaves and other plant material from which the roots absorb nutrients. These epiphytes appear to be rooted in the air and are often

Bromeliads

"Air plants" are popular indoor ornamentals. They are unusual in needing no soil. If they are placed on a secure surface, such as a small piece of a tree branch, and sprayed with a mist of water from time to time, they will thrive. That is all they need.

Many air plants are *bromeliads*—among more than 2,100 species belonging to the family Bromeliaceae. One bromeliad species, *Pitcairnia feliciana,* grows naturally in West Africa, but all the other species are American, occurring from the southern United States to central Argentina and Chile. The most widespread species is Spanish moss (*Tillandsia usneoides*), also known as Florida moss and old man's beard, with a range extending from Florida to Argentina. It hangs from forest trees in festoons, looking very much like a lichen. The pineapple (*Ananas comosus*) is also a bromeliad. Now grown in many parts of the world, it came originally from tropical and subtropical America and the West Indies.

A few species of bromeliads grow in the ground, with conventional roots, but many are epiphytes and adapted to dry conditions. They have only rudimentary true roots that are not important in absorbing nutrients and water.

Their stiff leaves, often with sharp spines and very wide bases, form a rosette around the base of the plant. Pineapple is a typical example, although it grows on the ground and has a few conventional roots. The rosette of leaves acts as a tank, holding water and humus made from decaying plant matter. Adventitious roots growing upward from the base of the leaves absorb moisture and nutrients from the tank. Most species have specialized leaf hairs called *trichomes* growing from the leaves. The trichomes also absorb water and nutrients from the tank.

Bromeliad tanks can be large. Many species have tanks that hold more than 1.3 gallons (5 L) of water. Small plants, insects, and even frogs inhabit these tanks.

The flower is produced at the end of a stalk that grows from the center of the tank. Many bromeliads die after flowering. In the pineapple the individual small fruits fuse to form a multiple fruit.

called "air plants." Many of those found in the Americas are bromeliads (see the sidebar).

Not all air plants are bromeliads, however. Some cacti live as epiphytes in American forests. These include the popular Christmas cactus (*Schlumbergera bridgesii*) and mistletoe cactus (*Rhipsalis baccifera*).

There are approximately 17,500 species of orchids, and almost half of these live as epiphytes in tropical forests. They include the vanilla orchid (*Vanilla planifolia*) of tropical America, which is the source of the flavoring vanillin, obtained from the pods. Their attractive flowers make orchids popular as ornamental plants, and many of the epiphytes are cultivated. The moth orchids (*Phalaenopsis* species) of Asia have attractive leaves as well as flowers that are spectacular in some species. The white and yellow flowers of *P. amabilis* are four inches (10 cm) across and grow as a group up to three feet (90 cm) long. The gray-green leaves of *P. gigantea* from Borneo can grow up to 24 inches (60 cm) long.

There are at least 900 species of *Dendrobium* orchids. They are among the most widely cultivated of all orchids, and many of the 1,200 species of *Bulbophyllum* are also popular as ornamentals. Both *Dendrobium* and *Bulbophyllum* grow in the Asian forests.

With their bright flowers, many epiphytes bring splashes of color to the tropical forests.

Parasitic plants

Orchid flowers are spectacular, but the biggest flower in the world, if not the most attractive, belongs to *Rafflesia arnoldii*—a plant that has no common name. Its reddish-brown flower is up to 42 inches (106.7 cm) across and smells of rotting meat. The smell, which people find revolting, attracts the flies that pollinate the plant.

Rafflesia grows on other plants, but it is not an epiphyte. Epiphytes use their host plants only for support; they take nothing from them. *Rafflesia* is different. It relies on its host for nourishment. It is a parasite, one of a number of parasitic plants that live in tropical forests.

There are approximately 500 species in the *Rafflesia* family (Rafflesiaceae), and most of them grow in tropical American and Asian forests, although there are a few in southern Europe, North Africa, and southern Africa. All of them are parasites that attach themselves to the roots or stems of other plants, especially vines and lianas (see "Lianas and other climbers" on pages 176–177). They have no leaves or true roots, so they are unable to perform photosynthesis (see the sidebar on page 168). Instead, they produce fine filaments that penetrate the host and draw nutrients from it, in some species reaching the growing tips of roots or stems. The flower bud develops inside the host and then breaks through the surface.

This type of growth harms the host plant but does not kill it. Parasites seldom kill their hosts. They merely rob them.

Rafflesia is not the only plant to produce a flower smelling of carrion—so do the 12 *Hydnora* species found in the tropical forests of Madagascar and Africa and the six *Prosopanche* species of South America. All 18 species belong to the family Hydnoraceae, which is closely related to the Rafflesiaceae. These plants have neither roots nor leaves but feed from the roots of their hosts. Their flowers are borne on a thick underground stem, and the flower is the only part of the plant that appears above ground.

More than 100 species of even more curious parasites belong to the family Balanophoraceae. At one time people thought they were fungi. They parasitize a wide variety of plants, but most of their hosts are trees growing in the moist montane forests (see pages 85–88) of tropical America and Asia. They also occur in Africa but are less common.

The parasite lives below ground in the form of a bulbous tuber, sometimes the size of a soccer ball, attached to the root of the host plant. In some species the tuber consists only of tissue belonging to the parasite, but in others it contains some parasite tissue and some tissue derived from the host. The *inflorescence*—mass of individual flowers—develops inside the tuber and then bursts out from it and pushes its way above the ground surface. This is the only part of the plant that appears above ground, and at a quick glance it looks very much like the fruiting body of a fungus. In most species the inflorescence is club-shaped with the individual flowers borne on the "club." The hundreds of tiny flowers making up the inflorescence include some of the smallest flowers in the world.

A parasite that can live in no other way is said to be an *obligate* parasite. Mistletoes, of which there are approximately 1,300 species, have green leaves and manufacture sugars by photosynthesis. They are *hemiparasites*. Most mistletoe plants grow on the branches of trees, but some grow on shrubs or lianas, and the flame tree (*Nuytsia floribunda*) of Western Australia attaches itself to the roots of grass and grows into a tree up to 40 feet (12 m) tall with brilliant orange flowers. A few mistletoe species have conventional roots that grow in soil, but most produce modified roots. Some of these are suckers that anchor the parasite to its host. Others called *haustoria* (singular haustorium) penetrate the tissues of the host and extract nutrients. Mistletoe species belong to the family Loranthaceae, and most are found in the tropical forests of all continents, although a few species grow in the warmer temperate regions.

Stranglers

Most tropical climbers grow upward from seeds that germinate in the soil, but many of the 500 *Philodendron* species found in the American tropics are different. They grow downward. The process begins when a bird drops a seed in the crown of a tree. The seed germinates there and produces short stems bearing leaves and two types of root. The first roots grow away from the light, into crevices in the tree bark; they anchor the plant. The second type of root grows downward, hanging free from the tree, and it has an absorbent surface that collects moisture. The roots may reach the soil and become conventional roots, but those of *Anthurium gracile,* a close relative, never do. Its absorbent roots remain in contact with the tree and absorb water and nutrients from its bark. This plant is a true epiphyte (see pages 183–185).

There are other epiphytes that begin life in this way but change character when their roots reach the ground. They strangle their hosts.

Some relatives of common ivy (*Hedera helix*) are stranglers, especially *Schefflera* species found throughout the Tropics, and so are certain *Clusia* species that grow in the American tropical forests. The best-known stranglers, however, are certain figs (*Ficus* species). The banyan (*F. benghalensis*) is an epiphyte, but it does not become a strangler (see "Seasonal forest" on pages 83–85). Neither does the epiphytic bo tree (*F. religiosa*), also known as the pipal, of India and Southeast Asia.

However, of the 800 species of figs, 200 are invariably stranglers or sometimes become stranglers.

The strangler's life begins when a bird drops a seed in the crown of a tree. If it is to germinate, the seed must fall onto a moss-covered branch or into the decaying plant material—*humus*—in a crotch where a branch joins the main trunk. Bacteria in the humus attack the seed coat, and only then is the fig seed able to sprout.

Using the humus as an initial source of nutrients, the young fig sends vine stems in all directions, even to adjacent trees. The vines produce stems that grow leaves and roots that absorb whatever moisture and nutrients they can find on the surfaces they cross. Like all epiphytes, the fig takes nothing from its host. Eventually, the fig finds a place where it is able to establish itself and grow a trunk.

Once established, the fig sends out thin roots that grow down the trunk of the host until they reach the ground. The roots penetrate the soil and produce branches. Now obtaining its moisture and nutrients from the soil and manufacturing sugars by photosynthesis in its leaves, the fig is ready to grow bigger. The roots it has attached to its host's trunk thicken, and it sends down more to add to them. Where adjacent roots touch, the bark between them disappears and the roots merge; the scientific term for this process is *anastomosis*. More and more of the roots anastomose until the host tree is completely surrounded by the roots of the fig.

The fig has taken nothing from its host, but it finally envelops it. This prevents the host tree from expanding the width of its trunk, which is an essential part of tree growth. The host is then unable to grow. Up in the crown, meanwhile, the fig's trunk and branches cover those of the host, and its leaves form a crown of their own that may be as large as the host's. The host's leaves are shaded. Prevented from growing or even feeding itself, the host dies. In time the host tree rots away leaving a fig tree with a hollow "trunk" that in fact consists of roots.

Despite having strangled its host to death, the fig nevertheless makes a valuable contribution to forest life. Unlike most tropical trees, strangler figs produce fruits throughout the year, and these provide food for a number of species of birds. The birds eat the fruit, and their hard seeds pass unaltered through their digestive systems to be deposited on other trees. Although the fig roots form a complete cylinder, it is a cylinder with a very uneven surface. There are many holes and hollows that provide shelter for small animals.

A strangler fig can be very large because it may have encompassed more than one host tree. Consequently, the fruit and shelter it provides are extensive. They are also long-lasting because strangler figs have no commercial use, so no logging company is interested in them, and they are also very difficult to remove. Consequently, when an area of forest is cleared, strangler figs are often left behind.

Plants that catch insects

Most of the plant nutrients in a tropical forest are contained in the living plants. When dead plant and animal material falls to the ground, it decomposes fast, and plant roots soon absorb its chemical contents. Despite the luxuriance of its vegetation, a tropical forest is not rich in available nutrients, and competition for them is intense. Not surprisingly, some plants have difficulty obtaining the quantities they need and, also not surprisingly, some of those have evolved a very unplantlike way to feed: They have become meat eaters or, more correctly, insect eaters.

Insectivorous plants grow in many parts of the world. The bladderworts and butterworts (family Lentibulariaceae) are fairly common water plants found in ponds and moist places, but of the approximately 180 species, 120 are found only in the Tropics. The 16 *Genlisea* species of West Africa and eastern South America are typical. Rosettes of leaves grow at intervals along a slender horizontal stem that floats just below the water surface. The plant has no roots. What look like floating stems grow outward from the rosette. In fact, these are leaves that are modified to form containers shaped like bottles, which stand about one inch (2.5 cm) above the water. Insects are lured into the "bottle." Once inside they cannot escape. The victims drown and dissolve in digestive juices.

American pitcher plants belong to the family Sarraceniaceae. Most occur in temperate regions, but five

Pitcher plants feed on insects that fall into the "pitcher," from which there is no escape. Carnivorous plants such as these live in places where fierce competition among plants means ordinary plant nutrients are hard to obtain. (Courtesy of Amanda Rohde/Istockphoto)

Heliamphora species—the name means "swamp pitcher"—grow on marshy ground in the mountains of Guyana and Venezuela. They have strong roots and horizontal underground stems, or *rhizomes,* from which rosettes of leaves emerge at intervals so that the plants grow in dense tufts covering a wide area. All or some of the leaves grow into the shape of a funnel, up to 12 inches (30 cm) long, usually with a thick-walled, spoon-shaped structure at the top made from the edge of the leaf curled inward. The funnels are traps. Glands on the "spoon" and inside the funnel secrete sweet-tasting nectar that attracts insects. They cross the smooth surface of the "spoon" but encounter a very slippery surface on the inside of the funnel and slide down across downward-pointing hairs that make it impossible for them to climb out. The bottom of the funnel contains water in which the prey drowns. When the insect is dead, the plant releases acids and enzymes that digest it, absorbing the released nutrients by means of trichomes—specialized hairs.

The most famous of all pitcher plants are the 70 species of *Nepenthes* that grow in forests from Madagascar and the Seychelles, through Southeast Asia, and as far as northern Australia. They grow only in very wet climates. One species, *N. distillatoria,* grows in wet grassland in Sri Lanka, but all the others grow in tropical forests from sea level to more than 8,000 feet (2,450 m). Most are lianas (see pages 176–177) rising from a rhizome, and many are epiphytes (see pages 183–185) with climbing stems up to one inch (2.5 cm) in diameter.

Nepenthes plants climb by means of tendrils, which are extensions of the midribs of leaves, and the pitchers develop from the tips of some of the tendrils. The tip swells and curls to form first a lid and then the pitcher beneath it. As the pitcher develops, the lid rises, thereafter remaining stationary over the mouth of the pitcher and a little distance above it, like an umbrella. Pitchers are invariably upright.

Pitchers vary in length from two inches (5 cm) to 12 inches (30 cm). They contain water, and the biggest pitchers hold up to four pints (2 L). The pitchers are brightly colored, red or green depending on the species, and often mottled, and they secrete nectar around the lip. Insects climb over the lip in search of nectar but then encounter a slippery surface and downward-pointing hairs and are trapped. They drown in the water at the bottom of the pitcher and the plant then digests them.

Some *Nepenthes* species are grown as ornamentals, mainly for their curiosity value but also because they are attractive plants. Their pitchers are colorful, and some cultivated varieties have pitchers of two sizes on the same plant. They produce spikes of small red, yellow, or green flowers, the color depending on the species.

CHAPTER 7

PEOPLES OF TROPICAL FORESTS

Peoples of the American tropical forests

Today the South American tropical forests have a mixed population. There are ranchers and their employees, farmers, mineworkers, construction workers, rubber tappers, and forestry workers—some engaged in logging and others in establishing and managing plantations. These workers and their families have entered the forest, or land that was formerly forested, from outside the forest area. They are of Hispanic, African, and Amerindian descent and they belong to the mainstream Latin American culture. That is to say, they come from the world of apartment buildings, cars, TV, telephones, washing machines, and all the everyday things that can be found in any modern city anywhere in the world.

There are also other inhabitants of the forest—people whose lives and culture are very different. These belong to the original Amerindian nations, and their ancestors had been living in the forest for countless generations before the first Europeans arrived. They fish and hunt game for meat, gather wild plants for food and medicine, and grow crops using slash-and-burn techniques (see pages 220–222).

The forest dwellers have not always lived the way they live today, and the idea that their way of life and forest environment have remained unchanged for thousands of years is wrong. Soil scientists have known since about 1880 that some of the soils in the Amazon region are dark in color and highly fertile, making them different from other soils. Scientists call them *terra preta de Indio* (which means "Amazonian dark earths" in Portuguese), or *terra preta* for short. For a long time no one knew the origin of the terra preta soils, but scientists now have clear evidence that they are the result of burning and cultivation that took place approximately 2,500 years ago. Terra preta soils cover an estimated 195 square miles (505 km²) in the center of the Amazon Basin (the region often called Amazonia).

The largest continuous area of tropical forest on the southern side of the Amazon is in the upper Xingu River region, to the north of the Mato Grosso highlands. There archaeologists have found evidence of settlements between 100 acres (40 ha) and 200 acres (80 ha) in area that were occupied from about 1250 C.E. until 1600 C.E. The people living in these villages supported themselves by farming and transformed the surrounding forest into farmland and parkland. Between 1600 and 1700 there was a sharp decrease in population, however. The farms and settlements were abandoned and the forest reclaimed the land.

A substantial area of what is now forest was once farmed, and traces of that way of life survive in the villages where the descendants of those farmers live today. Some of the Amazonian Indians live in the forest and some live along the riverbanks. Fishing provides much of the protein food for those who live beside rivers, and there is no need for hunters to trek long distances in search of meat. Fishing allows people to live in large and fairly permanent villages, with large gardens they tend carefully. Their most important crops are beans and corn (maize). Their settled lifestyles allow them to own possessions, and their large communities are well organized, with a clearly defined social order and recognized leaders.

Forest dwellers rely much more on making long treks in search of game. This makes them more mobile than the river dwellers. They spend up to 40 percent of their time on treks away from home, and while trekking they often divide into small groups to search for wild fruits and other foods such as honey. Their villages are smaller and less permanent than those of the river people, and their gardens are smaller and less intensively managed.

They grow many plants, but their principal crops include manioc, cocoyam, sweet potatoes, and bananas. Manioc (*Manihot utilissima*), known in other parts of the world as cassava or tapioca, is a small tree, six to seven feet (1.8–2 m) tall, that produces large tuberous roots that resist attack by insects because they contain high concentrations of cyanide. Once the trees have reached their full size, they can be left for up to two years without further attention and the tubers will not deteriorate. The tubers are peeled and either boiled to make a mash or grated to make a meal that can be baked into flat cakes. Cooking destroys the cyanide. Cocoyam or tannia (*Xanthosoma sagittifolium*) grows up to seven feet (2 m) tall. Its leaves are eaten like spinach and its swollen underground stem, or *corm*, is also edible, as are the secondary tubers that grow from the corm.

The Yanomami are the best-known of the Amazon Indians and form the largest group. They compose isolated communities living in the forests near the northern tributaries of the Amazon and the headwaters of the Orinoco. Their total population is uncertain but is believed to exceed 21,000, and they have more than 360 settlements, each with an average population of 50. The Yanomami are warriors. Warfare and feuding are common, and communities are sometimes divided by internal conflicts that can become violent. They are strongly egalitarian, however, and have no chiefs, although there are spokesmen who represent the interests of family groups.

The forest provides the Yanomami with all their materials. Their huts are made from timber and thatch, and the people sleep in hammocks made from split vines. Most of their plant food comes from their gardens, but they rely on hunting for their protein. The hunters use bows and arrows. The arrows, made from cane stems that grow wild but are also cultivated in their gardens, have heads shaped for particular targets. They use barbed heads for birds and long bamboo heads for large mammals such as deer and armadillos. When hunting monkeys they use extremely sharp heads, notched and coated with poison. Ideally, the head breaks at the notch, leaving the poisoned tip inside the victim. Their most important quarry, however, is the white-lipped peccary (*Tayassu pecari*).

The agricultural communities that existed until the 17th century along the valleys of the major rivers had a population density of 15–32 persons per square mile (6–12.5 per km^2). For comparison, the overall population density in the United States is approximately 81 persons per square mile (31 per km^2). The modern Yamomami need an average 3.5 square miles (9 km^2) for each person—one square mile supports 0.29 of a person (0.1 person per km^2). With their hunting, gathering, and gardening lifestyle, that is the greatest population density the forest can sustain. As pressures on the forest continue, it is uncertain how long that way of life can continue to survive.

Peoples of the African tropical forests

Asante, also called (incorrectly) Ashanti, is a region of Ghana, in West Africa. It is also the name of the predominant people of that region and adjoining areas of Togo and Ivory Coast. They are forest dwellers, and although nowadays some Asante live in towns, most live in villages and are farmers. They produce plantains, bananas, cassava, yams, and coco yams for local markets and grow cocoa seeds for export. Plantains are a starchy variety of bananas that are grown for cooking, usually by roasting or steaming.

Theirs is a peaceful life, but in the 17th century the expansion of trade in firearms in southern Ghana—then known as the Gold Coast—led to the rise of two rival states. Four other nations struggled for power farther north and the resulting wars ended with victory for the Asante and the establishment of an Asante state, with its capital at Kumasi (6.67°N 1.58°E)—now a city of about 611,000 people. Asante villages were grouped into territorial divisions. Each village had a chief, and the chief of the most important village was the paramount chief of the division. The paramount chief of Kumasi was the chief of the confederation. The symbol of Asante unity was the Golden Stool, which was the equivalent of the throne of a European kingdom. It was believed to have descended from the sky, and all chiefs acknowledged allegiance to the person occupying it.

The Asante fought the British in the 19th century, and some Asante sought an independent Asante monarchy at the time of Ghanaian independence in 1957. The majority favored the degree of autonomy granted to them under the new constitution, however, and with the creation of the Republic of Ghana the Asante state ceased to exist.

Farther east, the forests of Central Africa are home to the people who were formerly known as Pygmies; today they are called the Bambuti. There are several groups. The Mbuti live in the center of the Ituri Forest, in the northern part of the Democratic Republic of the Congo, and have probably lived in that area longer than any other people. The Efe live in the northern and eastern parts of the Ituri, and the Aka are in the northwest, extending into the Central African Republic, although few Aka remain. The Twa or Batwa people live around Lake Kivu, in the Democratic Republic of the Congo and neighboring Rwanda and Burundi. The Babinga people live to the north of the Congo River.

African forest people are smaller in stature than the people of the open grasslands, and the Mbuti are the smallest of them all. Few Mbuti are more than five feet (1.5 m) tall. Their small size brings advantages. They are able to move through dense forest more easily than larger people could, and their bodies lose heat more rapidly, which helps them keep cool. This is because the body loses heat through the skin, and the smaller people are, the greater their surface area—their total skin area—in proportion to the volume of their body. It is easy to calculate why this is. The volume of a cube that is two units long on each edge, will be eight cubic units (units^3) and its surface area will be 24 square units (units^2), giving a volume:surface area ratio of 8:24, or 1:3. If the length of each side is doubled, the volume will be 64 units^3 and the surface area 96 units^2, a ratio of 64:96, or 1:1.5. Compared with the larger cube, the smaller cube has twice the surface area in proportion to its volume. Small people keep cool more efficiently than large people.

Forest people are mainly nomadic, living in bands of 15–70 individuals, the size of the bands depending on local conditions. Approximately every three weeks the band moves to a different part of the forest, the people carrying their few possessions with them. When they arrive at a new site, they clear away the undergrowth and small trees but not the canopy trees. The forest canopy remains closed, sheltering the people from the fierce sun and frequent rain. They use the saplings they cut down to build the frames of their dome-shaped huts, which they then cover with large leaves, a task that is accomplished in a few hours.

The men hunt game and collect honey from the nests of wild bees. Honey is the most highly valued product of the forest—for all forest peoples, not only those of Africa—because of the burst of energy that a meal of almost pure sugar delivers. Men will climb 100 feet (30 m) to reach a nest. As they approach, they burn green wood that produces a great deal of

Mikea or Makoa people of Madagascar are descended from African slaves. Today they live in the forest, hunting game and gathering plant food. This man, equipped with a spear for hunting, carries tubers in his bag. (Courtesy of Frans Lanting/Minden Pictures)

smoke to quiet the bees. This allows the hunter to break into the hive and take the honeycomb, dripping with honey. Each group has its own preferred hunting methods. For example, the Efe hunt antelope and monkeys with bows and arrows, and they use spears to hunt buffalo, elephants, and giant forest hogs, while the Mbuti hunt only with nets. The women of all groups gather plant foods, such as nuts, fruits, and roots, carrying them in baskets on their backs.

Each group lives in association with a different tribe of agriculturists and frequently visits their villages to trade, a forest family having a close relationship with a village family. The forest people bring their surpluses of meat, honey, mushrooms, fruit, nuts—and also termites and caterpillars, which are eaten in this part of the world. They trade these for cultivated foods, cloth, salt, pots and pans, and metal tools. Bambuti women sometimes work for the farmers, receiving food as payment.

Singing, dancing, and storytelling are important in Bambuti life, and the Bambuti are accomplished musicians. Twa musicians sometimes become court musicians to the chiefs of other tribes. Because of their close relationships with villagers, however, most Twa and Babinga speak the languages of the agriculturists and have adopted much of their culture. The Bambuti, on the other hand, have remained little changed by their contact with villagers.

The peoples of the Congo Basin have not always lived as they do today. Archaeologists have discovered widespread evidence of cultivation, indicating that much of the Basin was farmed from about 3,000 years ago until about 1,600 years ago, when human numbers fell drastically and the farms were abandoned. There were iron foundries in the western part of the African forest from about 2,650 years ago until the fifth century C.E. Again the population suddenly declined. Together, this evidence suggests that much of the forest was cleared and that the present forest has grown up in approximately the last 1,600 years.

Peoples of the Asian tropical forests

The Andaman and Nicobar Islands lie in the Bay of Bengal, close to the traditional trading routes between India and

Myanmar (formerly known as Burma), and their existence and location have been known to travelers for centuries. The Nicobarese grew vegetables, although wild coconuts were their most important plant food. They also hunted wild pigs and birds and caught fish and turtles. Travelers had nothing to fear from them, although the Nicobarese did acquire a reputation for piracy.

Few foreigners landed on the Andaman Islands, however, for the very good reason that the islanders invariably killed any foreigner foolhardy enough to set foot ashore. This ensured their isolation. It was not until the 19th century that outsiders settled successfully, when the British established a penal colony at Port Blair, now the capital. Today India governs both groups of islands, and government officials have patiently established limited contact with the Jarawa and Onge, the only tribes still living in the traditional way and confined to the lesser islands of Little Andaman, South Andaman, and Rutland Island. They are protected from interference. Tourists are forbidden to land on these islands and no one may visit them without official permission.

The Andaman tribes may be the only people in the modern world who never discovered how to make fire. The islanders used fire but were able to do so only by lighting their fire from brands taken from a natural fire ignited by lightning and not allowing it to be extinguished.

The Jarawa and Onge grow no crops but live by hunting game, turtles, and fish, using bows and arrows, nets, and harpoons thrown from outrigger canoes. They collect iron from wrecked ships and use it to make arrowheads, knives, and adzes. (An adze is a tool for cutting wood, like an ax with its head at right angles to the shaft.) They also make pottery.

Andaman islanders are African in appearance and small in stature. Few are more than about 5.5 feet (1.7 m) tall, making them only slightly larger than the Mbuti of Africa. The Semang, people of similar appearance and stature, live in the forests of northeastern Malaysia. The men average 4.75–4.8 feet (1.4–1.5 m) in height, and the women are shorter. Traditionally the Semang lived by hunting and gathering, using blowpipes to kill small game, and made their homes in caves and beneath overhanging rocks. Where these were not available, they built simple shelters covered with leaves.

Today most Semang live settled lives in villages and grow crops. The Penan are also small people of African appearance. They live as nomadic hunters and gatherers in the forests of northern Borneo. Their most important food is starch that they obtain from the stem of the giant wild palm *Eugeissonas utilis*. Few still practice their traditional way of life, however; most now live in villages.

The forest dwellers of the Philippines are called the Aeta (or Ayta, Agta, Atta, Ata, Ati, or Ita) and they live on the northern island of Luzon, not far from Mount Pinatubo. They, too, are small. Most are less than five feet (1.5 m) tall. Traditionally they lived by hunting with bows and arrows and gathering wild plants, but today most Aeta are integrated into Westernized society. Mount Pinatubo is an active volcano, and many Aeta were driven from their homes in June 1991 when it erupted.

People of the Australasian tropical forests

The ancestors of the modern Aboriginal people sailed to Australia from the islands to the north. No one is certain when they arrived, but it was probably about 50,000 years ago, at a time when vast ice sheets, covering much of Europe and North America, held so much accumulated water that the sea level was far lower than it is today. Travelers would have been able to walk from the Malay Peninsula in mainland Asia through Sumatra and Java, but the final part of their journey to Australia must have been made by sea.

The first humans to set foot on the island continent would have arrived at Arnhem Land or the Cape York Peninsula in the far north of Australia, and they would have found themselves in a tropical rain forest. That is where the Native Australians first established themselves, expanding later into the grasslands and deserts to the south.

In those days there were no farmers anywhere in the world. Agriculture did not commence until approximately 14,000 years ago—and in the Middle East, not in what is now Indonesia. The new arrivals were hunters, fishers, and gatherers of shellfish, insects, honey, fruits, seeds, and edible leaves and roots. That is how they remained, for Australia had no animals that could be domesticated and no grasses that could be grown as cereal crops. As they adapted to their new environment the Aboriginal people developed a way of life that still survives.

Knowledge of that way of life is passed from each generation to the next in the form of stories, and the forest people of Northern Queensland preserve an oral history older than that of any other people without a written language. People also paint pictures, and the most extensive display of Aboriginal rock painting in Australia was made by the Kuku Yalanji people in rock shelters at Battlecamp Road, near Laura in the Queensland forest. Nowadays tourists can visit the forest and meet Aboriginal rain forest people.

At about the time the Aboriginal people reached Australia, migrants from the Indonesian archipelago were arriving on the island of New Guinea. Migrations such as these seldom occur as single events. Usually there are several waves of migrants, arriving over many years or even centuries, and that is the way people reached New Guinea.

New Guinea is rugged. A ridge of mountains called the Highlands occupies the center of the island, dividing the country into densely forested mountains and deep valleys. The territory is so difficult to cross that the settlers formed groups that were completely isolated from each other. Each group developed its own culture and its own language. Almost 800 languages are spoken in New Guinea. Ethnically, the people form four groups: New Guineans live in the north of the island, Papuans in the south, Highlanders in the mountains, and Islanders on approximately 600 offshore islands. There is considerable cultural and linguistic variety within each of these groups. At one time the Papuan tribes living along the south coast were notorious for being headhunters and cannibals.

Today the western half of New Guinea is the Indonesian province of Irian Jaya. Australia administered the eastern half until it became independent in 1975 as Papua New Guinea. Many people live in small villages and continue to observe tribal customs, but nearly 15 percent of the Papua New Guinean population lives in 10 cities; Port Moresby, the capital, has more than 250,000 inhabitants. The Highlands are the most densely populated region of the country and the valleys are extensively cultivated. Nevertheless, tropical forest still covers 85 percent of the area of New Guinea.

Explorers of the Tropics

Spanish and Portuguese explorers reached the Americas in the 15th century. Pope Alexander VI issued a series of bulls—edicts with the force of law—in 1493, and in 1494 Spain and Portugal agreed to the Treaty of Tordesillas. Between them, these gave Spain all the newly discovered territory to the west of a line drawn from the North Pole to the South Pole 370 leagues west of the Cape Verde Islands, and gave Portugal all the territories to the east. The pope stipulated that the native peoples must be converted to Christianity. This division gave Brazil to the Portuguese, but until the Portuguese navigator Pedro Álvares Cabral (1467 or 1468–c. 1520) landed there on April 22, 1500, on his way to India, there is no reason to suppose the Portuguese government knew that land existed.

By the middle of the 16th century there were colonial settlements on many Caribbean islands and in parts of Central and South America, but none of these were located in the forested regions. A few expeditions penetrated a little way inland in search of commercially valuable forest products, but the settlements were established on the coast.

In 1541, however, the Spanish explorer Gonzalo Pizarro (c. 1502–48) led an expedition across the Andes from Quito, Peru, in search of cinnamon. His party reached the Amazon, where they built several boats to help them find food. Francisco de Orellana (c. 1511–c. 1546), a member of the group, took the boats and sailed down the river, reaching the Atlantic on August 26, 1542. On his journey he heard stories about a tribe of warrior women, and he claimed to have encountered them. He named the river after the Amazons—warrior women of Greek mythology.

Early explorers were not motivated by scientific curiosity. They sought precious metals and valuable commodities with which to make their fortunes—*Río de la Plata* means "River of Silver"—and the conversion of Indian tribes to Christianity. Scientific exploration began in the 19th century, and the most distinguished explorers of South America were the Prussian geologist and meteorologist Alexander von Humboldt (1769–1859) and his companion the French botanist Aimé Bonpland (1773–1858; see the sidebar).

Europeans began settling in southern Africa in the 17th century, but they had little interest in the dense forests of central Africa. It was not until the early 19th century that hunters, traders, missionaries, and adventurers seeking their fortunes began to venture into the forest, where they met fierce resistance from the residents.

In 1851 the Scottish missionary David Livingstone (1813–73) traveled from Bechuanaland (now Botswana) to the upper reaches of the Zambezi River and from there went westward to the Atlantic coast. He then traveled eastward, encountering and naming the Victoria Falls. In subsequent journeys he became the first European to see Lake Nyasa and the southern end of Lake Tanganyika. His final exploration was in search of the source of the Nile, which he believed rose close to the source of the Congo.

Livingstone struggled against ill health, especially dysentery, and was seriously sick when he returned from the upper Congo to the town of Ujiji on the eastern side of Lake Tanganyika, in what is today Tanzania. That is where he was met by Henry (later Sir Henry) Morton Stanley (1841–1904), a Welsh-born soldier, sailor, journalist, and explorer who was then a U.S. citizen (Stanley was renaturalized a British subject in 1892 and became a member of Parliament). Nothing had been heard of Livingstone for some time, and the *New York Herald* had sent Stanley to find him. Stanley reached Ujiji in November 1871, found Livingstone, and met him with the famous greeting: "Dr. Livingstone, I presume."

Livingstone refused to leave, however, and Stanley departed in 1872, leaving Livingstone to continue his search for the source of the Nile. After Livingstone's death in 1873, Stanley determined to continue with the exploration of equatorial Africa. He traced the Congo River to its source, built a series of stations along the river and launched steamboats to develop commerce, and assisted the Belgian government to establish the Congo Free State (now the Democratic Republic of

Alexander von Humboldt

In the early 19th century Friedrich Wilhelm Heinrich Alexander, baron von Humboldt (1769–1859) was one of the most famous men in Europe. It was said that Napoleon's was the only name more people knew.

Born in Berlin, then the capital of Prussia, and educated at the University of Göttingen and the Freiberg School of Mining, von Humboldt became a geologist. In 1793 he obtained the post of director of mines in Bayreuth. During his years there he established a school of mining and invented a safety lamp.

On the death of his mother in 1796, von Humboldt inherited the large family fortune, which allowed him to travel. In 1799 he went to Madrid, accompanied by the French botanist Aimé Bonpland (1773–1858), where he won the support of the Spanish prime minister for his plan to visit the Spanish colonies in South America. The two companions embarked from La Coruña, arriving first at Cumaná, New Andalusia (now Venezuela). They sailed from there to Caracas, and in 1800 they headed inland.

Their aim was to discover whether the headwaters of the two great rivers of South America, the Amazon and Orinoco, were linked. They crossed the *llanos*—savanna grasslands—and continued by canoe when they reached the Orinoco, paddling through the rain forest and eating cocoa beans to survive after insects destroyed their food stores. Near the source of the Orinoco they found and followed the Casiquiare canal, a natural waterway that led them to the Río Negro and then into the headwaters of the Amazon. They had proved that the rivers are linked. Von Humboldt and Bonpland returned to the Orinoco and sailed back to Cumaná. They had journeyed 1,725 miles (2,775 km).

the Congo), ruled by King Leopold II of Belgium. Kisangani, a city of more than 400,000 people, was formerly called Stanleyville.

Several ancient kingdoms occupied tropical Asia for many centuries before the first Europeans began trading with this part of the world. The civilizations of the Malay Peninsula and the islands now comprising Indonesia were strongly influenced by Indian religion and culture. This influence did not extend to New Guinea, however. The first European to set eyes on New Guinea was probably António de Abreu (whose dates of birth and death are unknown), a Portuguese sea captain, in the fall of 1511, but he did not land there.

The two men then spent some time in Cuba, where von Humboldt spoke out against the slavery he saw there, and in March 1801 they returned to South America, landing at Cartagena, Colombia, with a plan to explore the Andes. They reached Lima, Peru, after a delay caused by Bonpland falling sick at Bogotá, then returned by sea. In 1803 they sailed for Mexico and on June 30, 1804, they finally departed for Europe.

During their travels, von Humboldt and Bonpland became the first Europeans to describe electric eels (*Electrophorus electricus*) and Amazon river dolphins (*Inia geoffrensis*). They collected more than 3,000 previously unknown species of plants, including the Brazil nut tree, which Bonpland named *Bertholletia excelsa* in honor of his friend the French chemist Claude-Louis Berthollet (1748–1822). Both men suffered from mountain sickness while in the Andes; von Humboldt was the first person to recognize that it is caused by lack of oxygen. Von Humboldt discovered the Peru Current, also known as the Humboldt Current, and sent samples of guano—dried bird droppings—for chemical analysis in France. Local people used it to fertilize their crops. The French chemist found it to be rich in plant nutrients, thereby launching a valuable trade exporting guano from Peru to Europe. Von Humboldt noted that Andean volcanoes lie in straight lines and found that this is because they form above faults in the crust. As he traveled, von Humboldt mapped the Earth's magnetic field and kept careful records of the weather.

Back in Europe, von Humboldt befriended Simón Bolívar (1783–1830) and helped inspire him to liberate much of South America from Spanish rule. Von Humboldt became a diplomat but spent much of his time writing about his travels and discoveries. He died in Berlin, aged 89, and was given a state funeral.

The first European to set foot on shore is believed to have been another Portuguese navigator, Jorge de Meneses, in 1526. Adverse weather forced him to seek shelter at a place he called Isla Versija—either Warsia on the northwestern coast or the island of Waigeo. De Meneses stayed there several months and named the country Ilhas dos Papuas—Land of the Fuzzy-Haired People, from the Malay expression *orang papuwah*, "fuzzy-haired man." Spanish, Dutch, German, and English explorers visited Ilhas dos Papuas in subsequent years, and on June 13, 1545, a Spanish sailor, Inigo Ortiz de Retes, landed on three northern islands. He named these La Sevillana (now Supiori Island), La Callega (Biak Island), and

Los Martyres (Numfor Island, also spelled Noemfoor and Numfoor). De Retes then landed on the mainland, at the mouth of the Bei River, to the east of Mamberamo River, naming the site San Augustin.

De Retes, who claimed the territory for Spain, thought the land resembled Guinea, another Spanish possession on the West African coast, so he renamed it Nueva Guinea: New Guinea. He did not know that it is an island; that discovery was not made until 1606, when the Spanish navigator Luis Váez de Torres found the strait, now named after him, that separates New Guinea from Australia. Even then, the existence of the Torres Strait was kept secret until 1764.

The British were the first Europeans to attempt to settle in New Guinea, in 1793 establishing a military garrison at Restoration Bay on behalf of the British East India Company. The Dutch East India Company also claimed New Guinea, and Germany also claimed land on the island. In 1884–85 the contesting powers finally agreed that West New Guinea west of longitude 141°E should be Dutch, and the remainder of the island British. In 1884 Germany annexed the northeastern part of the island, calling it Kaiser-Wilhelmsland and passing its administration over to the Neu-Guinea Kompanie. In 1899 the German government assumed direct control of the administration. German New Guinea, together with the Solomon Islands and several other groups of islands that were also ruled by Germany, were occupied by Australian forces during World War I and the territory was mandated to Australia when the war ended. The Australians gave the name Papua New Guinea to the territory under their control.

CHAPTER 8

BIODIVERSITY AND TROPICAL FORESTS

What is biodiversity?

Tropical rain forest, monsoon forest, mangrove forest, and elfin forest are evocative names. They conjure images of luxuriant vegetation, trees festooned with lianas, bright flowers, swamps, mists, and diminutive trees covered with lichens. Everywhere trees are the predominant plants, but there are many kinds and sizes of trees and by no means are trees the only plants. There are the epiphytes—plants that grow on the trunks and branches of trees, using their hosts for support. There are parasitic plants, such as the stranglers (see pages 185–187), and insect-eating plants. There are also the many animals that feed on the plants, the insects that pollinate them, and the predators that hunt the plant eaters—and one another.

Such an abundant variety of living organisms is nowadays described as an example of *biodiversity*—a contraction of *biological diversity*. It is easy to see what it means—or is it?

In 1987 the U.S. Congress Office of Technology Assessment (OTA) proposed that:

> *Biological diversity refers to the variety and variability among living organisms and the ecological complexes in which they occur. Diversity can be defined as the number of different items and their relative frequency. For biological diversity, these items are organized at many levels, ranging from complete ecosystems to the chemical structures that are the molecular basis of heredity. Thus, the term encompasses different ecosystems, species, genes, and their relative abundance.* (Technologies to Maintain Biological Diversity. *Washington, D.C.: U.S. Government Printing Office, 1987.*)

This remains the most widely quoted definition of biodiversity, but the term remains difficult to pin down precisely. Does it mean the whole of life? In *The Diversity of Life* (Cambridge, Mass.: Harvard University Press, 1992), the eminent biologist E. O. Wilson extends the definition to include the habitats and physical conditions under which organisms live.

At the smallest level, the OTA definition refers to "the chemical structures that are the molecular basis of heredity." These structures are genes, and since every individual is genetically distinct this would seem to suggest that biodiversity means the sum of all the genes in all the individual organisms. If that is so, then preserving biodiversity may be impossible unless we can find a way to prevent individuals from dying.

Most people would accept that the term refers to the number of species, either in the world as a whole or in a particular area. But even that is difficult, because biologists are uncertain of the best way to define a species and there are several competing definitions. Biologists do not equate biodiversity with the number of species. In the end, while everyone has an idea of what the term means, the concept of biodiversity is so wide and so complex as to be almost undefinable.

Despite the problems, however, scientists are developing ways to measure biodiversity. Diversity arises from genetic differences, which can be measured very precisely within and between populations. Measuring differences allows biologists to arrange organisms into groups that reflect the variety among them.

Why it matters

It seems obvious that wild plants and animals should be protected and that preventing damage to the areas in which they live is the only practical way to achieve this. When conservation is expressed in this very general way, few people could disagree that it is desirable.

Unfortunately, this is not the way issues arise in real life. Suppose, for example, that poor people need land to grow food for their families, and that trees are growing all over the only land they can find. Should they be prevented from felling those trees, even if it means they go hungry? Should mining companies be permitted to extract valuable minerals

The Biodiversity Convention

In June 1972 the United Nations sponsored the largest international conference held until that date. Called the UN Conference on the Human Environment, it was held in Stockholm, Sweden, and was known informally as the Stockholm Conference. Delegates to the conference resolved to establish a new United Nations agency, to be called the UN Environment Program (UNEP). UNEP came into being in 1973. Its tasks are to collect and circulate information about the state of the global environment and to encourage and coordinate international efforts to reduce pollution and protect wildlife.

UNEP sponsored several major conferences over the years, and in 1992, 20 years after the Stockholm Conference, it organized the UN Conference on Environment and Development, also known as the Earth Summit and the Rio Summit because it took place in Rio de Janeiro, Brazil. It was the largest meeting of world leaders ever held. The aim of the 1992 conference was to relate environmental protection to economic development, and to this end the delegates agreed on the provisions that were set down in the Convention on Climate Change and the Convention on Biological Diversity—also known as the Biodiversity Convention.

A convention is a binding agreement between governments. Government representatives sign the convention, and when their own legislatures have accepted it, the governments ratify it by signing it again, confirming their willingness to abide by its terms. The lawmakers must then translate those terms into national law. When a majority of signatory governments have ratified the convention, it becomes part of international law and is known as a treaty. By the summer of 2005, 157 countries had ratified the Biodiversity Convention.

The Biodiversity Convention reminds governments that natural resources are not infinite and promotes the principle of using resources in sustainable ways that ensure future generations will also be able to enjoy them. The convention requires governments to develop national strategies and plans of action to measure, conserve, and promote the sustainable use of natural resources. National plans for environmental protection and economic development should incorporate these strategies and plans, especially in respect of forestry, agriculture, fisheries, energy, transportation, and city planning. As well as protecting existing areas of high biodiversity, governments should restore degraded areas. The convention strongly emphasizes the need to involve local communities in its projects and to raise public awareness of the value of a diverse natural environment.

Many countries have now taken positive steps to implement the Biodiversity Convention.

from inside forests? Mining will involve clearing part of the forest and building roads through the forest to provide access to the mine, but it will provide jobs and earn money—some of which may be spent on conservation projects. Governments face such dilemmas every day.

Conservationists might argue that the forest is beautiful and the species inhabiting it have a right to live undisturbed. But someone might ask which species should be left undisturbed. Birds, butterflies, and monkeys, certainly, but what about mosquitoes that transmit diseases, slugs, slime molds, rats, and venomous snakes? People may not find such organisms attractive, but they have the same right to live.

Each case has to be decided on its merits, but there are more compelling arguments for protecting tropical forests against which competing demands should be weighed. Among the wild plants and animals there may be some that could be useful. Maybe an insect living in obscurity among the plants has an insatiable appetite for another insect that is a devastating crop pest and could be recruited to control that pest as an alternative to spraying pesticide. There might be plants that manufacture compounds that chemists could convert into medicines. Might a cure for some dread disease be awaiting discovery deep in the forest? Or perhaps there are plants that might be cultivated as commercial crops to provide food, fiber, or industrial materials.

Beyond such potential economic opportunities, there are subtler reasons for preserving tropical forests. Scientists have identified and named only a small fraction of the plant and animal species that inhabit them. We cannot understand our world unless, at the very least, we have a list of its living contents. Ecologists still have much to learn about the way an ecosystem, such as a forest, functions and how it relates to the other ecosystems around it. Scientists know, for example, that clearing lowland wet forest can alter the local climate. One day, scientists may be in a position to make reliable predictions about the consequences of clearing natural habitat, but they will be able to do so only if those habitats survive long enough to be studied. The need to acquire this knowledge is another reason for preserving natural habitats.

Scientists have succeeded in persuading governments of the importance of biodiversity and its protection. This was one of the principal topics discussed in 1992 at a conference in Rio de Janeiro held under the auspices of the United Nations (UN). The UN Conference on Environment and Development, also called the Earth Summit and the Rio Summit, was the largest meeting of heads of government ever held. One outcome was the Convention on Biological Diversity, also known as the Biodiversity Convention, which commits governments to the protection of natural habitats and sets out practical measures that will help them achieve it (see the sidebar).

Why there are so many species in tropical forests

Tropical forests contain more plant and animal species than any other type of environment. Although taxonomists—biologists who name, classify, and identify organisms—have studied only a small proportion of the inhabitants of tropical forests, most believe that these forests, and especially lowland wet forests, contain more species than all other habitats combined.

How can they be so sure? In the first place, the biodiversity is immediately visible. A person standing almost anywhere in a lowland forest will be surrounded by a huge variety of plants: One acre of forest may contain as many as 120 species of trees (300 per hectare), as well as all the shrubs and herbs.

This is interesting, but there is more persuasive evidence. Entomologists are biologists who study insects. Entomologists collecting insect specimens in lowland forests always find that at least some of the insects that fall into their nets and traps are unknown to science. This clearly indicates that there are many insect species still to be discovered, classified, and added to the list of known species. Most of the birds are known because birds are much easier to observe than insects, but from time to time scientists find previously unknown mammals. It is these surprises that lead scientists to believe in the high biodiversity of tropical forests.

Why this should be so is less certain, but the diversity must be linked to the tropical climate. Warm, wet weather throughout the year every year encourages plants to grow very vigorously. Competition is intense.

Few tropical plants are self-pollinating, and so plants compete for pollinators—the animals that carry pollen from male flowers to the female flowers. There is such a variety of pollinators that plants have evolved flowers to attract particular classes. "Bird" flowers open by day and are brightly colored, but have no scent. "Beetle" flowers open at night and are strongly perfumed. "Moth" flowers open at night, are sweet-scented, and have long tubes so that only the long tongue of a moth can reach the nectar at the bottom. "Fly" flowers smell of carrion or dung. There are also butterfly flowers, bee flowers, and bat flowers. This specialization results in a wide variety of flower designs within a small area—and, of course, each flower design denotes a particular plant species. Specialization also encourages close relationships between the plants and their pollinators, which results in the pollinators, especially the insects, becoming adapted to the plants on which they depend. As plant diversity increases, so does diversity among pollinators.

Plants also rely on animals to disperse their seeds, and this too leads to specialization. Many of the trees produce fleshy fruits in the forest canopy or below it in the subcanopy. In the lowland wet forests of South America, for example, 94.5 percent of trees produce fleshy fruit high above ground. Again, the fruits vary according to the animals they attract. Bats eat brown or yellow fruits with a strong, musty odor that ripen on the tree. Monkeys, rodents, civets, and mongooses feed on fruit, and each species finds particular fruits attractive while ignoring others.

Animals do more than pollinate flowers and feed on fruit, of course. They also eat leaves. This damages the plant, and plants have evolved defenses against it. Many plants have developed close relationships with ants (see "Tropical ants" on pages 115–118). The plant provides the ants with food and shelter and the ants attack any animal that attempts to eat the leaves.

Other plants produce substances such as latex, resins, and gums, called *secondary metabolites,* that have an unpleasant taste or are poisonous. These deter most plant eaters, but an insect that can tolerate the poison has an unlimited food supply. The plant therefore modifies the poison and the insect modifies its response. The resulting "arms race" leads to a highly specialized plant and an equally specialized insect that depends on it; both plant and insect may then become distinct species.

The "arms race" protects the plant, but trees have another means for evading herbivores. Fructivores—animals that feed on fruit—often carry food items some distance before consuming them in a place where they are safe from predators and would-be thieves. This is not practicable with small fruits, such as berries, so animals eat those fruits where they find them. As they do so, however, they also swallow the indigestible seeds and void them later, by which time they have traveled far from the tree. Dispersing its seeds in this way disperses the young plants, and in most types of rain forest many of the tree species occur as widely scattered single individuals. Insects that feed on the leaves of a particular tree species may harm an individual tree, but they cannot devastate an entire stand of trees, as they could if the tree dropped its seeds directly onto the ground.

Some tropical trees do drop their seeds in this way and consequently occur in dense family groups composed of parent trees and their seedlings and saplings. These are the species most likely to resort to chemical defenses.

Soils may also determine where particular trees grow. Research by the Wildlife Conservation Society, based in New York, has found that of four mahogany (*Khaya*) species growing in the 1,700–square mile (4,400-km²) Dznagha-Sangha Dense Forest Reserve in the Central African Republic, three will grow only in soils with a particular mix of plant nutrients. These species occur only where the soil is suitable for them, and if this is true of *Khaya* species it may also be true of others.

Such fierce competition drives plants and animals to evolve countless ways of obtaining the resources they need and avoiding their enemies. It also provides countless opportunities for organisms that can assist others or evade their defenses. These are the processes that lead to such a huge variety of animal and plant species in tropical forests.

CHAPTER 9

THREATS TO TROPICAL FORESTS

Clearing forest to make farms

Tropical forests cover a vast area, but that area grows smaller year by year. During the 1990s, tropical forests were decreasing in size by 0.8 percent each year. "Less than 1 percent of the total area" sounds quite small, but it amounts to approximately 59,000 square miles (153,000 km^2)—slightly more than the area of Florida—*every year.* The rate of deforestation varies from year to year. In 2003, for example, satellite observations by the Brazilian National Institute of Space Research shows that the forest area in the Brazilian Amazon Basin fell by about 9,170 square miles (23,750 km^2), compared with a loss of 8,983 square miles (23,266 km^2) in 2002.

The destruction is not confined to lowland wet forests. Mangrove forests (see pages 96–99) are the most severely threatened, but they receive less publicity because they occupy a fairly small area—approximately 85,000 square miles (220,000 km^2). Since 1960, Thailand has lost more than half of its mangrove forests, and the Philippines now has less than one-quarter of the mangrove forest area that it had in 1920. Mangroves are vulnerable to pollution from oil spills that clog their lenticels—pores in the root surface through which gases are exchanged. They are also harmed by changes in land use that result in prolonged flooding and increased silting that submerge their aerial roots (see "Growing in mud: peg roots" on pages 108–111).

Up to half of the loss of mangroves, however, is due to the growing worldwide demand for shrimps. The forests are cleared to provide space for ponds in which commercially valuable shrimps are raised for export. Shrimp farms are highly profitable, while mangrove forests are often regarded as useless swamps, ripe for "improvement."

Food production is the primary reason for forest clearance in temperate as well as tropical regions. Of the 59,000 square miles (153,000 km^2) of tropical forest cleared annually, approximately 55,000 square miles (142,000 km^2) is converted to other uses, principally to food production.

Poverty is widespread in tropical countries and the population is predominantly rural. People need a small patch of land to grow food for themselves, with a little surplus to sell. Often, the only land they are able to acquire is at the edge of the forest.

In South America, farmers move into cleared forest, or clear the land themselves, and establish homesteads, on average 120 acres (48 ha) in area. In the first year they grow a crop of rice, but in subsequent years they grow pasture grass, which is easier, and raise a few cattle on the pasture. Raising cattle makes sense. There is a high and rising demand for beef and milk. Where the roads are so bad that trucks cannot use them, cattle can be walked to market. If prices are low the animals can be kept alive until they improve. Cattle can die from diseases, but the risk of losing a crop to plant diseases and pests is very much greater.

Soybeans have long been grown on the savanna grasslands bordering the South American tropical forests. Now there are fears that the rising demand for soybeans is encouraging savanna farmers to increase output by clearing forest to provide more land. The demand for soybeans comes mainly from Europe, where fears arising from bovine spongiform encephalitis (BSE), or "mad cow disease," are forcing farmers to use alternative feedstuffs. Soybeans are grown in many countries, but South American farmers are able to exploit a further European fear, of genetically modified (GM) crops, by guaranteeing that their soybeans have not been genetically modified.

Many South American livestock farms are modest in size, but there are also big commercial ranches. It is not true, however, that the tropical forests of Central and South America are being cleared to supply cheap beef to the North American fast food industry. Brazilian beef is exported mainly as corned beef, sausages, and other processed meats, and all the beef from the Amazon Basin is consumed within Brazil. Central

American countries used to export beef to the United States, but the amount was always small, and the trade has almost ceased owing to rising domestic demand.

Hispanic people have a tradition of raising cattle and eating beef. It is part of their culture and many people consider it more socially prestigious to be a rancher, even on a very small scale, than to be a farmer. Ranching is less significant in Africa and Asia, where commercial crop-growing and slash-and-burn farming (see pages 220–222) are the principal causes of deforestation.

Logging

Tropical forests produce timber of the very highest quality. Ebony is a heavy, fine-grained, jet-black wood from *Diospyros* species of trees that grow in the forests of Africa, Madagascar, and Asia. It was formerly used to make the black keys on pianos and the backs of hairbrushes and for inlaid work.

Iroko, also known as African teak, is used to make furniture, stair treads, and shop counters. It is the wood of *Chlorophora excelsa,* a tree with buttress roots (see "Drip tips, buttress roots, and stilt roots" on pages 104–108) that grows to a height of up to 160 feet (49 m) in African tropical forests. "True" teak is the wood of *Tectona grandis,* a tree that grows in the forests of southern Asia from India to Laos, and that is naturalized in Indonesia, where it was introduced 400–600 years ago.

Several trees produce timber sold as mahogany, a pink wood that darkens as it matures, eventually to a deep red color. African mahogany is the wood of *Khaya* species of trees, and Central American mahogany is from *Swietenia* species. The finest 18th-century furniture was made from Cuban mahogany (*S. mahagoni*).

Nowadays these very costly woods are used only as veneers—thin sheets glued onto the surface of inferior material. Those listed above are just a few of the most famous names, but tropical forests abound in tree species and many of them provide commercially valuable timber that is used as timber rather than veneer. Harvesting timber from tropical forests—the operation known as *logging*—causes serious damage.

A new road cut through natural lowland rain forest to provide access for logging also allows people to penetrate the forest and clear land for farming. (Courtesy of Gerry Ellis/Minden Pictures)

Merchants specify the timber they want and logging companies supply it. They cannot do this by clearing a block of forest, however, because the desired trees are often scattered over a wide area (see "Why there are so many species in tropical forests" on pages 211–213). The forest workers therefore find the trees they need and mark their location. Machines then enter the forest to fell and remove individual trees—one tree here, another there, often removing no more than one tree per acre (2.5/ha). This leaves small clearings in the forest that should fill naturally as young trees grow to replace those that were removed.

In practice, however, the damage is greater than this. The loggers must make a road into the forest to provide access for their machines. When a mature tree is felled, it brings down with it the lianas and epiphytes that were using it for support (see "Lianas and other climbers" on pages 176–177 and "Epiphytes" on pages 183–185). As it falls, the tree is liable to damage other vegetation nearby, including other trees. The forest recovers, but recovery takes years and there is a serious risk that if loggers enter an area of forest too frequently the damage may become permanent. The giant machines also damage the forest by compacting the soil in the clearings and along the tracks between the felling site and the access road.

Selective logging is expensive, however, and it is used only to obtain the most valuable timber. If the wood is to be processed into chipboard or similar products it is obtained by clear-felling an area of forest. A high proportion of the wood taken from tropical forests is used locally as fuel and this is also extracted by clear-felling. Clear-felling removes all the trees, saplings, and shrubs, and crushes or uproots the herbs, leaving the ground bare. The appearance is of total devastation, but because it affects only a limited area the overall damage may be no greater, or even less, that that caused by selective logging.

Satellite monitoring of Indonesian forests has revealed an additional hazard. During the extensive forest fires in 1997 and 1998, when drought resulting from an exceptionally severe El Niño (see pages 68–70) had made the vegetation tinder-dry, not all areas of forest were affected equally. Scientists from the European Space Agency (ESA) compared data from the ESA's *ERS-2* satellite with a land-use map produced from NASA's *Landsat* satellites to study the effect of the fires in East

Kalimantan, Borneo. This showed that only 5.7 percent of the area of undisturbed forest was damaged by fire, compared with 59 percent of the forest that had been logged. The damage was also more severe in the logged forest, where all the vegetation was destroyed in 48 percent of the burned area, compared with total destruction over only 4 percent of the undisturbed area. The scientists concluded that when forest regenerates in areas that have been selectively logged, the resulting forest is less fire-resistant than is undisturbed rain forest.

They also found that fire leaves the ground covered with dead, flammable wood and that an area of forest that has burned once is more likely to catch fire again. The combined effect of logging and fire can eventually destroy large areas of forest entirely.

Logging produces timber sold as *roundwood*—wood of all kinds removed from forests—and it is measured in cubic feet or cubic meters. Some is used to make timber products, but a large amount is burned as fuel or made into charcoal. The industry is huge. The table compares the total output of four countries in 1990 and 2000, in each case giving the proportion of the total that was used for firewood or for making charcoal.

Roundwood production, 1990 and 2000

Country	1990 Output (million cu. ft.)	1990 Output (million cu. m.)	1990 % for fuel	2000 Output (million cu. ft.)	2000 Output (million cu. m.)	2000 % for fuel
Brazil	9,154	259	71.9	6,990	198	57.6
Democratic Republic of the Congo*	1,374	39	92.7	1,800	51	93
Indonesia	6,057	171	82.2	6,700	190	83.5
Malaysia	1,802	51	17.1	1,040	29.5	26.2

*Known as Zaire in 1990

Logging is now permitted only under government license, but unfortunately it is proving extremely difficult to enforce the law. Illegal logging is widespread throughout the Tropics. Public servants approve illegal contracts with private companies; companies harvest protected tree species; raw materials are processed without a license; and forest products are smuggled across frontiers. The high value of tropical timber, combined with the low salaries paid to officials, poorly drafted regulations, and weak implementation of them, makes illegal logging profitable, attractive, and safe. Nongovernmental organizations have publicized the problem and are now working with some governments and intergovernmental institutions such as the Food and Agriculture Organization (FAO) of the United Nations to address it. Together they are striving to overcome resistance from powerful interests behind those who profit from crime and corruption. That will allow them to act effectively by improving the monitoring of the forests, simplifying the laws, and enforcing the laws strictly.

Slash-and-burn farming

Logging companies make roads to gain access to the parts of the forest where they will find the trees they are seeking. Large-scale farmers also encourage the building of roads to link their farms to the ports from where their produce, such as soybeans, is exported. Governments expand their road network to link towns and cities. Some or all of those roads may cut through the forest.

Roads occupy only a small area and have no harmful effect in themselves, but in addition to the logging companies and commercial farmers, they provide routes into the forest for people looking for land to farm. Many of these are peasants who were driven from their holdings by the expansion of commercial farms and who are now landless and extremely poor. There are also people who are better off and wish to acquire a small farm within easy reach by car that they can tend on weekends and during vacations.

Most of the poor farmers use a method known as *slash-and-burn* or *swidden* farming; it is also called *shifting cultivation,* and in Indonesia, where it is very widely practiced, it is called *ladang.* A farming family begins by making a clearing in the forest. In areas with a seasonal climate they clear the land as the rainy season is coming to an end. They fell the trees and saplings and uproot the tree seedlings and shrubs. If they can use any of the timber, they remove it. Then they leave the remaining plant material to dry out through the dry season. By the end of the dry season the material is tinder-dry and they set fire to it. The fire destroys the vegetation and leaves the ground covered with a layer of ash. Using very simple implements—often nothing more than a sharpened digging stick to scratch the soil—the family prepares the site for sowing and plants its crops. These usually include a wide variety of plants including all their staple foods.

The rainy season is just beginning and the ground is fertile. Wood ash is rich in potassium, an essential plant nutrient. The land produces satisfactory harvests, but after a time the site shows signs of deterioration. Weeds become difficult to control and tree seedlings appear, showing that the land is reverting to forest, and yields start to fall. It is then time to move on. Everyone begins work to prepare another site nearby. By the time crops on the first site are being seriously choked by weeds and shaded by trees, the next site is ready for sowing. A site may last for only one year or as many as six, but rarely for longer than that.

Each family moves in this way from site to site, eventually returning to the first site. By then the land will have fully recovered its fertility and the trees will be big enough to provide useful amounts of wood. It is a sustainable farming method, but its one great disadvantage is that it requires a very large area of land. The time needed for a site to recover varies from place to place, but it is at least four years and may be up to 20 years. In effect, a family needs not one plot of land, but up to 20 plots.

Families arriving at the forest edge to farm in this way must clear a substantial area of forest in the course of their first farming cycle. The road that might have been lined by family holdings up to about five acres (2 ha) in size instead provides access to 50-acre (20-ha) slash-and-burn holdings as, inevitably, each newly arrived family encroaches farther into the forest. Slash-and-burn farming is now the principal cause of deforestation in Latin America and Africa and the second most important cause in Asia after commercial farming.

Reducing the damage due to this type of farming means improving farming methods to allow families to feed themselves from much smaller holdings. This is partly a matter of education, but it also requires much more extensive reforms. The landless peasants need access to credit so they can buy better tools, fertilizer, and improved seeds. They also need access to markets where they can sell their surpluses for a fair price in order to repay their loans. Helping the small farmers will also help protect the forest.

Soil erosion

When the tropical rain beats down on the forest, leaves break the fall of the water. It bounces off their surfaces, drips from leaf tips that are adapted to shed surplus water (see "Drip tips, buttress roots, and stilt roots" on pages 104–108), and runs down tree trunks. A great deal of the rain evaporates before it reaches the ground, and the water that does reach the ground drips quite gently onto the surface.

When the vegetation is cleared, the ground loses its protection. The torrential rain then lashes the surface, washing soil particles down hillsides and into streams and rivers. This is *soil erosion* and its effects can be devastating. The eroded soil moves downhill, carried by water flowing across the surface. Any obstruction will trap soil behind it, reducing the severity of the erosion, but nevertheless a substantial amount of soil will be washed into rivers, turning the water a muddy brown. Muddy water harms aquatic animals, and as the soil settles to the riverbed it buries some of the organisms that live there. Forest dwellers who live beside a river depend on fishing to provide them with high-quality protein. If eroded soil pollutes the river, killing fish, these people suffer just as surely as those living on higher ground whose crops fail because their topsoil has disappeared.

All soils lose some soil by erosion. This is a natural process. Undisturbed tropical forest on rolling terrain loses an average 0.09–4.5 tons of soil from each acre (0.2–10 tonnes per hectare) annually, and up to 18 tons per acre (40 tonnes per ha) on sloping land. This sounds like a great deal, but it is equivalent to only 0.0004–0.02 inch (0.01–0.5 mm) a year. On a slope that has been cleared and plowed, the annual rate of erosion can be as high as 500 tons per acre (1,122 tonnes/ha), or up to 2.4 inches (60 mm). Growing crops on the land reduces the rate of erosion dramatically because the plants protect the ground surface and their roots bind soil particles, making the soil less likely to move. Many tropical soils are suffering badly from erosion, but the erosion rate varies widely. In Brazil, for example, some soils are eroding annually at eight to nine tons per acre (18–20 tonnes/ha), while the rate on some soils in Ecuador is 89–267 tons per acre (200–600 tonnes/ha) and in Peru it is seven tons per acre (15 tonnes/ha).

Fortunately, soils vary in their susceptibility to erosion. Erosion occurs when rainwater washes soil down a slope, and the steeper the slope, the more severe the erosion will be. Erosion has caused considerable harm where forests growing on steep hillsides have been cleared. Land has eroded badly following forest clearance on the eastern slopes of the Andes and in Nepal in the Himalayas.

Hillside erosion is likely to be serious in mountainous regions, but lowland forest lies mainly on level ground and

Once the plants have gone, soil erosion often accelerates. This deeply eroded pathway crosses deforested land in the Atlantic rain forest of Brazil. (Courtesy of Frans Lanting/ Minden Pictures)

this is the forest—the typical tropical rain forest—that covers most of the Amazon and Congo Basins. Soil erosion is of minor significance in these forests. In the Amazon Basin, for example, only 8 percent of the soils are susceptible to erosion, and 94 percent of those are found on ground with a slope steeper than 30°, which is a very steep gradient.

Heavy weights compact the soil, pressing the mineral particles closer together and squeezing out the air and water filling the tiny spaces between particles. Plant roots have difficulty penetrating compacted soil, so soil compaction reduces plant growth. This increases the risk of erosion by slowing the rate at which vegetation returns naturally to land that has been cleared and then abandoned. It seems obvious that the heavy tractors used to cultivate cleared ground and the still heavier tree-crusher that slices through tree trunks and crushes the wood to splinters must cause the greatest damage. A Caterpillar tractor weighs 20–40 tons (18–36 tonnes) and a tree-crusher approximately 70 tons (64 tonnes).

Surprisingly, without careful management, herds of cattle and horses can cause more damage than heavy machines can. A Caterpillar tractor or tree-crusher is much heavier than a horse, but it is also much bigger and has a great deal more surface area in contact with the ground. The machine's weight is distributed over the area in contact with the ground. So is the weight of the horse, but only its hoofs are in contact with the ground; therefore the horse's weight presses onto a smaller area. In fact, the pressure a horse exerts on the ground, measured as pressure per unit area, is 400 times greater than that of a big tractor and 300 times greater than that of the tree-crusher. Cattle are lighter than horses and exert less pressure, but this is still about 370 times greater than the pressure exerted by the tractor and 250 times greater than that exerted by the tree-crusher. The effect is evident, even in temperate regions of the world, where the hillside paths livestock routinely follow have turned into deep gullies, scoured by the rain.

Soil erosion can be reduced to an acceptable minimum. Sloping land should be stabilized, for example by terracing or planting rows of trees or shrubs at intervals parallel to the contours, and the land should always be cultivated at right angles to the slope, never directly up and down it. Crops should be sown as soon as possible on cleared ground so that the ground is left bare for the shortest possible time. Livestock should be grazed on level ground, not on steep slopes, and animals should never be allowed to remain on an area of pasture for so long that they destroy the plant cover, leaving the soil exposed.

Soil exhaustion

Tropical soils are often deeply *weathered*. That is, chemicals dissolved in water flowing through the soil have reacted with the underlying rocks to release the mineral nutrients plants need, and these have drained—the technical term is *leached*—out of the soil. Consequently, the remaining plant nutrients are concentrated in the vegetation itself and in the upper layer of soil, where dead plant and animal matter decays. Such soils are said to be old (see "How soils age" on pages 38–42) and they often contain few plant nutrients. In the Amazon Basin, for example, 90 percent of the soils contain too little phosphorus and 56 percent too little potassium to sustain healthy plant growth. Phosphorus and potassium are two of the nutrient elements that plants need in relatively large amounts.

Deeply weathered soils also tend to be acidic, and acid soils tend to be infertile owing to the effect of aluminum. Aluminum is very abundant in all soils, but it is tightly bound chemically to mineral particles, especially in clay. As the water moving through the soil becomes increasingly acid due to the substances dissolved in it, the acids dislodge some of the aluminum, which reacts with the water, making it still more acid. The high acidity slows the rate at which dead plant and animal material decomposes. Since tropical plants depend for nutrients on the rapid decomposition of organic matter, slowing the rate of decomposition reduces the amount of nutrients available to them. Aluminum toxicity affects 75 percent of soils in the tropical lowlands.

When the forest is cleared, the soil is already acidic and inherently infertile. Most of the plant nutrients are contained in the living vegetation, and if this is removed those nutrients are lost. Burning the vegetation, which is the usual way to prepare the ground, deposits a layer of ash containing most of the nutrients, although some is blown away and lost.

Crop plants have higher nutritional requirements than the natural plants of the forest, therefore they take nutrients from the soil in greater amounts. When the crop is harvested, the edible parts—the tubers, leaves, stems, fruit, or seeds—are taken away. The residue is left to decompose, but the most nutritious parts of the plants are eaten away from the site where the crop was grown. The kitchen scraps may be returned to the site, but inevitably there is a progressive loss of nutrients from the soil. Since the soil contained few nutrients to begin with, before long it is depleted to such a degree that the crops fail. Sometimes within a single year and rarely after more than six years, the farmers have no choice but to abandon the land and begin again at a different site (see "Slash-and-burn farming" on pages 220–222).

Some tropical soils are *lateritic*. That is, on exposure to the air they tend to turn into laterite (see the sidebar on page 37). Laterite forms a layer of brick-hard material below the surface. It prevents water from draining efficiently, thereby increasing the risk of flooding, and because plant roots are unable to penetrate the laterite layer, lateritic soils are thin and support few plants.

Plowing a lateritic soil is likely to destroy it as a medium for plant growth. Fortunately, however, such soils are not very widespread. Approximately 4 percent of Amazon Basin soils suffer from this problem—although in this vast region 4 percent of the area amounts to 81,000 square miles (210,000 km^2).

Farmers need to identify lateritic soils and avoid them, for they are agriculturally useless. Soil exhaustion is a problem that can be surmounted by careful farming, the recycling of organic matter, and the judicious use of fertilizer. As history shows (see "Peoples of the American tropical forests" on pages 192–206), farming on tropical soils is possible.

CHAPTER 10

MANAGING TROPICAL FORESTS

Ecotourism

Forests are cleared to create land for farming. This is overwhelmingly the principal reason for forest clearance and it has been so throughout history, in temperate as well as tropical regions. It is true that trees are felled to provide timber, and therefore it is often logging companies that clear the forest, but clear-felling alone would not remove the forest. More trees would grow, and the forest would regenerate and in time provide more timber. The forest disappears because farmers move onto the cleared land, convert it to farmland, and destroy tree seedlings to prevent regeneration. Loggers merely provide access.

Obviously, people need land to grow food, but agricultural products are also commodities, which are bought and sold. The fact that agricultural products have market value means that the land producing them also has a value. The two values—of the produce and the land—are clearly related. Land that will produce good yields of almost any crop is more valuable than land capable of sustaining only pasture grasses. When farmers talk of "good" and "poor" land, they are referring to the productive capability of the land.

Farmland has a value that can be calculated; once people recognize this, they can value any land that is not being farmed on the basis of its agricultural potential. By comparing that value with the land's value in its present use, landowners can decide whether it would be profitable to convert the land to farmland. If the land is forested, the comparison is between the value of forest products and farm products calculated on an annual basis and averaged over a number of years.

The result of the calculation is always the same: Farmland is worth more than forested land. Timber and wood products are valuable, of course, but trees grow slowly. If the forest is mature (most of its trees are fully grown), then the existing trees, known as the *standing crop,* can be sold for a high price. If the forest is then replanted or left to regenerate naturally, however, many years will pass before a second crop can be taken from it. On the other hand, if the land were sown with corn, soybeans, or some other field crop, it would produce a much less valuable crop, but it would produce it year after year. If trees take 30 years to reach marketable size, during that time the field crops will produce 30 harvests. Farmland is bound to win.

Even in tropical forests, where some of the trees sell for extremely high prices, the outcome is the same. Those trees are usually widely scattered (see "Why there are so many species in tropical forests" on pages 211–213), so the value of each tree is the value of a large area of land.

It is easy to say that tropical forests are part of our heritage, that they should be preserved for future generations, that they belong to all the people of the world, or even that removing them might unleash some terrible natural calamity. But the fact is that forests are actual stands of real trees in particular locations, and local people will decide their future—comparing the value of the trees with that of the farm crops they could grow on the land. If forests are to survive, ways must be found to make the land beneath them more valuable than farmland.

One way to increase the value of the forest is to encourage people to visit it and charge them for doing so. Visitors will travel long distances to enjoy walking through a tropical rain forest, feeling the heat and humidity, smelling the odors, listening to the cries of the birds and monkeys and the mysterious rustlings perhaps made by other animals. Tropical forests are famous and romantic places, and visiting one is a big adventure for someone who lives in a northern city.

At one time, only wealthy explorers could travel thousands of miles to the tropical forests. Today, affordable air travel brings the forests within the reach of many more people, who arrive not as explorers but as vacationers. They come to see, to appreciate, and to enjoy the experience.

Visitors require local transport, accommodation, and restaurants. They need guides. They may need to buy special clothing or equipment, and before they depart they will want to buy souvenirs to take home and gifts for their friends and families. Providing these goods and services creates jobs for local people, and the income from tourism transforms the economics of the forest, making it more valuable than farmland. The most profitable use for the forest is then to leave it just as it is.

Naturally, this requires that the visitors do not gradually destroy the forest they have journeyed so far to see. They must travel through the forest on foot or by boat, not by car or bus because building roads through the forest would lead to its destruction. Visitors must follow prescribed routes for their own safety and also to minimize the disturbance to wildlife. The paths must be kept open, but they need not be wide, and if there are enough of them they will not be rapidly eroded by trampling.

The visitors respect the forest, and by visiting—and paying for it—they ensure the forest's survival. This is *ecotourism*, and it is a rapidly expanding branch of the global tourist industry. The United Nations (UN) declared 2002 the International Year of Ecotourism.

The UN supports ecotourism, which it defines as "sustainable tourism." More specifically, the UN says ecotourism should contribute actively to the conservation of natural and cultural heritage. It should include local and indigenous communities in its planning, development, and operation, contributing to their well-being. For the tourist, it should interpret the natural and cultural heritage of the destination and lend itself better to independent travelers, as well as to organized tours for small size groups.

The International Ecotourism Society, founded in 1990 and based in Washington, D.C., exists to promote ecotourism and disseminate information about it. This is an organization anyone can join. Its members include scientists, individuals, and companies directly involved in providing ecotourist facilities, government organizations, and individual tourists. There are also Web sites through which people can arrange and book ecotourism vacations.

Agroforestry

Converting tropical forest to farmland begins with the felling and removal of all the trees and shrubs. Farming begins when the ground is clear, and the farmer aims to keep the ground clear so far as that is possible. Trees have no place on farms.

This conventional view of tropical farming is now known to be wrong. Trees can help the farmer, but the tree species need to be chosen carefully. Farming with trees, or *agroforestry,* is now being practiced on every continent, in rich industrial countries as well as poor, less industrialized ones, but there are several reasons why the technique is especially beneficial in the Tropics.

Many tree species have roots that penetrate the soil more deeply than do the roots of crop plants, so the trees are able to obtain nutrients that crop plants cannot reach. Dead leaves and branches that fall from the tree contain those nutrients, and decomposition returns them to the upper layer of soil, where they are accessible to crop plants. Trees supply crop plants with nutrients that are otherwise unavailable. Some tree species are *legumes*—plants with colonies of bacteria that convert atmospheric nitrogen into soluble nitrogen compounds, living in nodules attached to their roots. These trees add nitrogen, an essential plant nutrient, to the soil.

Each plant species has particular nutritional requirements. That is, it requires nutrients in certain proportions, like the ingredients for a recipe. It is therefore important to select tree and crop species that do not have very similar requirements because they would compete for nutrients and the tree, having a more extensive root system, would win. In that case the crop plants would not grow well. Provided the species are compatible, however, the trees help the crops nutritionally.

Trees and shrubs that are grown among other crops, for example in alternate rows with them, help in other ways. They form barriers that make it more difficult for insect pests and the roots of weeds to move from one crop row to the next. They also bind soil particles together, reducing the risk of erosion. This is extremely valuable on hillsides.

Tall trees provide shade for livestock and also for crop plants. Plants need sunlight for photosynthesis (see the sidebar on page 168) and usually the rate of the photosynthetic reactions increases as the sunlight becomes more intense. Beyond a certain level of intensity, however, photosynthesis slows down, because very intense light stimulates reactions that alter some of the substances involved in photosynthesis. This is called *solarization,* and shade-loving plants are particularly susceptible to it. Photosynthesis also accelerates with rising temperature. The rate doubles for every 18°F (10°C) rise in temperature between 32°F (0°C) and 95°F (35°C). But between 77°F (25°C) and 95°F (35°C) the increased rate is sustained for only a few minutes, after which it decreases to its previous value. Photosynthesis becomes progressively slower as the temperature rises above 95°F (35°C), and most plants die when the temperature reaches 113°F (45°C). Shade is therefore helpful to crop plants that would otherwise be exposed to intense tropical sunlight and very high temperatures.

For centuries, farmers in temperate regions have used woody plants to make hedges that mark field and farm boundaries and enclose livestock. Hedges can perform the same function in the Tropics, and hedges that are strong and dense enough to contain livestock will also prevent animals from invading crops.

Trees do more than provide useful services, however. They also produce fodder for livestock and food such as fruit and nuts for people. Some species have roots, bark, or fruits with medicinal properties and produce them in quantities far in excess of the needs of the farming family. The surplus can be collected, dried, and sold to pharmacies in the nearest town.

Wood from fast-growing trees is usually too weak to be much use in construction, but it makes excellent fuel. Slow-growing trees produce much denser wood. This can be used to make household articles and articles for sale, and for building.

With careful management and the use of some fertilizer for the crop plants, agroforestry will provide the farming family with food, medicines, and raw materials for their own needs, as well as goods for sale. Most important of all, perhaps, the method can be sustained indefinitely and, once the "agro-farm" is established, the farmer need clear no more areas of forest. As well as helping the people, agroforestry helps protect the forest.

New products from natural forest

Tropical countries export timber from their forests. Scientists explore the forests for plants that might be the source of therapeutic drugs. Ecotourists visit the forests for recreation (see "Ecotourism" on pages 227–230). Local people clear land to grow crops or run cattle ranches, producing food almost entirely for domestic consumption. These are the only uses made of tropical forests. It sounds paradoxical, but far from being overexploited, the forests are hugely underexploited. Realizing their full commercial potential would greatly increase their value—as forests.

The true value of the forests lies not in the land on which they grow, but in the plants and animals they contain. Removing wild specimens is obviously harmful and in many cases banned under international law, but it is possible to exploit tropical species without depleting wild populations. This means cultivating the plants and raising the animals in captivity.

Certain tropical insects are already popular. People love and are fascinated by butterflies and moths, for instance, and those of the tropical forests are far bigger and more spectacular than the species that flutter across the temperate countryside (see "Beetles and butterflies" on pages 111–115). Exotic live insects such as these are highly sought by collectors and exhibitors in Europe and North America, who keep them in large enclosures where they can be seen flying.

Farmers can harvest butterflies and moths from the forests without depleting the natural population. Butterfly farmers need to know the plants on which their chosen insect species feed and lay their eggs. They grow these plants from seed in large cages, and when the plants are established the farmers go in search of mated female insects. The captured female is placed in the cage to lay her eggs, which are collected and placed in a small container until they hatch. After hatching, the caterpillars are transferred to another cage where they feed and grow until it is time for them to pupate. The farmer collects the live pupae, which are the commercial product, exported by air to butterfly farms all over the world. It is a profitable business, and increasing numbers of farmers are turning from subsistence agriculture to butterfly farming. The next step will be for the farmers to raise the butterflies in captivity, rather than catching them. This would be more efficient and it would remove any risk of depleting the natural population if the trade in pupae should expand.

The forests also contain plants that could earn money for local people. Burití palms (*Mauritia flexuosa*), known in different parts of the species' range as *miriti, muriti, moriche, muriche, canangucho, ité, aetí,* and *aguaje,* may be the most abundant palm trees in South America. There are millions of them in the Amazon Basin, and they are cultivated locally. Some Indian tribes call the burití the "tree of life" because it supplies them with food, a fermented drink, wood for rafts, clothing, and leaves for thatching. The burití palm grows to a height of about 80 feet (24 m), and its leaves are 10 feet (3 m) long. Its fruits are about the size of an egg, have a pleasant sweet taste, and are believed to contain as much vitamin C as citrus fruits. These would probably prove popular in other parts of the world, but the tree could produce much more than that. Its potential products include oil and starch for industrial use, timber, cork, and fiber suitable for making twine, hammocks, nets, and sacking.

Cauassú (*Calathea lutea*), also known as *casupo, hoja blanca,* and *bijão,* is a tall herb that grows along riverbanks in tropical South America: There are dense stands of it on the banks of the Amazon. It is easy to find and to harvest, but it could also be cultivated and grown more widely; one acre of land will support 30,000 plants (75,000 per ha). The plant's value lies in the *cauassú* wax that forms a thin layer coating the underside of each leaf. The wax is suitable for use in high-quality polishes.

Pequí (*Caryocar brasiliense*), also called *piqui* or *piqui-á,* is a tree about 33 feet (10 m) tall that is common throughout the Amazon Basin. Its fruits, called "chocky apples," contain seeds known as souari nuts, which are coated with a layer of pale yellow fat from which edible oil is obtained. This oil is sweet and can be used as a substitute for butter or in the manufacture of cosmetics. Wood from the tree is tough enough to be used in shipbuilding. The babassú palm (*Orbignya barbosiana*), also called *babaçú, aguassú,* and *coco de macaco,* grows in northern South America and throughout the Amazon Basin. A handsome tree up to 65 feet (20 m) tall, it produces nuts resembling small coconuts containing up to 72 percent by weight of an oil similar to coconut oil, used in soapmaking, and a single tree produces up to 1.5 tons (1.4 tonnes) of nuts a year. Babassú palms are grown commercially, but only on a small scale, and the industry could be developed further.

There are several tropical fruits that are eaten by local people but are rarely exported. Durian (*Durio zibethinus*) is a fruit up to 12 inches (30 cm) long, six inches (15 cm) across, and weighing up to eight pounds (3.6 kg). It has a strong, disagreeable odor, but its flavor is said to be delicious. It is grown widely in Malaysia, Indonesia, southern Thailand, and the Philippines, but despite its being one of the most famous fruits in the world, few people outside those countries ever have an opportunity to taste it. Alfred Russel Wallace (1823–1913), the English naturalist, wrote that it was worth traveling to Asia simply to taste the durian. Although its flesh deteriorates rapidly after harvesting and it must be consumed fresh, it surely has commercial potential.

There are dozens more plants found in tropical forests that are used locally but which could find much wider markets, and doubtless many more with a potential that remains to be discovered. In most cases there are technical problems to overcome before the industries can be launched, but these should not prove insurmountable.

The existence of known plants that might form the basis of profitable industries suggests that the forests probably contain other plants with useful properties. It follows that when tropical forests are cleared, those opportunities for profit are lost and that if the commercial potential is to be exploited, the forests must remain undisturbed while the species growing in them are fully explored.

Timber plantations

Tropical forests produce timber that is in great demand in countries outside the Tropics. That demand cannot be met simply by logging in natural forests because the supply would soon be exhausted and the attempt to meet it would cause large-scale destruction of the forests.

Increasing public concern over the fate of tropical forests led to the International Tropical Timber Agreement (ITTA), reached in 1994 between exporting and importing countries. Its aim is to promote the sustainable use of tropical forests while promoting trade in forest products. As of 2005 the ITTA has 30 members from producing countries and 25 importing countries (including the European Union). Together these account for almost 90 percent of all trade in tropical timber, calculated by value, and 76 percent of the total area of tropical forest. The implementation of ITTA policies is coordinated by the International Tropical Timber Organization (ITTO), established in 1986.

The ITTO operates a certification scheme that aims to ensure that all exported tropical timber is taken from forests that are being managed in a sustainable way. Anyone buying imported tropical timber can discover where and how the timber was produced. The scheme is far from perfect because sometimes timber obtained by illegal logging is falsely certified or is mixed with timber from genuinely sustainable sources. Nevertheless, certification is helping to reduce illegal logging.

Even sustainable management, in which trees of the same species are planted to replace those taken, is insufficient to meet all of the demand. Orders can be met only if a substantial proportion of tropical timber is grown in plantations. A plantation forest is different from a natural forest. It contains only trees with a commercial value, and these are grown as a crop to be harvested when they attain marketable size.

According to Patrick P. Durst, senior forestry officer for the Food and Agriculture Organization of the United Nations, plantations now supply 22 percent of all the wood used industrially, although they account for only 3.5 percent of the global forest area. The proportion is small, but worldwide it represents an area of approximately 478,000 square miles (1.2 million km^2).

Plantations are not distributed evenly. As the table shows, China, the United States, the Russian Federation, India, and Japan account between them for 65 percent of all the world's forest plantations.

Distribution of plantations

Location	Square miles	Square kilometers
China	83,000	214,000
United States	71,000	184,000
Russian Federation	66,000	171,000
India	48,000	124,000
Japan	41,000	107,000
Other Asia	48,000	124,000
South America	32,000	82,000
Oceania	10,400	27,000
Europe	34,000	87,000
Africa	22,000	57,000
Former USSR except Russia	20,000	51,000
Other North and Central America	3,089	8,000

Source: Durst, Patrick B., and Chris Brown. "Current Trends and Development of Plantation Forestry in Asia Pacific Countries," in *Proceedings of the International Conference on Timber Plantation Development*. Rome: FAO, 2002.

Most plantations produce fast-growing trees. One acre of natural forest produces an average 14 cubic feet of timber a year (1 m³/ha). An established plantation can yield 140–280 cubic feet per acre per year (10–20 m³/ha), and yields of 700 cubic feet (50 m³) are not unknown.

Teak (*Tectona grandis*) plantations cover approximately 2.5 million acres (1 million ha) in India and up to 500,000 acres (200,000 ha) in Bangladesh, although mangroves are the most abundant trees in Bangladeshi plantations. Commercial considerations mean that plantation trees are not necessarily those that grow naturally in the area. *Acacia* and *Eucalyptus* species, native to Australia, are popular plantation trees elsewhere in the Tropics because they grow rapidly and produce timber of high quality. Hickory wattle (*A. mangium*), also known as black wattle and silver leaf acacia, is one of the most popular plantation species. Japanese larch (*Larix leptolepis*), Caribbean pitch pine (*Pinus caribaea*), Korean pine (*P. koriaensis*), and Sumatran pine (*P. merkusii*) are also grown extensively, and in Fiji there are plantations of Mexican mahogany (*Swietenia macrophylla*).

In addition to timber, plantation forests also supply other products, such as palm oil, used to make margarine, soap, and candles, and in some countries used as a substitute for diesel oil. It is obtained from the oil palm (*Elaeis guineensis*), a tree originally from West Africa that is now grown throughout the Tropics.

Plantation forestry is controversial because it involves introducing exotic tree species—species that do not grow naturally in the area. If introduced species escape from cultivation and become naturalized, as many plant species have done in Europe and the United States, there is a danger that one or more of them will become invasive weeds that outcompete and suppress native species. This would harm the forests that plantations are meant to help protect. Given the profits to be made from fast-growing timber trees, some commentators fear that companies might accelerate the clearing of natural forest to provide land for plantations.

So far as possible, plantations are sited on degraded land that is otherwise useless. This is often land with secondary forest that is regenerating after being deforested and is deemed unlikely to develop into valuable natural forest.

Plantations should be designed and managed in collaboration with the local population and with its needs in mind. Plantations produce commodities for export, whereas local people rely on the natural forests for food, fiber, construction materials, and fuel. Those needs must be met, perhaps by devoting areas within the plantation to trees planted for that purpose to which communities have access.

If the worldwide demand for tropical forest products is to be satisfied, eventually most will have to be obtained from trees grown in plantations. Plantation forestry brings very real dangers, especially from the introduction of exotic species, but with careful planning and good management the risks can be minimized—and there is no realistic alternative.

Providing jobs outside forests

Loggers cut roads into the forest and people follow them, carving out land on which to grow food. These farmers are extremely poor and they attempt to farm in the forest because it is only there that they can find land. They possess only the most basic of tools and cannot afford to buy fertilizer. Consequently they have no choice but to practice slash-and-burn farming methods (see pages 220–222). Slash-and-burn farming is a major cause—and in some places *the* major cause—of tropical deforestation.

Farming methods could be improved and new products developed to allow the forests to be exploited more efficiently, more profitably, and less harmfully. But any improvement will require investment, and there is a long list of things the farmers who implement the changes will need. These include credit facilities and improved roads, transport, and storage facilities—and they will need to be paid a wage that will support them and their families. And that is not all they will need. Far from the nearest city, the rural communities will need power supplies, schools, hospitals, stores, and a range of other services and amenities. If rural families have cooking stoves that burn kerosene or bottled gas, they will not depend on the forest for fuel.

Protecting tropical forests is possible, but only if living standards rise for the poorest section of the rural population. Raising living standards is possible only if national economies grow and if governments act to ensure that the poor enjoy a share in the resulting prosperity.

There is an even more important way in which economic development will help protect the forests. Schools need teachers; hospitals need doctors, nurses, and other staff; stores need shopkeepers; and schools, hospitals, and stores are buildings that must be constructed and maintained by additional workers. These are jobs with no direct link to farming, and the people doing the jobs have to be trained by others. That is how economic development generates jobs outside agriculture and, once it begins to do so, the process accelerates. People with jobs have money to spend, so more people must work to supply the things they want to buy. If villagers can pay for the food they eat, farmers can buy better tools—which someone must make. Steadily the economy shifts away from agriculture and into manufacturing and the provision of services.

National economic activity is measured as the *gross domestic product* (GDP) and expressed in U.S. dollars. GDP is the monetary value of all the goods and services produced within a nation during a specified time—usually one year. Values are calculated at market prices, and the GDP includes taxes on expenditure, such as sales taxes; subsidies, for example to farmers, are counted as negative taxes. Comparing the GDP for one year with that for previous years provides a measure of economic growth or decline.

GDP is a measure of national income, and dividing it by the size of the population gives a figure for the *per capita GDP,* or GDP per person. This is not a very reliable guide to prosperity, however, because currencies vary in value, so the same goods or services may cost more in one country than in another, simply because one currency is undervalued or overvalued compared with the other. The per capita GDP then gives an inaccurate idea of the average living standard. *Purchasing power parity* (PPP) is a much better measure. It attempts to equalize currencies on the basis of the cost of a specified "basket" of goods and services priced first in the national currency and then in U.S. dollars.

The table lists the PPP and annual rate of economic growth in a number of tropical countries, with the PPP and growth rate in the United States for comparison. The table shows that the citizens of all these countries are poor and that some are very poor indeed. Malaysians have the highest PPP and on average they earn less than one-quarter the average U.S. income. People in the Republic of the Congo earn 1.7 percent of the U.S. average.

Economic development

Country	Purchasing power parity (US$ per person)	Rate of economic growth (per person per year %)
Bangladesh	1,530	3.1
Brazil	6,840	1.5
Colombia	5,580	1.4
Republic of the Congo	540	−3.3
Ecuador	2,820	0
Gabon	5,280	0.6
Indonesia	2,660	3.0
Malaysia	7,640	4.7
Papua New Guinea	2,260	2.3
United States	31,910	2.0

(Figures for 1999. Source: *2004 Book of the Year.* Chicago: Encyclopaedia Britannica, 2004.)

These figures are averages, and in nonindustrialized countries there is a wide gap between the income of the rich—some of whom are exceedingly rich—and the desperately poor. Averaging masks the plight of the rural poor, who earn much less than the PPP data suggest.

Reducing poverty and aiming eventually to eliminate it should be an urgent priority. Fortunately, as the figures show, the situation is improving in some tropical countries. Average prosperity is increasing by an annual 4.7 percent in Malaysia and by 3 percent in Bangladesh and Indonesia. Improvement is much slower in South America: 1.5 percent in Brazil and 1.4 percent in Colombia, while in Ecuador there is no improvement at all. The situation is worst of all in Africa, with prosperity increasing by a mere 0.6 percent in Gabon and decreasing by 3.3 percent in the Republic of the Congo.

If tropical countries can be assisted economically, making it easier for them to sell their goods for a fair price in world markets and thereby earning money for investment, living standards will rise. That will allow farmers to increase output, and therefore income, without cultivating still more of the forest. At the same time, economic development will generate employment outside agriculture, further easing the pressure on the forests.

CONCLUSION

What future for tropical forests?

Tropical forests are being cleared at an alarming rate. Deforestation is due less to the greed of wicked corporations than to the desperate poverty of rural people whose only means of feeding themselves involves farming land that was formerly forested. If the rate at which the forests are shrinking is to slow, rural poverty in tropical countries must be reduced.

It is unrealistic to suppose that all of the world's tropical forests can remain unchanged forever. Some will have to disappear because the land they occupy is needed for other uses. It is not unrealistic, however, to imagine that substantial areas can be protected and preserved in their present form and that these areas will represent all of the different types of tropical forest.

So far as possible the forests should be preserved because their value is unique. They support a wider variety of plant and animal species than any other land biome (tropical coral reefs may be equally rich in species). Their richness makes the forests very complex, constructed of several horizontal layers of plants and animals one above the other (see "Forest layers" on pages 166–167). Scientists have identified and studied only a fraction of the species to be found in the forests. Some of the species that are known may one day be of great commercial value to the people living in and near the forests (see "New products from natural forest" on pages 232–234), and products from those awaiting discovery may be of still greater value.

Because they are so complex, tropical forests can teach society much about the way ecosystems—communities of living organisms and their nonliving environment—function. People need to learn as much as possible as quickly as possible about the way the world works if the environment is not to be damaged. Tropical forests are one of the classrooms in which scientists acquire that knowledge.

Despite the rate of clearance, however, the tropical forests will not vanish from the Earth. Forests will survive that have no mineral resources worth mining and are located in regions too remote or too mountainous to be farmed economically. Not all of the forests, and perhaps not even most of them, will be cleared. But if the present deforestation is allowed to continue unchecked there will be no way of ensuring that the most important areas are the ones that survive. The only thing left might be a substantial area of poor forest when a smaller area of rich forest would be more valuable. This compels people to attempt to regulate the process, to encourage by all the means available the sustainable management of the forests and, so far as possible, to provide the rural populations of tropical countries with alternatives to inefficient and unsustainable farming.

The task seems daunting, but it is not impossible. Some tropical countries, such as South Korea, have already developed economically to such a degree that they are no longer classed officially as "less industrialized," but are now said to be "newly industrialized." Other countries, including Malaysia, Indonesia, and Brazil, may be approaching that level. Economic development eases the pressure on forests by providing nations with alternative sources of income, some of which can be used to increase the economic value of their forests.

At present we have no way of knowing whether in years to come we will be able to identify and preserve the most important forests. All we know is that they can be preserved.

SI UNITS AND CONVERSIONS

UNIT	QUANTITY	SYMBOL	CONVERSION
Base units			
meter	length	m	1 m = 3.2808 feet
kilogram	mass	kg	1 kg = 2.205 pounds
second	time	s	
ampere	electric current	A	
kelvin	thermodynamic temperature	K	1 K = 1°C = 1.8°F
candela	luminous intensity		
mole	amount of substance	cd	mol
Supplementary units			
radian	plane angle	rad	$\pi/2$ rad = 90°
steradian	solid angle	sr	
Derived units			
coulomb	quantity of electricity	C	
cubic meter	volume	m^3	1 m^3 = 1.308 $yards^3$
farad	capacitance	F	
henry	inductance	H	
hertz	frequency	Hz	
joule	energy	J	1 J = 0.2389 calories
kilogram per cubic meter	density	$kg\ m^{-3}$	1 $kg\ m^{-3}$ = 0.0624 lb. $ft.^{-3}$
lumen	luminous flux	lm	
lux	illuminance	lx	
meter per second	speed	$m\ s^{-1}$	1 $m\ s^{-1}$ = 3.281 $ft\ s^{-1}$
meter per second squared	acceleration	$m\ s^{-2}$	

(continues)

(continued)

UNIT	QUANTITY	SYMBOL	CONVERSION
mole per cubic meter	concentration	mol m^{-3}	
newton	force	N	1 N = 7.218 lb. force
ohm	electric resistance	Ω	
pascal	pressure	Pa	1 Pa = 0.145 lb. in^{-2}
radian per second	angular velocity	rad s^{-1}	
radian per second squared	angular acceleration	rad s^{-2}	
square meter	area	m^2	1 m^2 = 1.196 yards^2
tesla	magnetic flux density	T	
volt	electromotive force	V	
watt	power	W	1W = 3.412 Btu h^{-1}
weber	magnetic flux	Wb	

Prefixes used with SI units

PREFIX	SYMBOL	VALUE
atto	a	$\times 10^{-18}$
femto	f	$\times 10^{-15}$
pico	p	$\times 10^{-12}$
nano	n	$\times 10^{-9}$
micro	μ	$\times 10^{-6}$
milli	m	$\times 10^{-3}$
centi	c	$\times 10^{-2}$
deci	d	$\times 10^{-1}$
deca	da	$\times 10$
hecto	h	$\times 10^{2}$
kilo	k	$\times 10^{3}$
mega	M	$\times 10^{6}$
giga	G	$\times 10^{9}$
tera	T	$\times 10^{12}$

Prefixes attached to SI units alter their value.

SOIL CLASSIFICATION: ORDERS OF THE SOIL TAXONOMY

Entisols   Soils with weakly developed horizons, such as disturbed soils and soils developed over alluvial (river) deposits.

Vertisols   Soils with more than 30 percent clay that crack when dry.

Inceptisols   Soils with a composition that changes little with depth, such as young soils.

Aridisols   Soils with large amounts of salt, such as desert soils.

Mollisols   Soils with some horizons rich in organic matter.

Spodosols   Soils rich in organic matter, iron, and aluminum; in older classifications known as a podzol.

Alfisols   Basic soils in which surface constituents have moved to a lower level.

Ultisols   Acid soils in which surface constituents have moved to a lower level.

Oxisols   Soils rich in iron and aluminum oxides that have lost most of their nutrients through weathering; old soils often found in the humid Tropics.

Histosols   Soils rich in organic matter.

Reference Soil Groups of the Food and Agriculture Organization of the United Nations (FAO)

Histosols   Soils with a peat layer more than 15.75 inches (40 cm) deep.

Cryosols   Soils with a permanently frozen layer within 39 inches (100 cm) of the surface.

Anthrosols   Soils that have been strongly affected by human activity.

Leptosols   Soils with hard rock within 10 inches (25 cm) of the surface, or more than 40 percent calcium carbonate within 10 inches (25 cm) of the surface, or less than 10 percent of fine earth to a depth of 30 inches (75 cm) or more.

Vertisols Soil with a layer more than 20 inches (50 cm) deep containing more than 30 percent clay within 39 inches (100 cm) of the surface.

Fluvisols Soils formed on river (alluvial) deposits with volcanic deposits within 10 inches (25 cm) of the surface and extending to a depth of more than 20 inches (50 cm).

Solonchaks Soils with a salt-rich layer more than six inches (15 cm) thick at or just below the surface.

Gleysols Soils with a sticky, bluish gray layer (gley) within 20 inches (50 cm) of the surface.

Andosols Volcanic soils having a layer more than 12 inches (30 cm) deep containing more than 10 percent volcanic glass or other volcanic material within 10 inches (25 cm) of the surface.

Podzols Pale soils with a layer containing organic material and/or iron and aluminum that has washed down from above.

Plinthosols Soils with a layer more than six inches (15 cm) deep containing more than 25 percent iron and aluminum sesquioxides (oxides comprising two parts of the metal to three parts of oxygen) within 20 inches (50 cm) of the surface that hardens when exposed.

Ferralsols Soils with a subsurface layer more than six inches (15 cm) deep with red mottling due to iron and aluminum.

Solonetz Soils with a sodium- and clay-rich subsurface layer more than three inches (7.5 cm) deep.

Planosols Soils that have had stagnant water within 40 inches (100 cm) of the surface for prolonged periods.

Chernozems Soils with a dark-colored, well-structured, basic surface layer at least eight inches (20 cm) deep.

Kastanozems Soils resembling chernozems, but with concentrations of calcium compounds within 40 inches (100 cm) of the surface.

Phaeozems All other soils with a dark-colored, well structured, basic surface layer.

Gypsisols Soils with a layer rich in gypsum (calcium sulfate) within 40 inches (100 cm) of the surface, or more than 15 percent gypsum in a layer more than 40 inches (100 cm) deep.

Durisols Soils with a layer of cemented silica within 40 inches (100 cm) of the surface.

Calcisols Soils with concentrations of calcium carbonate within 50 inches (125 cm) of the surface.

Albeluvisols Soils with a subsurface layer rich in clay that has an irregular upper surface.

Alisols   Slightly acid soils containing high concentrations of aluminum and with a clay-rich layer within 40 inches (100 cm) of the surface.

Nitisols   Soils with a layer containing more than 30 percent clay more than 12 inches (30 cm) deep and no evidence of clay particles moving to lower levels within 40 inches (100 cm) of the surface.

Acrisols   Acid soils with a clay-rich subsurface layer.

Luvisols   Soils with a clay-rich subsurface layer containing clay particles that have moved down from above.

Lixisols   All other soils with a clay-rich layer within 40–80 inches (100–200 cm) of the surface.

Umbrisols   Soils with a thick, dark colored, acid surface layer.

Cambisols   Soils with an altered surface layer or one that is thick and dark colored, above a subsoil that is acid in the upper 40 inches (100 cm) and with a clay-rich or volcanic layer beginning 10–40 inches (25–100 cm) below the surface.

Arenosols   Weakly developed soils with a coarse texture.

Regosols   All other soils.

Note: A *basic* or alkaline soil is one containing more hydroxyl ions (OH^-) than hydrogen ions (H^+); an *acid* soil contains more H^+ ions than OH^- ions. Acidity is measured on the pH scale, a logarithmic scale expressing the activity of H^+ ions in solution, where pH 7.0 is a neutral reaction. A basic soil has a pH greater than 7.0; an acid soil has a pH lower than 7.0.

GLOSSARY

adiabatic   a change in temperature that involves no exchange of heat with an outside source

adventitious   arising from an unusual part of the plant. Roots that emerge from NODES are said to be adventitious

adze   a woodcutting tool with an axelike blade mounted at right angles to the haft

aerenchyma   plant tissue containing large air spaces

aerial root   a root that emerges high on the trunk of a tree and grows downward beside the trunk until it reaches the ground

agroforestry   farming combined with forestry, with crops and trees growing on the same land

air mass   a large body of air, covering most of a continent or ocean and extending to the TROPOPAUSE, in which atmospheric conditions are fairly constant throughout

alpine meadow   grassland that grows above the TREE LINE on mountainsides

anastomosis   the linking and eventual merging of the branches of woody plants

angiosperm   a flowering plant

anthracite   a very hard, black coal that burns with a hot flame and very little smoke

anthropoid   pertaining to monkeys, apes, and humans

artiodactyl   an UNGULATE with an even number of toes

bamboo   a plant with a woody stem belonging to the grass family

bituminous coal   black coal, intermediate in quality between ANTHRACITE and LIGNITE that burns with a smoky flame

bivouac   a temporary nest made by migratory army or driver ants

bole climber   a climbing plant that attaches itself to the base of a tree and climbs up the trunk (bole)

brachiation   a method of locomotion, used by gibbons and to a lesser extent by spider monkeys, in which the animal hangs by its hands below a branch and advances by swinging hand over hand

248

brasile   *see* BRAZIL

brazil (brasile)   a red dye obtained from the brazilwood tree after which the country was named

breathing root   *see* PNEUMATOPHORE

brown coal   *see* LIGNITE

bryophyte   strictly speaking, a moss, but the name is often extended to include hornworts and liverworts

buttress root   a root that emerges from the trunk of a tree some distance above the ground and grows outward and downward, attached to the trunk at its inner edge, resembling a buttress and helping to support the tree

callow   an army or driver ant WORKER that has recently emerged from its pupa

canopy   the forest cover, more or less shading the floor, formed by the touching and overlapping branches and foliage of adjacent trees

capillarity (capillary attraction)   the movement of water against gravity through a fine tube or narrow passageway

capillary attraction   *see* CAPILLARITY

capillary fringe   the region immediately above the WATER TABLE into which water rises by CAPILLARITY

carnivore   an animal that feeds only on other animals

catarrhine   having nostrils that are close together and open downward, as in Old World monkeys, apes, and humans

cauliflory   bearing flowers directly on the trunk

charcoal   a form of impure carbon used as a fuel that is made by heating wood in airless conditions

charge separation   the process by which a CUMULONIMBUS acquires a positive charge near the top and a negative charge near the base

chlorophyll   the pigment present in the leaves and sometimes stems of green plants that gives them their green color. Chlorophyll molecules trap light, thus supplying the energy for PHOTOSYNTHESIS

clear-felling   removing all the trees from an area of forest

climber tower   a narrow column of vegetation made from climbers growing up and completely enclosing a dead tree trunk

climbing root   a small, nonfeeding root produced by certain climbing plants that penetrates crevices in the bark of a tree, giving support to the climber

cloudburst   a brief but very heavy shower of rain that occurs when the currents of rising air in a storm cloud are suppressed and the cloud starts to dissipate, releasing all of its water

cloud forest   forest growing on mountainsides that is shrouded in low cloud for most of the time

condensation   the change from gas to liquid

conditional instability   the condition of air when the ENVIRONMENTAL LAPSE RATE is lower than the DRY ADIABATIC LAPSE RATE but greater than the SATURATED ADIABATIC LAPSE RATE. Dry air that is forced to rise cools faster than the surrounding air and so tends to sink to its former level (it is stable), but when its moisture begins to condense it cools more slowly than the surrounding air and so tends to continue rising (it is unstable)

consumer   an organism that obtains nourishment by ingesting other organisms

continental drift   the movement of the continents in relation to one another across the Earth's surface

continentality   the extent to which a climate resembles the most extreme type of continental climate, that is, dry with extreme summer and winter temperatures

convection   the transfer of heat by vertical movement within a fluid

convergent evolution   the process by which unrelated organisms evolve to resemble one another because they have adapted in similar ways to the similar conditions under which they live

CorF   *see* CORIOLIS EFFECT

Coriolis effect (CorF)   the deflection due to the Earth's rotation experienced by bodies moving in relation to the Earth's surface; bodies are deflected to the right in the Northern Hemisphere and to the left in the Southern Hemisphere

corm   a underground plant storage organ

cortex   an outer layer

crown   the branches and foliage at the top of a tree

culm   the stem of a grass plant

cumulonimbus   a dense cloud with a low base that often extends to a great height; it produces heavy precipitation and can generate thunderstorms and TORNADOES

cumulus   a fleecy, billowing, white cloud

cyanobacteria   bacteria that possess CHLOROPHYLL and manufacture sugars by PHOTOSYNTHESIS

cyclone   a midlatitude depression. Also, a TROPICAL CYCLONE that occurs in the Bay of Bengal

deciduous   describes parts of a plant or animal that are shed at the same season each year

dew-point temperature   the temperature at which water vapor condenses to form dew or cloud droplets

disjunct distribution   the occurrence of related species in places separated by major geographical barriers, such as an ocean or mountain range

doldrums   a sea area, inside the INTERTROPICAL CONVERGENCE ZONE, where the winds are usually light and variable

dry adiabatic lapse rate   *see* LAPSE RATE

ecological pyramid (Eltonian pyramid)   a diagram representing feeding relationships within an ECOSYSTEM as a series of bands, all the same thickness but varying in width, with PRODUCERS at the base and CONSUMERS stacked above them

ecology   the scientific study of the relationships among organisms inhabiting a specified area and between the organisms and the physical and chemical conditions in which they live

ecotourism   tourism by visitors who wish to see an area of natural habitat while causing the least possible disturbance to it

elfin forest   forest consisting of stunted, gnarled trees that grows high on mountainsides and elsewhere in very exposed places

El Niño   a weakening or reversal of the prevailing easterly winds over the tropical South Pacific Ocean that happens at intervals of two to seven years. This weakens the wind-driven surface ocean current, allowing warm water to accumulate off the South American coast and producing weather changes over a large area

Eltonian pyramid   *see* ECOLOGICAL PYRAMID

elytra (sing. elytron)   the hardened forewings of a beetle, which give the beetle its characteristic appearance when not flying and that rise to allow the hind wings to open when the beetle is in flight

emergent   a forest tree that stands taller than those around it

endodermis   the innermost layer of plant CORTEX, surrounding the STELE

endosperm   material in a seed that surrounds the embryo and supplies it with nourishment between germination and the time the young plant begins to obtain its own nutrients

ENSO   the full cycle of EL NIÑO and its opposite, LA NIÑA, associated with the SOUTHERN OSCILLATION

environmental lapse rate   the rate, in degrees F or C per thousand feet or C per kilometer, at which the atmospheric temperature decreases with increasing altitude

epidermis   the outermost layer of cells in a plant or animal

epiphyte   a plant that grows on the surface of another plant, but without obtaining nourishment from that plant

equatorial trough   the region of low pressure where the TRADE WINDS from either hemisphere converge, causing air to rise

equinox   March 20–21 and September 22–23, when the noonday Sun is directly overhead at the equator and day and night are of equal length everywhere in the world

erosion   *see* SOIL EROSION

estuary   a region near the mouth of a river where the tides carry seawater upstream and where freshwater and seawater meet

evergreen   describes a plant that bears leaves at all times of year; although it sheds its leaves, it does not shed all of them at the same time

exoskeleton   the horny casing that covers all arthropods (insects, spiders, mites, scorpions, crustaceans, and others) protecting the soft parts of their bodies and providing mechanical support

floodplain   the lower part of a river where the surrounding ground is inundated from time to time, either because the river overflows its banks or because a system of meanders advances across it

floret   *see* INFLORESCENCE

fog oasis   a local area, usually in a valley in a coastal mountain range, where clouds moving inland from the sea provide enough moisture to sustain forest in an otherwise arid region

food chain   a set of feeding relationships in which each in a sequence of organisms feeds on the preceding member

food web   a diagram that shows the inhabitants of an ECOSYSTEM linked by lines between species and the species on which they feed; a series of FOOD CHAINS

forb   a herbaceous plant other than a grass

forest limit   *see* TREE LINE

fructivore   an animal that feeds exclusively on fruit

gallery forest   forest that grows along river valleys where the soil is moist even during the dry season

GDP   *see* GROSS DOMESTIC PRODUCT

geotropism   movement in response to gravity

glacial   a period when polar ice sheets advance; an ice age

gross domestic product (GDP)   the value of all the goods and services produced within a country during a specified time (usually one year)

groundwater   water that flows underground through permeable rock or gravel

gutta-percha   a rubbery latex produced by *Palaquium gutta,* a tree that grows in the rain forests of Malaysia and Indonesia

gymnosperm   a seed plant in which the OVULES are carried naked on the scales of a cone. Coniferous (cone-bearing) trees are the most abundant gymnosperms.

Hadley cell   the tropical part of the general circulation of the atmosphere. Air rises over the equator, moves away from the equator at high altitude, subsides over the subtropics, and flows toward the equator at low altitude

haustorium an outgrowth from the root of a parasitic plant that penetrates the tissues of the host

hemiparasite a parasitic plant that possesses CHLOROPHYLL and makes sugars by PHOTOSYNTHESIS, but augments its food supply by taking nutrients from its host

herbivore an animal that feeds exclusively on plant material

horse latitudes regions around latitude 30°N and S, where winds are light and sailing ships are liable to be becalmed. When supplies of drinking water ran low, horses sometimes died and were thrown overboard

humidity the amount of water vapor present in the air

humus decomposed plant and animal material in the soil

hurricane a TROPICAL CYCLONE in the North Atlantic or Caribbean

hypha one of the minute threads that form the main part of a fungus

igapó an extensive area of SWAMP or marsh in the Amazon Basin

inflorescence a mass of small but complete flowers (called florets) growing together and giving the appearance of a single flower. Sunflower and grass "flowers" are inflorescences

insectivore an animal that feeds exclusively on insects

interglacial a period of warmer weather between two GLACIALS

internode the part of a plant stem between two NODES

intertropical convergence zone (ITCZ) the region where the TRADE WINDS from either hemisphere meet (converge)

ischial callosity an area of hardened skin on the buttocks of certain monkeys

ITCZ *see* INTERTROPICAL CONVERGENCE ZONE

jungle an impenetrable tangle of vegetation, often formed by secondary growth on either side of roads

keratin the tough, fibrous protein from which hair, skin, and horn are made

knee root a loop of tree root that emerges above the surface of ground that is waterlogged for most or all of the time

La Niña the opposite of EL NIÑO, when the TRADE WINDS and east-to-west ocean currents strengthen and the sea surface is warmer than usual in the western tropical South Pacific Ocean and cooler in the east

lapse rate the rate at which the air temperature decreases (lapses) with increasing altitude. In unsaturated air the dry ADIABATIC lapse rate is 5.38°F per thousand feet (9.8°C/km); in saturated air the saturated adiabatic lapse rate varies, but it averages 2.75°F per thousand feet (5°C/km)

last glacial maximum   the time, about 20,000 years ago, when the most recent GLACIAL was at its most extreme

latent heat   the heat energy that is absorbed or released when a substance changes phase between solid and liquid, liquid and gas, and solid and gas. For water at 32°F (0°C) the latent heat of melting and freezing is 80 calories per gram (334 J/g); of vaporization and condensation 600 calories per gram (2,501 J/g); and for sublimation and deposition 680 calories per gram (2,835 J/g)

laterite   a rock rich in oxides and hydroxides, chiefly of iron and aluminum, found in lumps or a continuous layer in some tropical soils

leaching   the removal of soluble chemical compounds dissolved in water draining from the soil

lenticel   a pore in the stem of a woody plant through which plant cells exchange gases

liana (liane)   a woody climbing plant

lichen   a composite organism consisting of a fungus and an alga or cyanobacterium

lifting condensation level   the altitude at which the air is at the DEW-POINT TEMPERATURE and water vapor begins to condense to form cloud; the lifting condensation level marks the cloud base

lignite (brown coal)   coal intermediate in quality between PEAT and BITUMINOUS COAL in which plant remains are clearly visible

logging   the felling of forest trees for timber

lowland wet forest   forest that occurs close to the equator from sea level to about 4,000 feet (1,200 m)

mangrove   a tree that grows in tropical, shallow, coastal waters with its roots immersed in mud. Depending on the classification, there are up to 75 species of mangroves

mantle   that part of the Earth's interior lying between the outer edge of the inner core and the underside of the crust

marsupium   a pouch in which a female animal carries eggs or young

monsoon   a reversal in wind direction that occurs twice a year over much of the Tropics, producing two seasons with markedly different weather

montane   pertaining to mountains

Müllerian body   a structure at the base of a leaf stem of certain tropical trees that contains starch, fats, and protein as food for ants

mutualism   a relationship between two species that benefits both

mycelium   the mass of HYPHAE that make up the main part of a fungus

node   the point at which a leaf attaches to the plant stem

obligate   having no alternative. An obligate PARASITE can live only as a parasite; an obligate anaerobe cannot tolerate oxygen

oceanicity   the extent to which a climate resembles the most extreme type of maritime climate; that is, moist with cool summers and mild winters

omnivore   an animal that feeds on both animal and plant material

opposable   describes a thumb or great toe that can be turned so its pad is able to press against the pads of other digits on the same hand or foot

parallel evolution   evolution in which two species with a common ancestor continue to resemble one another because they are both adapted to similar environmental conditions

parasite   an organism that lives in close association with another, usually much larger, organism from which it derives food, shelter, or some other requirement. Parasites often harm their hosts but seldom kill them

parent material   the underlying rock from which the mineral content of a soil is derived

peat   partly decomposed plant material forming a distinct SOIL HORIZON; peat of suitable quality is dried and burned as fuel

pedology   the scientific study of soils

peg root   a tree root that rises vertically from the main root to project above the surface of ground that is waterlogged for much or all of the time

pericycle   the outermost layer of the STELE

perissodactyl   an UNGULATE with an odd number of toes

permeability   the ability of a material to allow water to flow through it

phellogen (cork cambium)   a layer of tissue beneath the outer bark of a tree comprising cells that divide to produce new cork and new bark; in PNEMATOPHORES they give rise to AERENCHYMA tissue

phloem   tissue through which the products of photosynthesis and hormones are transported from the leaves to all parts of a vascular plant

photosynthesis   the sequence of chemical reactions in which green plants and cyanobacteria use sunlight as a source of energy for the manufacture (synthesis) of sugars from hydrogen and carbon, obtained from water and carbon dioxide, respectively. The reactions can be summarized as

$$6CO_2 + 6H_2O + light \rightarrow C_6H_{12}O_6 + 6O_2 \uparrow$$

The upward arrow indicates that oxygen is released into the air; $C_6H_{12}O_6$ is glucose, a simple sugar

pioneer species a plant species that appears early in the succession of plants colonizing bare ground

plane of the ecliptic the imaginary disk with the Sun at its center and the Earth's orbital path around the Sun as its circumference

plantation a forest consisting of trees that have been planted to provide a crop of timber that will be harvested

plate tectonics the theory holding that the Earth's crust consists of a number of rigid sections, or plates, that move in relation to one another

platyrrhine describes nostrils that face to the sides and are widely separated. All New World monkeys have platyrrhine nostrils

plywood a product made from thin sheets of wood that are glued together in layers, with the grain in each layer running at right angles to the grain in the layers on either side

pneumatophore (breathing root) a root with sections that project above the ground surface, the projections having many pores through which the root exchanges gases

pore space the total interconnected space between the mineral particles in a soil

porosity the percentage of the total volume of a material that consists of spaces between particles

predator an organism that obtains energy by consuming, and usually killing, another organism

prehensile capable of grasping

producer an organism that synthesizes food from simple compounds. Green plants and certain bacteria are producers

propagule any structure, such as a spore or seed, by means of which a plant reproduces (propagates itself)

prop root a root that provides mechanical support to a tree, such as a BUTTRESS ROOT or STILT ROOT

prosimian pertaining to lemurs, bush babies, lorises, and pottos

purchasing power parity (PPP) GROSS DOMESTIC PRODUCT per person, corrected for over- or undervaluation of the local currency by pricing a basket of goods and services first in the local currency and then in U.S. dollars. This yields a fairly true valuation of the local currency against which the GDP is adjusted

rain shadow the drier climate on the lee (downwind) side of a mountain range caused by the loss of moisture as air approaching the mountains is forced to rise, resulting in the condensation and precipitation of its water vapor on the windward slopes. Compression raises the temperature of the subsiding air, further reducing its RELATIVE HUMIDITY

refugium (pl. refugia) an isolated area in which plants and animals survive major climatic changes taking place elsewhere

relative humidity the amount of water vapor present in air at a particular temperature expressed as the percentage of the water vapor needed to saturate the air at that temperature

relict an organism that has survived while related species became extinct

respiration the sequence of chemical reactions in which carbon in sugar is oxidized with the release of energy; the opposite of PHOTOSYNTHESIS. The reactions can be summarized as

$$C_6H_{12}O_6 + 6O_2 \rightarrow 6CO_2 + 6H_2O + energy$$

$C_6H_{12}O_6$ is glucose, a simple sugar

rhizome a horizontal underground stem

roundwood wood of all kinds that is taken from a forest commercially

ruminant an ARTIODACTYL that has a stomach with three or four chambers, one of which, the rumen, contains bacteria that break down the cellulose in plant cell walls

saturated adiabatic lapse rate *see* LAPSE RATE

savanna tropical grassland with varying densities of drought-resistant trees and shrubs

seafloor spreading the theory that the ocean floor is created at ridges where MANTLE material rises to the surface and the crustal rocks move away from the ridges on either side, causing the ocean basin to widen as the seafloor spreads

secondary metabolite a product of plant metabolism that contributes nothing to the growth or maintenance of the plant but may help protect the plant from competing plants, PARASITES, or HERBIVORES

selva tropical rain forest, especially that of the Amazon Basin

slash-and-burn farming an agricultural system in which an area is cleared of vegetation, dead plant material is burned, and crops are grown for several seasons until weeds become unmanageable and crop yields fall. The operation is then repeated on another site

snow line the level on a mountainside above which the ground remains covered by snow throughout the year

soil erosion the loss of soil particles through the action of wind and/or surface water

soil horizon a horizontal layer in a SOIL PROFILE that differs in its mineral or organic composition from the layers above and below it, and from which it can be clearly distinguished visually

soil profile a vertical section cut through a soil from the surface to the underlying rock

solarization   the inhibition of PHOTOSYNTHESIS that occurs when the light is very intense, due mainly to the breakdown of some of the substances involved in photosynthesis by reactions driven by light energy

solstice   one of the two dates each year when the noonday Sun is directly overhead at one or other of the Tropics and the difference in length between the hours of daylight and darkness is at its most extreme. The solstices occur on June 21–22 and December 22–23

soredium   a microscopic structure formed by a LICHEN for the purpose of reproduction, comprising a few fungal HYPHAE together with cells from the alga or cyanobacterium

southern oscillation   a change that occurs periodically in the distribution of surface atmospheric pressure over the equatorial South Pacific Ocean

statary period   a time when army or driver ants remain in one place, sending out foraging parties to find food

stele   the part of a root that contains PHLOEM, XYLEM, and PERICYCLE tissue

stilt root   a tree root that emerges from the trunk some distance above the ground and grows outward then downward until it reaches the soil; it provides mechanical support for the tree

stoma (pl. stomata)   a small opening, or pore, on the surface of a plant leaf through which the plant cells exchange gases with the outside air. Stomata can be opened or closed by the expansion or contraction of two guard cells surrounding each stoma

storm surge   a rise in sea level, accompanied by large waves, that is caused by sea storms and especially by TROPICAL CYCLONES

stratosphere   the region of the atmosphere that extends from the TROPOPAUSE to an altitude of about 31 miles (50 km)

subduction   the movement of one crustal plate beneath another, returning the crustal rock to the Earth's MANTLE

sucker   an ADVENTITIOUS shoot that arises from the horizontal root or base of a plant and grows into a new plant

supercontinent   a landmass formed by the merging of previously separate continents as a result of CONTINENTAL DRIFT. Pangaea was a supercontinent comprising all the present-day continents

supercooling   the chilling of water to below freezing temperature without triggering the formation of ice

superorganism   a group of organisms that behave in a coordinated fashion as though they were a single organism

swamp   an area of forest (or, in European usage, of herbaceous vegetation) growing on land that is covered by water for most or all of the time and that does not dry out during a dry season

thermal equator the line around the Earth where the temperature is highest. It moves with the seasons, but its average location is at about 5°N

three-cell model a representation of the general circulation of the Earth's atmosphere as a system of three sets of compartments (cells) in which air rises in one latitude and subsides in another. HADLEY CELLS circulate in the Tropics, and polar cells operate at high latitudes; together these drive the Ferrel cells of midlatitudes

timberline *see* TREE LINE

tornado a rapidly spinning spiral of air that descends as a column from a large storm cloud

trade winds the winds that blow toward the equator in equatorial regions, from the northeast in the Northern Hemisphere and from the southeast in the Southern Hemisphere

tree line (timberline, forest limit) the elevation or latitude beyond which the climate is too severe for trees to grow

trichome an outgrowth, resembling a hair and including root hairs, from a surface plant cell

trophic pertaining to food or feeding

tropical cyclone a violent storm, with heavy rain and sustained winds of more than 74 MPH (120 km/h), that develops over a tropical ocean

tropical depression an area of low surface pressure caused by the convergence of air over a tropical ocean

tropical disturbance a local change in the wind direction and pressure distribution over a tropical ocean

tropical storm a TROPICAL DEPRESSION that has deepened until it generates winds of 38–74 MPH (61–119 km/h)

tropopause the boundary separating the TROPOSPHERE from the STRATOSPHERE. It occurs at a height of about 10 miles (16 km) over the equator, seven miles (11 km) in middle latitudes, and five miles (8 km) over the North and South Poles

troposphere the layer of the atmosphere that extends from the surface to the TROPOPAUSE; it is the region where all weather phenomena occur

tuber a swollen plant stem or root that serves as an underground storage organ for nutrients

typhoon a TROPICAL CYCLONE that occurs in the Pacific Ocean or China Seas

understory the trees that are shorter than the trees forming the forest CANOPY

ungulate a mammal with hoofs

várzea a region of tropical forest, especially in the Amazon Basin, that is flooded once each year

vegetative reproduction   the growth of a new plant from the stem, leaf, or root of another plant, rather than by sexual reproduction

veneer   a thin layer of high-quality wood that is glued to the surface of an inferior wood to improve its appearance

vine   a nonwoody climbing plant

viviparous   producing live young

Walker circulation   a movement of air between the equator and about 30°N and S in which air rises, moves to the east or west, and subsides. Changes in this circulation are linked to the SOUTHERN OSCILLATION

water table   the upper margin of the GROUNDWATER; soil is fully saturated below the water table but unsaturated above it

wattle   a name for *Acacia* shrubs producing wood that was once used, plastered with mud, in a type of construction called wattle-and-daub

weathering   the breaking down of rocks by physical and chemical processes

worker   a sterile member of an ant, bee, wasp, or termite colony that raises the brood, maintains the nest, or forages for food

xylem   plant tissue through which water entering at the roots is transported to all parts of the plant

BIBLIOGRAPHY AND FURTHER READING

Print

Allaby, Michael. *Dangerous Weather: Hurricanes.* Rev. ed. New York: Facts On File, 2003.

———. *Encyclopedia of Weather and Climate.* 2 vols. New York: Facts On File, 2002.

———. *Ecosystem: Deserts.* New York: Facts On File, 2001.

Ashman, M. R., and G. Puri. *Essential Soil Science.* Malden, Mass.: Blackwell Science, 2002.

Foth, H. D. *Fundamentals of Soil Science.* 8th ed. New York: John Wiley, 1991.

Hancock, Paul L., and Brian J. Skinner, editors. *The Oxford Companion to the Earth.* New York: Oxford University Press, 2000.

Hora, Bayard, consultant editor. *The Oxford Encyclopedia of Trees of the World.* New York: Oxford University Press, 1981.

Oliver, John E., and John J. Hidore. *Climatology: An Atmospheric Science.* 2d ed. Upper Saddle River, N.J.: Prentice Hall, 2002.

Willis, K. J., L. Gillson, and T. M. Brncic. "How 'Virgin' Is Virgin Rainforest?" *Science* 304 (April 16, 2004): 402–403.

Wilson, E. O. *The Diversity of Life.* Cambridge, Mass.: Harvard University Press, 1992.

Web sites

"About Ecotourism." UNEP. Available online. URL: www.uneptie.org/pc/tourism/ecotourism/home.htm. Last updated February 7, 2003.

"The Alex Foundation." Available online. URL: www.alexfoundation.org. Accessed February 12, 2004.

"Amphibian Facts." AmphibiaWeb, April 25, 2002. Available online. URL: http://elib.cs.berkeley.edu/aw/amphibian/facts.html. Accessed January 30, 2004.

Butler, Rhett. "Tropical Rainforest: Soils and Nutrient Cycling in the Rainforest." Mongabay.com. Available online. URL: www.mongabay.com/0502.htm. Accessed July 10, 2003.

Canadian International Development Agency. "Tropical Forests." Available online. URL: www.rcfa-cfan.org/english/eforests.htm. Last modified June 15, 2000.

Durst, Patrick B., and Chris Brown. "Current Trends and Development of Plantation Forestry in Asia Pacific Countries," in *Proceedings of the International Conference on Timber Plantation Development.* Rome: FAO 2002. Available online. URL: www.fao.org/docrep/005/ac781e/AC781E03.htm. Accessed August 19, 2004.

"Facts About Tropical Rainforest." Available online. URL: www.westy.dk/manona/rainforest.htm. Last changed December 15, 2001.

Felter, Harvey Wickes, and John Uri Lloyd. "Gutta-Percha." Affinity Laboratory Technologies. Available online. URL: www.altcorp.com/AffinityLaboratory/guttahistory.htm. Accessed May 12, 2005.

"Forest Types: Ecoregions." Tropenbos International. Available online. URL: www.tropenbos.nl/DRG/ecoregion.htm. Accessed January 21, 2004.

"Goliath Beetles." Available online. URL: www.ivyhall.district96.k12.il.us/4th/kkhp/1insects/goliathbeetle.html. Accessed January 28, 2004.

Haemig, P. D. "Birds and Mammals Associated with Bamboo in the Atlantic Forest." *Ecology.Info* # 5, 2003. Available online. URL: www.ecology.info/birds-bamboo-atlantic-forest.htm. Accessed January 20, 2004.

Henniger, Scott. "*Actias selene* (Indian Moon Moth)." Available online. URL: http://pooh.unl.edu/~scotth/samantha/selene/selene.html. Accessed January 29, 2004.

"The International Ecotourism Society." Available online. URL: www.ecotourism.org. Accessed August 18, 2004.

Lauri, Bob, and Judy Gibson. "Mangrove Wetlands." *Ocean Oasis Field Guide.* San Diego Natural History Museum, 2000. Available online. URL: www.oceanoasis.org/fieldguide/mangroves.html. Accessed January 22, 2004.

Lehmann, Johannes. "Terra Preta de Indio." Cornell University. Available online. URL: www.css.cornell.edu/faculty/lehmann/terra_preta/TerraPretahome.htm. Accessed August 6, 2004.

Myers, Phil. "Order Chiroptera (Bats)." *Animal Diversity Web.* University of Michigan Museum of Zoology, 2001. Available online. URL: http://animaldiversity.ummz.umich.edu/site/accounts/information/Chiroptera.html. Accessed February 5, 2004.

———. and David L. Fox. "Family Tayassuidae (Peccaries)." *Animal Diversity Web.* University of Michigan Museum of Zoology, 2001. Available online. URL: http://animaldiversity.ummz.umich.edu/

site/accounts/information/Tayassuidae.html. Accessed February 5, 2004.

Nagypal, Tony. "An Introduction to the World of Birdwing Butterflies." Available online. URL: www.nagypal.net. Accessed January 29, 2004.

———. "Check-list of the Birdwing Butterflies." Available online. URL: www.nagypal.net/foerstes.htm. Accessed January 29, 2004.

Njiro, Esther I. "The Montane Ecosystems: Characteristics and Conservation." Mountain Forum On-Line Library Document. Available online. URL: www.mtnforum.org/resources/library/njire97a.htm. Accessed January 20, 2004.

Nowak, Ronald M. "Pigs, or Hogs." *Walker's Mammals of the World.* Johns Hopkins University Press, 1997. Available online. URL: www.press.jhu.edu/books/walkers_mammals_of_the_world/artiodactyla/artiodactyla.

Oehlke, Bill. "*Coscinocera hercules* (Miskin, 1875)." Available online. URL: www.silkmoths.bizland.com/sample5.htm. Accessed January 29, 2004.

Protected Areas Programme. "World Heritage Sites: Lorentz National Park, Indonesia." Cambridge: United Nations Environment Program World Conservation Monitoring Centre. Available online. URL: www.unep-wcma.org/protected_areas/data/wh/lorentz.html. Last revised February 21, 2001.

Quarto, Alfredo. "The Mangrove Forest." *The Ramsar Convention on Wetlands.* Available online. URL: www.ramsar.org/about_mangroves_2.htm. Accessed January 22, 2004.

"Rainforest Relationships: The Strangler Fig (*Ficus spp*)." Singapore Zoological Gardens Docent. Available online. URL: www.szgdocent.org/ff/f-stfig.htm. Accessed February 18, 2004.

"Rain Forests." Available online. URL: www.geocities.com/RainForest/Canopy/1806/page2.html. Accessed July 10, 2003.

Salaverri, Jorge. "Cloud Forests: The Kings of the National Park System." *Honduras This Week; Special Edition: The Environment.* Available online. URL: www.marrder.com/htw/special/environment/5.htm. Accessed January 19, 2004.

Scotese, Christopher R. "Paleomap Project." Available online. URL: www.scotese.com. Last updated February 2, 2003.

UN Environment Program. "Convention on Biological Diversity." Available online. URL: www.biodiv.org. Updated June 10, 2004.

Washington Park Zoo. "Poison Dart Frog." Washington Park Zoo, Michigan City, Indiana. Available online. URL: www.

emichigancity.com/cityhall/departments/zoo/animals/poison dartfrog.htm. Accessed January 30, 2004.

Wiles, Chris. "Fact File: Papua New Guinea." Available online. URL: members.aol.com/prwiles/page7.htm. Last modified April 8, 1998.

Wings, R. Grey. "Learning with Parrots: Recognizing Intelligence." Conservancy of the Phoenix Inc., 2001. Available online. URL: www.trib.com/~phxcon/PARROTLEARN.html. Accessed February 12, 2004.

"World Agroforestry Centre." International Centre for Research in Agroforestry. Available online. URL: www.worldagroforestry.org. Accessed August 18, 2004.

Note: *Italic* page numbers refer to illustrations.